Verdicts on Social Work

P. R day

Verdicts on Social Work

Stuart Rees and
Alison Wallace

Edward Arnold

© copyright 1982 Stuart Rees and Alison Wallace

First published 1982 by
Edward Arnold (Publishers) Ltd
41 Bedford Square, London WC1B 3DQ

British Library Cataloguing in Publication Data

Rees, Stuart
    Verdicts on social work.
    1. Social science—Great Britain
    I. Title   II. Wallace, Alison
    361.3′0941   HV245

ISBN 0-7131-6279-1

Printed in Great Britain by Richard Clay
(The Chaucer Press) Ltd, Bungay, Suffolk.

Contents

Acknowledgements

This work was generously supported by the Scottish Social Work Services Group through their Principal Research Officer John Tibbitt. We owe a great deal to John's trust and patience even though he always knew that the project was meant to have an application not only to Scotland but well beyond its borders. All the Scottish Directors of Social Work cooperated in tape-recorded interviews in which they spoke spontaneously. They gave us hospitality and imposed no conditions on our analysis.

Thanks are also due in the early stages of the project to Moyra Turnbull who typed the first transcripts and to Joan Oldman who provided important support through her interest and constructive criticism.

Janice Whittington and Karen Honey had the skills and cheerful stamina required to type final drafts, including more than the usual number of references. Dr Rosamund Thorpe and Professor Wyatt Jones read the final manuscript and offered invaluable advice and criticism. We have heeded their observations but the responsibility for any typical authorship sins, of omission or repetition, of sacrificing controversy for coherence or vice versa, remains ours.

Stuart Rees,
Alison Wallace
Sydney, July, 1981

To our parents

Part I
Evaluation Comes of Age

1

Accusers and Accused

Introduction

At the beginning of the 1980s, many governments have made substantial cutbacks in health and welfare services. They have been motivated by a desire to balance their budgets and spend the welfare dollar only where they think it is absolutely necessary. They have been disquieted by the accumulation of information alleging that certain services are ineffective and do not reach those who need help most.

In social work and social policy circles there is considerable debate about the nature of social work practice. Some critics of social work have assumed that social workers act as therapists and partly in consequence of such assumptions these critics have stressed the desirability of social workers engaging in a taken-for-granted way in alliances with other professionals such as doctors (Brewer and Lait 1980). Such a view has been attacked, rightly in our view, for ignoring the role of social work in social policy and for attempting to make social workers carry the can for the hypocrisy of other professions and for the callousness of governments (Jordan 1980).

In some recent confident accusations of social work it is never absolutely clear who or what is on trial. Social workers have been a focus of attention not merely because some are said to be repeating the esoteric professional aims which Barbara Wootton criticized so scathingly in the late 1950s (Wootton 1959) but, in many instances, because social workers can easily be scapegoated by politicians searching for explanations of economic recessions and their consequences. Governments which value economic independence at all costs, almost inevitably are reluctant supporters of services concerned to deal with conditions of human dependence.

Nevertheless, politicians of several countries have been making a case which needs to be answered. The Australian Senate Standing Committee on Social Welfare argued for greater accountability in health and welfare services (Commonwealth of Australia 1979). The United States General Accounting Office made sweeping criticism of the limited attainments of community development type programmes for urban youth (Singer 1979). In Britain, the Secretary of State for Social Services announced a national enquiry into 'the social work task' by telling a conference of the Association of Directors of Social Services that the time had come for a 'clear-headed look' at social work and in particular how it is defined (Fry and Cockburn 1980).

At a time when welfare has become a subject of public debate, researchers have been accumulating evidence concerning the uses and usefulness of social work and social workers. But there is usually a separation between professional researchers' private world and the arena of public debate, except where certain critics are prone to select information to bolster their particular version of the truth. The time is opportune, if not overdue, to relate the volume of researchers' evidence to current questions about the evaluation of social work services.

This book identifies the meaning of the criteria used to evaluate social work. It identifies criteria of evaluation used by different people, but mainly clients and social workers, involved in providing personal social services. Our task involves both a description of the activities which prompted evaluations and an account of the contexts in which these judgements were being made. In an attempt to reach verdicts about the achievements and shortcomings of social work and social workers we have confronted two issues. The first concerns the variety of the evidence. This has involved us in a dragnet operation amounting to a detailed review of the social work research literature. The second issue concerns the need to place this evidence in some kind of organizational and political context. To do this we have interviewed civil servants and politicians who hold responsibilities for the administration of social work. We paid particular attention to the views of Directors of Social Work in Scotland, since that was where we began and ended our enquiry. The themes identified by these Directors are shared by managers in similar positions elsewhere and these concerns are often addressed directly in the findings of independent research.

The importance of questioning the possible motives of those who doubt the value of continued financial support for welfare services has been hinted at in our use of metaphors such as accusers and accused, the search for evidence and verdicts on social work. Our motives in writing this book should also be made clear.

Motives and interests

In discussions about social work it is frustrating to hear people who select only the evidence which justifies their predetermined conclusions. The criteria of evaluation of social work tend to be known only in an *ad hoc* way by people who can remember, if nothing else, the hardly surprising conclusion, from a project carried out in the USA before the Second World War, that counselling neither prevented delinquency (Powers and Witmer 1951) nor, when followed up several decades later, did the treated group show any positive effects from having been in this delinquency prevention programme. (McCord and McCord 1959; McCord 1978).

Apart from the summaries of the findings of such experimental projects, the conclusions of research have not been collected or compared, let alone been the basis for arguments about changes in policy. We want to place in one volume the research evidence which relates to what social workers have done, to whom and with what consequences.

A second sense of frustration is prompted by some oversimplified versions of social work. A familiar, almost stereotype conclusion, derived from experimental studies, was that casework was ineffective (Fischer 1973, 5–20; Fischer 1976). From this well researched conclusion, it is an easy step to make judgements about all social work. This is often done (Brewer and Lait 1980) without asking about the differences between casework and everyday social work, or about the circumstances of the activities being measured in experimental trials. We are not apologists for casework. We want to avoid drawing oversimplified or unjustified conclusions about social work.

The current concern with cost effectiveness and related political controversies, has arisen simultaneously with a new tradition of radical criticism about the relationship between welfare and the state.* This radical analysis has emphasized and criticized the social control functions of social workers (Piven and Cloward 1971; Cockburn 1977). More cautious critics have related the difficulties of doing social work to society's ambivalence about having the job done at all (Rees 1978). Simpkin argues that social work can achieve little on its own terms without attempting to move the world of which it is itself only a small part (Simpkin 1979). We also want to see how research-based information concerning social workers' day-to-day activities, squares with some of the conclusions of both the radical and Marxist criticisms of social work's alleged uncritical support of state institutions at the expense of ordinary people's interests.

Momentum of interest in evaluation

We are involved in evaluating social work by weighing the conclusions of others' research. Our interest follows a wider development of ideas about evaluation. Our interpretation of this notion is influenced by our understanding of some important historical events which were prompted and promoted by insights from the social sciences and by some major political considerations. Sarri observes that in the USA, an increasing interest in evaluation occurred from the 1960s onwards when a sense of optimism about the changes which might be achieved by social experiments was replaced by a sense of dismay when dramatic changes did not occur (Sarri

---

* By radicalism we mean a linking of immediate policies and practices to objectives concerned with social change as influenced by socialist principles. Radical short-term practices would be characterized by redefinitions of agency goals to match client interests and by a refusal to work in terms of traditional professional/client relationships. Radical practice would include an analysis of the ways in which capitalist economies sustain certain patterns in power relationships and other inequalities. It would involve social workers in effecting alliances with groups with similar long-term objectives. (For a useful discussion of these issues, see Galper 1980.)

1979, 60–74). That social reformers were often more concerned with liberating ideas than with foreseeing outcomes, did not change some people's
hopes for a new society. The evaluation of such processes did at least identify
the dilemmas, of 'giving form to so many new initiatives at once' and of
raising poor people's aspirations without the accompanying political means
of ensuring wider social changes to guarantee any social project's temporary
achievements (Marris and Rein 1973).

If social workers and others benefited in career terms from the optimism of
the 1960s, then professional evaluators of various kinds are reaping the
benefits of the conservative pragmatism of the 1980s. Evaluators are often
both the midwives of projects and the respectable undertakers when financial life-support systems are to be turned off.

In Australian social policy circles there is a year-round ritual known as
submission writing – agencies' carefully worked out attempts to obtain
financial sponsorship for cherished health and welfare initiatives. The
prologues and epilogues of such submissions find common themes in references to evaluation.

The American literature on this subject has now reached encyclopaedic
proportions (Guttentag and Struening 1975). A new industry and accompanying profession has emerged: the assessment of effects and effectiveness
by professional evaluators. Nothing is sacred. Attempts to decrease dog
litter (Jason 1980) to compare community corrections and incarceration
(Gray *et al.* 1978, 375–400) to contrast the differences in objectives and
performance in school programmes (Jemelka and Borich 1979, 236–76) all
can be evaluated.

Decisions to evaluate are usually an expression of political decision
making. Value judgements are at the hub of evaluative-type decisions
whether to continue an activity, redirect or terminate it. Some evaluations
may be carried out as though they are private organizational and professional concerns. Ultimately, however, they are likely to appear in a public
arena and be acknowledged to be as much a part of a political process as a
consequence of scientific endeavour. In this respect, verdicts on social work
can hardly be formulated without their being linked to wider social and
economic issues.

Even in apparently affluent countries, poverty and homelessness persist.
Some commentators see large pools of unemployment as a permanent feature of economic order. The persistence of such problems affects the most
vulnerable citizens, the social worker's potential clients. In our sifting of
others' research, we shall assess the appropriateness of social workers'
reported activities in relation to the interests of the most powerless groups.

However, our discussion of the criterion of appropriateness comes later.
Before that discussion we shall clarify the research evidence which we have
examined and what we mean by evaluation.

Evaluation defined

Evaluation is a judgement-passing activity. It involves criteria to differentiate´ one thing from another, these criteria depending on values which form a baseline in relation to which judgements can be made. Galtung's (1967) definition, in which he links judgements to values yet distinguishes between them, should be helpful.

> *Evaluation is an act* . . . and consists in the allocation of objects or stimuli of any kind to an element corresponding to 'good', 'neutral', 'bad'. To evaluate is to sort and order stimuli. A value, however, is the principle according to which this sorting or ordering is done.

The values involved in the evaluation of welfare often include a mixture of references to accountability, appropriateness, effect, cost-benefit/cost effectiveness and effectiveness. Although these concerns could be placed at different points along a continuum representing different values and increasing sophistication in research measurements, they often conflict. For example, the home help who socializes with the old people with whom she works takes longer to complete her domestic tasks than a second home help who is not so concerned to establish friendly relationships. Agency managers judge the first home help's activities not cost effective but from the point of the old people, this first home help's intervention may be preferable. Some non-monetary consequences of home help should therefore be considered along with monetary ones.

Rothman stresses that any time the state intervenes in the lives of any of its citizens, it has the obligation to do so in ways that are humane, just and fair. (Rothman 1978). If such a concern with equity becomes the yardstick for assessing social workers' activities, questions about cost effectiveness might be relegated as less important considerations, so that some forms of social work, such as long-term care for the lonely aged, might be assessed in terms of their effectiveness irrespective of costs.

Even the current use and apparent respect for the notion 'cost effectiveness' represents a statement of values. The development of this particular form of evaluation could not have been sustained without politicians and other influential individuals having high regard for notions of financial accountability. But the notion of accountability, as we shall see, is not limited to cost effectiveness. In this respect Senator Baume, the Chairman of the Australian Senate Standing Committee on Social Welfare, described how his interpretation of the purpose and meaning of evaluation had changed.

> I imagined when I got into this evaluation business that we were looking at cost effectiveness . . . some people still think it is about cost effectiveness, punishing bad people, rewarding good ones. I only gradually came to realize that we were looking at something far more basic than that, where power rests and how it is denied to some people.

Senator Baume introduces a key issue, power relationships, into the debate about the place and purpose of health and welfare services in society. In this debate, evaluation can be a sensitive tool or a clumsy threat. Some of the current concern with evaluation sees some politicians and senior administrators in entrenched positions but making assaults – under the guise of evaluation – on activities of which they disapprove.

Evaluations concern not only assessments of outcomes but also involve judgements about the worthiness of objectives. For example, although the esoteric goals of certain professionals might be attained, in terms of the aspirations of ordinary people, outside observers might judge these professionals' activities as an irrelevant luxury. That raises the controversy about appropriateness. There are, however, other usually more immediate conflicts concerning the relationship between objectives and evaluation. These include the issues whether different people have different objectives and/or whether their objectives change in the course of a programme being implemented.

Evaluation requires agreement about the nature of social work and some discussion of its diverse objectives, a task which has some resemblance to wading through a quagmire. Before we embark we ought to make the distinction between evaluation and research and identify the research to which we have referred in this book.

The research material

We have made little use of agency-based evaluations. These involve usually an accounting of resources, cases and costs in relation to programme goals. Unfortunately, the results of such evaluation are seldom completed *and* published, or they exist only as in-house reports and are difficult to obtain. In consequence we have used mostly the studies of researchers who were independent of governments or agencies. Such research is wider than evaluation. In Graycar's terms research represents a probe of reality, as compared with evaluation which he regards as being programme and policy orientated. Researchers tend to have more freedom to decide on their objectives whereas appointed evaluators have to make the most of a programme already existing (Graycar 1979, 460–71).

We have tried to have the best of both worlds. If the objectives of a piece of research aimed, among other things, to identify the effects of a particular social work activity, this suited our purposes. This is not as simple as it sounds. For example, the study *Motherless Families* (George and Wilding 1972) was not preoccupied with social work. But these authors provide valuable information about some fathers' experiences of social work.

We examined research which seemed likely to facilitate our goal of identifying the meaning of the criteria of evaluation used by clients, social workers and others. We have not attempted to review the experimental studies of the effectiveness of certain forms of social work intervention, an exercise which has already been carried out at length on several occasions (Mullen and

Dumpson 1972; Fischer 1976; 1978). There is no point in merely repeating these authors' conclusions but in Chapter 9, in our discussion of the different views of the effects of social work as identified in the disagreements of clients, practitioners and researchers, we will refer to the conclusions of some experimental work.

In examining the findings from non-experimental qualitative research we have been concerned with two main issues. First, we identify the contexts in which social work occurred and in which the research was carried out. For example, if the enquiry referred to a particular ethnic group seeking private casework services in a Manhattan-based agency staffed with highly trained professional specialists, then we say so. A second issue involves a searching for comparability in findings within countries and between them.

Already in this discussion we have referred only loosely to clients and their difficulties and to the types of social work which they encountered. There were a few activities which some might regard as social work which we excluded.

The nature of social work

We regarded social work as involving some service related primarily to individuals' welfare needs. The essential aspects of this description are the provision of a service, from an agency base and provided by someone identified as a social worker. This would not necessarily be a social worker identified by a client. The question of whether the service resulted in change in people's welfare, as seen by the client and others, was among the criteria of evaluation we were looking for.

Our research studies have usually excluded references to community development but they have included a range of other diverse activities, from studies of probation and residential care in Britain to accounts of walk-in mental health centres in the USA, from enquiries into the local authority social work services in England, Wales and Scotland to descriptions of the activities of social workers in government and non-government agencies in Australia. A problem in evaluating the findings of diverse studies concerns the different objectives of outwardly similar activities. The common labels, personal social service or human organizations, or even social work, should not obscure diverse objectives.

Social work objectives

The debate as to whether social work possesses certain objectives because it is a profession or semi-profession is worn and threadbare, leading nowhere. However, the question whether social workers do things differently or more expertly than people not so labelled is not insignificant. It is not easy to answer, partly because people's welfare is not social work's exclusive domain and because social work's objectives are posed often in either extravagant or unexceptional terms.

In Scotland, social workers have been empowered to promote the welfare of all citizens not covered by previous legislation, (Social Work Scotland Act, 1968), whereas in England, Jordan describes the task of social work as 'helping people' (Jordan 1979). Social workers themselves have tried to operationalize such ideal goals in terms of enabling people to 'achieve happiness', 'be independent' or 'become settled' (Rees 1978).

Even if objectives are articulated in manageable terms, it is not always certain that they are carried out or are carried out in the ways originally planned. Williams says that implementation was the Achilles' heel of President Johnson's policy (Williams and Elmore 1975). Sarri concludes that the failure of many programmes has been due to faulty implementation rather than ineffective treatment. (Sarri 1979a, 64).

Our task involves taking no objectives for granted, avoiding professionals-only points of view and realizing that the objectives set at one point in time may change subsequently. Social work is often undertaken in association with the members of other professions and occupations, including sometimes, volunteers who may also be clients. It is not always clear whose objectives are to be assessed; to whom and by what criteria a social worker is held accountable.

Constraints

Consider the confusion of social workers when asked to make links between their objectives and related evaluation criteria. The following example illustrates why evaluation is seldom a simple linking of objectives to outcomes. The constraints of the job are likely to be inherent in any conclusions about performance.

The social worker was employed in a private agency concerned with services for mentally handicapped children. The agency's objective was to place children in long-term residential care. The social worker argued that there was a belief in the field generally that placement in residential care was inevitable for certain mentally handicapped children. Even the specific nature of the objective raised problems. It meant that there was little room to examine whether the child should be in residential care. The existence of the service apparently gave sanction to it. There was little room to question the desirability of separation from parents. The social worker described some problems in fulfilling her objectives.

> . . . I'm in isolation. I am a law unto myself. I am not required to exhibit to anyone in particular what I do. Communication is blocked between those who are in direct contact with clients and the senior executives of the organization who are not welfare trained. The constraints really are the sheer internal politics of it all! Everyone works by themselves. The physiotherapist is in charge. The occupational therapist is in charge. No one is very interested in what the other is doing. Evaluation which might bring the different groups together is not valued.

Such issues confront practitioners daily in trying to overcome some of the constraints of their jobs and in their attempts to discover whether their work is considered effective or whether anyone cares anyway.

Themes

In identifying the meanings of criteria of evaluation, several themes are given prominence. These concern the importance of saying whose views are being referred to and whether these amount to more than opinions. A second theme refers to contexts, an account of types of social work intervention in relation to the personal circumstances of particular clients or client groups. A third theme concerns the relativity of the evidence, including the point that the same things have different connotations for different people.

We have not been impressed by statements about effectiveness or ineffectiveness which did not make us any wiser about the good, indifferent or ill effects of social work on aspects of people's lives. In this respect we needed to know who was making a judgement, from what value base, in relation to what sort of activity. This is why we have separated the judgements of clients from those of social workers, from other criteria used by researchers. Part II is concerned entirely with clients' verdicts. Part III refers to social workers' evaluations of their own practice.

Without some focus on the different contexts of practice, it would be easy to give the impression that people's problems and their expectations of help had a lot in common or that an agency's resources were infinite and social workers' competence uniform. In Chapter 4 of Part II we talk about different clients and different outcomes. In Part III, Chapter 7 we refer to the constraints which, according to social workers, affected what they could achieve.

Pictures of practice, however, depend partly on the conduct of research. This does not mean that we have to give separate consideration to methodology. There are enough books on this subject to clutter many shelves and numerous minds. Even this observation misses the point that methods of research affect the data which they reveal. A description of the contexts of social work can be made clearer if it includes some account of how information was collected and where it came from.

The third theme is highlighted in Part IV. There we refer to a plurality of verdicts on social work. Numerous people reach conclusions. Some have opinions derived from conversations with 'those who know'. Others may pay attention to research. But they are aware of different pieces of evidence or they make different interpretations of the same evidence. In Chapter 9 we refer to the different criteria and the different judgements held by clients, social workers and researchers, apparently about the same things.

The theme, different things to different people involves us in reaching our own conclusions. We are not just sifting and reviewing others' work. We shall give our own verdicts on the achievements and shortcomings of social work. We shall pay attention to the notion of accountability to the most powerless groups, a criterion to which we return in summaries at the end of most chapters.

People with the same responsibilities have different commitments to and different ideas about evaluation. Some feel threatened by it. Some take it for granted. Some think it is a gimmick. This was readily apparent from our interviews with Directors of Social Work throughout Scotland. The notion evaluation was interpreted variously, depending on the activity in the respondents' minds and the criteria being used. These differences form the focus of the following chapter.

2

Managers Muddling Through

If evaluation is 'well done' it should reflect the idiosyncrasies of social work, its specific details in the eyes of some people, its vagueness in the minds of others. It is unwise to think of evaluation in monolithic, absolute and summative terms. Far better to identify what people mean when they talk about evaluation.

We interviewed all the Directors of Social Work in Scotland and also some Australian politicians who were interested in, or who had responsibilities for social welfare. They told us what they understood by evaluation. They portrayed the conditions of theirs and their employees' work. These conditions have much in common with those affecting most personal social service employees, whether in Australia, North America or Europe: the discretionary powers affecting social workers' responsibilities, their accountability to committees of elected local politicians, their sensitivity to media which report social service cutbacks with relish and make sensational headlines of social workers' alleged failures.

Differences in the terms of reference of the agencies in the countries referred to would affect evaluation, so too would regional variations, from one part of one country to another. For example, any researcher would be foolish to ignore consequences of demography in the Scottish regions. These ranged from the sense of isolation and intimacy among administrators and citizens in the far-flung Shetland Islands, (the only barrier to Newfoundland gales reaching eventually the Norwegian coast), to some people's sense of urban anonymity in the industrial Strathclyde region with Glasgow at its hub. They varied according to the biographies and values of the most powerful people in a region, from one Director of Social Work who cherished child-care and saw such activities as a priority, to another who saw the concern with evaluation as a gimmick, and emphasized that 'efficiency is our priority, giving the public value for money, avoiding unnecessary trouble or publicity'.

These references to geography, to rural/urban differences, to the preferences of individual directors, to the peculiar profiles of committees of elected politicians are some of the important dimensions of the contexts of social work. Any verdict about the attainments of social work and social workers should identify these contexts. That is a recurrent theme in this book. The activities of social workers, the assumptions of researchers, and

11

the criteria being used to evaluate social work are embedded in contexts. For example, assumptions about the importance of oil for the Shetlands, of religion in the Hebrides, of the scale of Strathclyde, of the constant tension between Federal and State agencies in Australia, the 'unpredictable' behaviour of politicians everywhere, were aspects of everyday life which affected the views of both professionals and citizens. As such they form part of the data of any evaluation.

In this chapter we discuss how contexts of social work might affect evaluation. We do so not only because our interviews provided interesting glimpses of public officials at work, but also because they provided the threads which recurred throughout our analysis of others' research findings. We use only certain quotes from our tape-recordings in order to illustrate certain points of view.

Our interviewees responded to questions about the meaning of evaluation, about the links between politics and evaluation, about the value of consumers' points of view, about the machinery for evaluating staff effectiveness. Their answers included comments on the differences between staff styles in providing a service and the actual nature and consequence of the service itself. This important distinction is referred to later in our discussion about the differences between process and outcome.*

The themes which the directors identified were of two kinds: those which referred to the constraints influencing their interpretations of evaluation and the conduct of evaluation research in their regions. Secondly, those which referred to differences in the use of 'evaluation', sometimes referring to appropriateness, sometimes to efficiency and effect, occasionally to effectiveness, almost always to accountability.

Different things to different people

The Scottish directors admitted to difficulty in saying what they meant by evaluation. It was a struggle for them to relate 'evaluation' to specific activities. One of them commented, 'in any organized, systematic way evaluation is totally absent'. Another director thought that evaluation was almost always a term depicting judgements of staff by staff:

> we had a survey of effectiveness of services. It was very much a trial and error operation. We told the staff this wasn't intended to be an evaluation of them. But personal evaluations came into it. We endeavoured to make the staff feel that this wasn't the spirit of the operation.

Asked to illustrate what they understood by evaluation, several activities were identified. Three ideas merged. Evaluation was sometimes synonymous with management. This referred to matters concerning the control of staff and resources and the visible consequences of certain specific activities. Secondly, evaluation was related to activities concerned with accountability.

* See Part II., in particular chapter 3 & 4.

This was a continuous concern but seldom deliberately planned. It was a permanent preoccupation yet only triggered into life by certain events. The third concern was with the constant business of assessing and being assessed. This referred to the evaluation of staff by staff. The directors admitted that to their minds the processes of everyday work and life involved evaluation. In this respect evaluation was implicit seldom explicit, inherent yet invisible, governing activities but not according to criteria which were acknowledged openly.

As a concern of management
The heads of numerous organizations like to run things efficiently: the headmaster wants a well disciplined school, the prison governor's survival depends on running a quiet institution, the University Vice-Chancellor hopes for outward signs of student and staff satisfaction. Each may have an abiding psychological need to run their own and others' lives according to timetables of tidiness and predictability.

Irrespective of their own self-images and individual needs and aspirations, the Directors of Social Work paid attention to the demands of other powerful audiences. They played their roles with outsiders in mind. These outsiders were not always individuals. More often they were a general 'them' or 'they': elected councillors, the general public, potential critics and supporters, the senior representatives of other agencies. Or, not surprisingly, some of the activities referred to as evaluation concerned the sense of being able to do things well, or at least to avoid being seen to do them badly.

Most of the following illustrations represent a concern with accountability. Acting as a good manager meant being accountable for the consequences of what they did. For example a director of a mainly rural region said:

> we are constantly trying to find ways, within the limits of our knowledge and resources, to evaluate whether what we think we're doing by the provision of services – fieldwork, residential day-care centres – is in any way achieved.

The same director explained the point that we made in the first chapter, namely that value judgements are linked inextricably with evaluation:

> How can you try and evaluate the personal social services without making explicit your own personal set of values that you are applying before you start. For me it's important to ask what's the point of all this activity apart from the fact that I earn my money, I go on holidays and have a nice time.

In a similar vein the director of the region serving people around Scotland's capital argued that evaluation was involved in consolidating after the massive reorganization of welfare services in 1968. Such consolidation was continuous, 'probably taking about three to four years'. His assessment of effects had to be a conservative check.

> Social work is never a repetitive service. It's always changing. Before you change you should evaluate even though it's not very systematic. It's haphazard. Often evaluation is a check that we are doing what we think we're doing. It leads simply

to a renewal of proven methods rather than a departure. There's always an implication that if you're doing something different you're doing something better. I
suppose the only way to resolve these pressures is through evaluation.

Some sense of accountability

Some employees' sense of accountability to important publics is usually
reflected in their preoccupation with certain priorities which, in Scotland,
were influenced by two concerns. Firstly, the influence of statute set down
by Parliament. Secondly, relationships with local people who were perceived as influential.

One director elaborated on the influence of statutes on evaluation: 'the
ground rules are set down by Parliament. As long as the local authority who
are our employers are satisfied that the statutory commitments are being met
all is quiet.'

This reference to statutory requirements illustrated a concern with some
standards of service and a concern not to be seen to be wasteful. But such
ideas about quality of service and cost-effectiveness were not used in the
sense in which business management might use them regarding commer-
cial products. Quality control in industry would refer among other things
to the attainment of optimum standards. By contrast in social work, minimum standards were sometimes regarded as all that could be realistically
achieved. For example, to some directors, cost effectiveness meant finding
enough staff and other resources merely to keep things going.

The sense of accountability through relationships with key local citizens
was illustrated by staff in rural areas which were often also remote. In these
contexts, accountability and evaluation merged as ways to sustain key relationships in particular ways of life. The director of an island region said:

> Evaluation is tied up with identification of needs and planning to meet particular
> needs. In a small community we have very close relationships with people, with
> elected members. Through our social work committees, our management teams,
> through the networks we've evolved in the community we feel we are pretty well
> able to know what the community feels about how we are operating. It works both
> ways. Accountability means not only general approval but also resistance to
> change as with that hospital for the mentally handicapped which we tried to build.

The directors' accounts of evaluation paint a picture of their managing some
of their tasks by muddling through. In no way does this imply a sense of
chaos. The alternative to muddling through would involve Brave New
World forms of control and predictability. (Huxley 1932) By contrast, social
work managers performed constantly some form of evaluation. They did so
by playing with and to different audiences: staff to staff; to the citizens who
were potential clients; to the influence of politics and politicians.

Assessing and being assessed

Staff to staff

Implicitly at least, employees assess one another's work. Occasionally this is systematic as in the review of frontline staff's work by their seniors, and as in the discussion of criteria affecting promotion. Mostly, staff evaluation is unsystematic rather than planned in the way that research might be. For example, some peer evaluation occurs in allocation meetings as when some social workers are considered more suitable than others to take certain responsibilities. At intake meetings in one area team in Strathclyde one social worker had an alleged habit of volunteering for certain cases. He said, 'I'll take that, I'm dealing with alcoholics.' A colleague responded, 'You're not dealing with alcoholics at all, you are collecting alcoholics.' In most agencies, in most countries, social workers are much more familiar with such unsystematic evaluation than they are with the findings of research, let alone with any consideration of how to apply such findings. Staff play to other audiences. Usually, the concern is with appropriateness and effect, almost always about the processes of social work rather than any judgement that one outcome would be better than another.

Most directors acknowledged that staff supervision was irregular. One director commented:

> Evaluation through supervision is a constant dilemma. It's a living process but no one gets put into a position of critically evaluating his colleague in case that person ever becomes his boss. So, everybody sits back and says nice things about each other. It's all duly recorded and put on file and really that has no meaning at all.

The routine irregularity of supervision was depicted by the director who said, 'review is something that takes place in a very uneven pattern, depending on the approach by the area controller.'

We have unearthed a lot of research which talks about the helpful and unhelpful attributes of social workers and related staff. Few papers have confronted the question whether certain practitioners, by providing one form of service rather than another, will be more effective than others, i.e. a distinction between the effect of the person and the effectiveness of the service.

Seldom is the question of effect or effectiveness an explicit criterion affecting promotion. Most directors had their own notions about the criteria of suitability for promotion. Few were as blunt as the one who said, 'the personal quality of a social worker is paramount. Their professional capabilities are secondary'. Asked to identify personal qualities, he replied, 'a certain level of intelligence, a certain capability to express themselves, a certain insight into people, a certain concern to help people who have problems.'

Apparently the criteria to evaluate who should or who should not be promoted were contained in the directors' heads. Intuitively, at least, several directors felt they knew why they would promote some people but not others. One admitted, 'it's all in the director's head. Any sensible director would know what he felt his staff could do and who's the best at doing what and who showed the most potential.'

Using clients' evaluations

In subsequent sections of this book we discuss the common denominators in clients' appraisal of social work and social workers. Contrary to what has been argued (Mayer and Timms 1970) far more research has been done on listing clients' expectations and appraisals than on social workers evaluating their own work. In addition to this research, several authors have advocated machinery for building in clients' opinion as an inherent part of agency evaluation. Some clients or client groups are seen as a taken-for-granted part of the decision making procedure of social service agencies (Giordano 1977; Rees 1978 Ch. 6). But problems remain. How do you elicit a client opinion? How do you ensure that it represents a cross-section of people who use services? How do you ensure that it has any subsequent effect on the distribution of resources, including professionals' time?

There was no consensus among the Scottish directors that clients' opinions were valued and important. Existing feedback was unsystematic, *ad hoc* and usually related to the business of complaints. Some evaluation occurred as a result of dissatisfied citizens 'going to the top'. Some aggrieved individuals wrote to their Member of Parliament. Others addressed complaints to the Chief Executive of the region, the senior administrative officer with responsibility to oversee all services including social work. More often than not, complaints came through elected councillors. One director explained, 'the usual source of complaint is through elected members holding their surgeries. People have a habit here of making complaints to their councillors. After that I have six councillors buzzing around me with little names on little lists and so on.'

Much of the research which we discuss later is concerned with the processes of social work, with identifying some intangible aspects of services. By contrast clients' complaints were said to be about two relatively tangible things: the unavailability of practical items; being in queues and on waiting lists.

One director explained, 'most of the complaints have been in connection with the refusal by social workers to provide practical things such as money to see about housing, to take a child into care, to provide a place in an old peoples' home.'

The second point of view is explained by the director who said, 'wherever you have waiting lists you have complaints, whether it is the day nursery, for day care centres for the aged, for home help etc.'

Only one director mentioned complaints other than the two items referred to above. Even then he was confirming what has been found elsewhere. (Mayer and Timms 1970). Some people he found were dissatisfied with social workers because they were not openly partisan in taking one point of view rather than another. Others, however, complained about social workers being one-sided!

The only way we get involved in trying to evaluate consumers' points of view is if complaints are investigated. We've discovered here that the complaints are mainly about rudeness or not taking care in marital disputes, complaints that the social worker takes one side or another.

The evaluations of clients, researchers and social workers can be complementary, though sometimes they are totally at variance. Each of the directors recognized not only the considerable difficulty in collecting consumers' evaluations but also in knowing what reliance to place upon them. The difficulties included the feeling that the famous 'silent majorities' were never heard, that only the assertive and articulate raised their voices.

In weighing the importance of clients' evaluations, the low expectations and passivity of the most powerless groups has been a strong theme in much literature, in Australia, (McCaughey and Chew 1977) in Scotland (Rees 1978) and in the United States (Perlman 1975). The directors recognized that, particularly with the elderly, this passivity affected such clients' views. If social workers were trying to elicit the points of view of the elderly who were already in care, a sense of fear and a reluctance to bite the hand that fed them affected such people's response to being asked their opinions: 'The elderly are inhibited almost always from saying what they really feel and would like to see because to a certain extent their lives are depersonalized when they come into residential care.'

Even in the most carefully selected client sample it would be foolish to claim that people would be wholly representative of those who obtain services, let alone of those who need them. The directors heard frequently of the well organized opinion of pressure groups. Such views could hardly be regarded as representing client opinion overall. One director explained this with reference to a certain Society for the mentally handicapped:

> Here I would say that they are something of a problem. It's almost as though there's no other client groups. The danger is that if you get a pressure group with an organization behind them and a very powerful advocate at the head it can distort policies. We do have a problem here of making sure that those who don't have a voice are not pushed aside.

Another group whom the directors claimed to have almost always paid attention to were foster parents. It seems that wherever professionals regard certain groups as resources to them and as potential colleagues, then machinery for eliciting those individuals' opinions is maintained. One director explained a point of view which was shared by others:

> Registering the usefulness of consumers' opinions is an area we have underestimated except probably regarding foster parents. When we are looking for service improvements we do try to get together with the foster parents and the natural parents to hear what they have to say. We need to listen to them and we do.

The meaning and merits of clients' views could be assessed in relation to the views of social workers and others, a point stressed by the director who said, 'Probably the best way to secure useful evaluation is to get a cross bearing on perceptions of different people.'

Those directors who valued clients' evaluations concluded that their being known to have such attitudes could have the effect of raising peoples' expectations unrealistically. Such a process was also thought to have been facilitated by other events. Publicity in the 1970s regarding expenditure on the personal social services may have raised public expectations. But there is a contrast between the optimism of some legislation and the pessimistic fatalism of some potential recipients of services. Some ambitious goals contained in legislation and in the minds of highly motivated social workers were regarded as having affected potential clients' evaluations. Such evaluations would also be affected by the low expectations of those relatively powerless people who had had poor experience of people in positions of authority and who had preferred to keep themselves to themselves. This final warning was given by the director who had held several different positions in Scottish regions since the reorganization of services in 1969: 'One of the great mistakes we made in 1969 was to over-sell ourselves. We more or less said that with our comprehensive agencies we can look after people from the cradle to the grave.'

The influence of politics and politicians

Unless the constraints of politics and politicians are built into evaluation studies, one important source of data will always be missing. The choice of what is to be evaluated and how has been influenced unduly by administrative politics within organizations and by the wider audience of elected representatives. Health and welfare managers' concern with evaluation is spasmodic, jerked into life on the occasions of budgets, applications for renewal of funds, sensational scandals and other forms of criticism in the media. Politicians and managers are not necessarily cynical. They are in the business of impression management. The sensitive politician demonstrates to his cabinet colleagues and through the media to a wider public, his department's concern with some forms of accountability, as, in New South Wales, through an evaluation of a Family Support Services Scheme. (Alexander and Sutton 1980). The manager of a large American voluntary agency has to dramatize staff virtues to the potential financial supporters of that agency. (Stanton 1970) The Director of an Australian Community Welfare Department or the Director of the Scottish Social Work Department present particular images to their political paymasters. These images concern politically sensitive aspects of evaluation, the visible demonstration that worthy work is being done in a worthy way. Such images don't necessarily reflect faithfully what is occurring in the department or what is a staff priority.

The political climate in which demands for evaluation are being made should be acknowledged. Directly and indirectly, evaluation is a political activity: directly because the values used toward a judgement stem from political considerations; indirectly because the motivation behind the evaluation and the digestion of results are influenced by the ebb and flow of what politicians consider to be public concerns. These would not necessarily involve answering the question whether needy and powerless people received appropriate services and whether such services made any permanent difference to these people's lives.

The Scottish directors knew that evaluation involved paying attention to their elected members. It was not done systematically but they did play carefully to political audiences, at certain times.

Election time interests

In local government, at least, politicians' interest in the efficiency or effectiveness of social work services was said to increase nearer election time. Even in an island region where elected members were described as having 'no political allegiances', the director acknowledged that in response to government circulars, 'Most fighting over issues occurs at election time. They try and find out which are the most important issues. They really take this very seriously.'

Contentious issues in most local elections and in most countries concern the allocation of money and the publication of budgets. But in Scotland in this respect social workers, let alone client groups, were relatively ignorant and without much influence. Almost by definition, powerless client groups did not have political platforms. Services with already few resources were usually at the bottom of politicians' league table of priorities. The director of a large rural region said poignantly, 'the overall sense of this council is like most other councils. They don't want to increase the rate but they want good services. Social services effectiveness is a hassle in between.'

Not all social workers' activities were regarded as a hassle. In between the concern with 'sound budget sense' and commitment to good services, only certain social work activities were selected as worth promoting. The things to be evaluated were the things to be valued. In this respect evaluation went hand in hand with the promotion of some services rather than others, usually for children and the aged, seldom over court and penal matters.

In an area which had always returned a socialist member to the Westminster Parliament, in which Trades Union membership was high, 'support for social work' usually meant 'care for the elderly'. The director explained,

> They support the aged here. This area has the strongest presence of the Scottish Old Age Pension Association. The General Secretary lives here. That's why on the social work committees there's always political pressure to maintain concessionary fares for the elderly.

The interests of the elected Social Work Committee in another region were described by the director,

> Anything to do with delinquents or penal matters doesn't have the same interest for this committee. Anything to do with the elderly, the disabled or child care generally then they will listen very attentively and very sympathetically.

Politicians' and social workers' priorities

Social workers have their own preferences and priorities. They also are reminded daily of the need to provide a continuity of care not influenced by financial considerations. But the managers of services were conscious of high watermarks at budget and election times when they were asked for evidence of the effects of only certain forms of care.

Different frames of reference and a different consciousness of the notion 'service' ensure a clash in perspectives over what should be evaluated and what should be a priority. In Scotland, local politicians were alleged to be more concerned with the visible effects of the personal social services. Social workers, conversant with some processes of change, were not so obviously concerned with the visible display of 'doing good works'. On the contrary they showed an almost inept disdain for handling the media. They didn't publicize what they thought should be the hub of social workers' activities. In consequence, diverse views of social work were maintained. For example, one social work committee was concerned with using some part of its departmental budget to have old peoples' lawns cut. By contrast the director commented, 'Professional social workers don't regard this as social work. It's not going to be a priority compared with making sure that old people maintain reasonable independence.'

Another director contended that broad principles and concepts seldom influenced local politicians. They were not trained to this way of thinking. They preferred to have figures demonstrating the effects of their administration. By contrast, concerns with quality not quantity were said to be social workers' criteria for assessing job effectiveness.

> Quality reasons are not acceptable to the local authorities in the main. Sometimes on our social work committees I think we get around to using statistics, sometimes pseudo statistics and sometimes statistics which were not a hundred per cent acceptable anyway, is that what evaluation means?

The same director said that 'proving cost effectiveness' gave him the most leverage with local authority committees. The only other form of evaluation which was acceptable to the committee concerned the telling anecdote on the individual deserving case. At that point a politician's adrenalin began to run: 'You have to come in with emotional arguments. "Someone is at risk of dying unless you do something".'

These contrasts will be discussed in later chapters. Different evaluators have different interpretations of what is social work let alone what is good social work. Political constraints influence the activities which were placed under some scrutiny. Often that scrutiny was concerned to produce statistics showing some link between the expenditure of money and the service provided. The only exception to this general conclusion concerns the fascination within individual cases which some observers, including politicians, may have chosen to regard as the tip of an iceberg.

It was apparent that in everyday terms, politicians, social workers and administrators differed in what they considered to be the objectives of social work. They also differed, therefore, in what they understood by evaluation. In consequence they produced different verdicts on different topics.

Directors' disagreements with elected members foreshadow other conflicts of view, as in the lack of common ground between social workers', clients' and researchers' evaluations. Other conflicting verdicts which we shall uncover are of a more subtle kind, as depicted in the creative tension which often exists between the alleged shortcomings of an overall programme and the outcome of any one particular event or case in that programme (Bryson 1979).

The meanings of different criteria of evaluation can be unravelled by identifying the contexts in which the judgements made by different people with different frames of reference exist. In this respect the views of the Scottish Directors of Social Work, that they had to keep several different audiences in mind and for that reason felt obliged to muddle through as efficiently and as sensitively as possible, provide a more apt view of the operation of on-going evaluation in social work than any image of careful flow charts, of contentions about cost effectiveness through management by objectives, or of apparently systematic hierarchical schemes to demonstrate accountability.

Summary

Managers of social work agencies and politicians in several countries have different interpretations of the meaning and purpose of evaluation. Yet, all are affected by the constraints and opportunities provided by evaluation-type activities: the preoccupation with running an organization with as little trouble as possible; the assessment of staff by their colleagues; the difficulties of collecting systematically and then using clients' opinions; the concern, in particular at election and budget times, with critical audiences of politicians and other interested outsiders.

These are only some of the events involving evaluation and the conditions affecting such activities. Later in this book we discuss what can be expected from evaluation and whether the time, money, print and paper spent on it has any desirable effect on overriding social issues, such as the prevalence of poverty, the permanence of unemployment. Before we get that far we should consider what can be learned from relatively powerless groups, those clients whose views have been sought by researchers in different countries. How have clients evaluated their experiences?

Part II
Clients Evaluate their Experiences

Introduction

The literature reporting clients' evaluations of the personal social services is the source and material of Part II. Our aim is to identify the criteria used by clients when they evaluate their experiences with social workers and social work agencies. All the material used is derived from research conducted within the last two decades in the following areas:

1 Studies in which the exploration of clients' views has been a central concern of the research
2 Studies in which clients' views have been only a peripheral concern
3 Biographical accounts by clients themselves (included for the purpose of illustration)
4 Material from research findings in fields closely related to the social services (e.g. medicine/law/psychotherapy)

Comparing material from related fields enables us to both identify any correspondence in findings, and to indicate social work conclusions which stand alone.

The studies and the methods utilized vary. They differ in sample size, the largest study involving over 3,500 people, the smallest fewer than ten. The depth of analysis also varies. The quality of information that can be derived from very intensive, semi-structured interviews repeated over a long period is different from that acquired by one-off structured questionnaires sent through the post, or in one case, administered over the phone in an estimated time of two minutes. The literature refers mainly to North American and British research but also includes material from Australia.

An appraisal of clients' verdicts defies simple analysis. This is not surprising given the diverse nature and scope of social work. Clients are not homogeneous. Different client groups need different kinds of help. The problems of the elderly, the mentally handicapped, probationers, the poor, are diverse. Apparently similar groups express different needs.

Clients' evaluations do not occur in a vacuum. Both between and within client groups, clients' expectations and their orientations to seeking help and solving problems differ. Some clients are seeking help for the first time in their lives. Others have had experience of contact with the social services – spanning years. Some are evaluating the social services in terms of one brief, initial contact. Others are concerned with evaluating social work of a long-term nature. The clients referred to in some studies have encountered a variety of social work agencies and personnel and the nature and content of social work experienced by the clients is not necessarily similar.

Two patterns emerge from the studies: (1) A common finding is that clients' feelings of satisfaction and being helped are related to characteristics of the social worker, to the relationship between clients and social workers and the general tone of the encounters as perceived by the clients. (2) The other recurrent criterion for evaluation used by clients relates to the outcome of their help-seeking experiences.

This distinction between clients' perception of the service, and that of their interpersonal experiences during the help-seeking process, is not new. For example, one researcher divided the comments of people approaching a British local authority Social Services Department for the first time into those referring to the personal quality of the encounter, the time and frequency of contact, and the actual outcome (Jordan 1976). A client seeking help with obtaining accommodation had mixed feelings about the department. Although the social worker's manner, and the advice given was appreciated, practical help did not materialize.

Other researchers have divided clients' comments on agency contact into 'outcomes', 'treatment process' and 'counsellor' (Beck and Jones 1973), into 'relationship-centred satisfaction' and 'problem-centred satisfaction' (Tessler 1975) and into 'client-worker relationship' and 'satisfaction with outcome' (Maluccio 1977). Goldberg (1970) has highlighted the importance to the elderly of their relationship with the social worker, whether or not they receive certain practical help. Similar findings have been found in studies relating to multi-problem families, the mentally and physically handicapped – indeed relating to all client groups.

The distinction made between comments pertaining to the social worker and his or her initiatives, and the actual outcome of contact, is important. But it is often blurred. The difficulty occurs when it is far from clear what exactly the client is referring to in his appraisal. In summarizing 300 clients' evaluations of their experiences with a Local Authority Social Services Department, the authors comment,

> The consumers' feelings of satisfaction were also bound up with attitudes towards their social workers. Although we tried to differentiate between the consumers' attitudes towards the Department, the services received and their individual worker, it proved difficult to achieve (McKay *et al*. 1973, 489).

Recognition of the difficulties in making these distinctions is not peculiar to social work. Freidson (1961) found that patients' satisfaction with medical care was bound up with how they perceived the physician. Another medical study (Caplan and Sussman 1966) of an outpatient service found that 'medical care' (the highest rated criterion of patient evaluation) was associated with a group of variables such as the physician's expression of interest and time spent with the patient. Such studies indicate the importance of the physician-patient relationship in patient assessment of medical services.

Part II is divided into three chapters. The first of these, Chapter 3, is concerned with clients' evaluative criteria which cannot be easily separated from the individual involved in the provision of service. It deals with aspects of social workers' personalities, styles and methods of working. It attempts to elucidate whether differences in how these are evaluated depend on such factors as the type of help being sought by clients, or on the particular stage of the help-seeking process. Chapter 4 includes clients' opinions of whether or not they had received a service as an *outcome* of the process of seeking help. It explores the extent to which the perceived value and nature of those outcomes depends on who the client is and the kind of problem he is faced with. Chapter 5 provides a critical evaluation of the material in the previous two chapters. It discusses the research findings on clients' evaluations in relation to matters of methodology and broad contextual features. In so doing it enables us to make some judgements about the meaning and merits of clients' views.

3

Helpful People and Initiatives

The manner or style in which social workers respond to their clients is important because it is often on the basis of this encounter that the latter make judgements about the help-seeking process. These judgements can make the difference between a person deciding whether or not it is worthwhile continuing contact, and whether or not he or she feels they are going to be helped.

In exploring what people are looking for in their encounters with social workers, and the styles of intervention they prefer, we found that two things are crucial. For clients to feel that social workers are helpful people, the latter have to display certain qualities that are often personal in nature. But people require further 'proof' of social workers' helpfulness. Social workers must also display a willingness to take various forms of action based on their experience and knowledge. It is the combination of the *personal* and the *professional* styles which forms the basis of this chapter.

Personal interest and concern

Perhaps not surprisingly, it is of great importance to clients that the social worker is personally interested in, and concerned with, their well-being. This concern is one common denominator appreciated by people seeking different forms of help. For example, clients of Southampton Social Services Department (Glampson and Goldberg 1976), whose problems prompting contact included physical handicap, child care, mental illness, housing and finance, thought that an ability to take an interest in people was one of the main desirable personal qualities of the social worker. Clients of other local authority departments, probation offices, specialized casework agencies, Family Service Unit etc. think likewise.

Personal services in other fields are evaluated similarly. Patients' perceptions of personal interest and concern for them by physicians have been significant in their evaluations of medical care (Freidson 1961). Young people's assessment of their job satisfaction in a variety of work places has been related to the concern and interest shown in them by the 'boss' or the foreman (Carter 1966). Patients have indicated favourable evaluations of similar qualities in psychotherapists (Orlinsky and Howard 1967). Why do clients feel these attitudes are desirable and how does the social worker communicate his or her personal interest and concern to the client?

People coming into contact with the social services hold differing views and expectations as to the nature of the personal encounter they will experience. Most are bewildered and confused largely due to their ignorance of the workings and functions of social work. Hazy and conflicting notions from referral agents and acquaintances of what can be expected contribute to this confusion. Contradictions and inconsistencies in the attitudes of previous 'helpgivers' compound this further. Previous and on-going help-seeking experiences with other official agencies, such as social security, housing departments and charity organizations are often far from pleasant. (Mayer and Timms 1970; Rees 1974; Sainsbury 1975). They are usually formal in nature and lacking in sympathy. Sometimes as a result of these experiences people feel stigma and shame in admitting to a formal agency that for one reason or another they have difficulty in coping with some aspect of their lives. This can give rise to expectations that are suspicious, hostile and even fearful. Together these experiences result in broadly two types of expectation. Either clients feel that their meetings with social workers are unlikely to be any more comfortable than their previous contacts with other officials, or they regard social workers as being their last hope of getting help. The pessimistic view appears to be the most prevalent. A typical comment being,

> I thought down there (at the FWA*) it would be like the Social Security. They are very abrupt there. Then they call your name out and you talk in front of other people. They don't really want to know about you (Mayer and Timms 1970, 104).

Unpleasant experiences like these are as likely to occur with Australian (Bryson 1979) and American (Varon 1962) social security officials as their British counterparts. But some clients have far more optimistic expectations about the quality of the personal encounter with the social worker. They hope that their contact will be different from the dismissive and routine experiences encountered with officials elsewhere (Jordan 1976). While it is unclear what accounts for the differences in these expectations, they go some way towards explaining why personal interest is such a concern of the client. What are the activities and behaviour which convey this interest to the client and convince him or her that the social worker is a helpful person? Three things are prominent – social workers treating clients as people not 'cases', helping them to feel at ease, and expending effort on their behalf.

People not cases

Repeatedly, clients emphasize how much they value a warm, informal and sympathetic approach by the worker. These attributes are equated with caring. The qualities described are those of a 'good friend'. The importance to clients of being treated as a person and not just another case depends partly on what they expect from social work departments in the first place. The variation in knowledge and expectations of people approaching a social work department suggests that the client's initial contact with the agency personnel can take on a special importance. It is sometimes overlooked that

* Refers to the voluntary, London-based, Family Welfare Association.

the first person a client will meet with is more likely to be a receptionist than a social worker. Part of Hall's (1974) study of the 'point of entry' to several English children's departments investigated the impact of the reception process on clients. Although he did not directly ask the clients involved their opinions of how they were treated, he did spend time observing this reception. Many clients suffered obvious discomfort. Some receptionists were hardened to tales of misery and misfortune and failed to react sympathetically. For example, insensitive to the fact that the room was full of waiting people, they would often request clients to speak up more loudly when discussing their personal problems. Although it is impossible to say how much this treatment affected later evaluations, there is evidence to suggest that the memory of what happens at this stage can remain in people's minds for some time. Having perhaps left the seeking of help until a crisis situation arises, at this point many people are no doubt particularly sensitive. This appeared to be the case amongst widowed and divorced mothers in America, seeking help from a variety of specialist helpers (Weiss 1972). Long after contact, these women recalled their dissatisfaction with the reception. Expecting a personal approach, they felt a loss of personal worth when they were subject to a kind of 'social invisibility' and were kept waiting for a long time before seeing anyone, all the while being ignored by the official personnel.

Researchers in the social work and medical fields are becoming increasingly aware of the potential significance of clients' reaction at this stage for their evaluations of later contact (Freidson 1961; White 1973). Just how significant they may be in the world of social work remains to be investigated, but one piece of research which included an analysis of the receptionists in a medical practice concluded:

> These personnel are (thus) inextricably connected with the patients' conception of the care they receive: as agents through whom the patient must pass before he reaches the doctor, they can colour the patients' relation to the doctor himself. (Freidson 1961, 78).

What does the client think is important once he or she actually meets the social worker? A number of studies have shown that people are more likely to evaluate this first contact according to the social workers' perceived 'personalities' rather than what the social workers actually do (Sainsbury and Nixon 1979). For example, people seeking counselling from a Catholic Family Service Agency in America felt that in the initial session the emotional aspect of the client-worker relationship was most important (Maluccio 1977). At this early stage of contact clients made fewer references to such things as the workers' skill and competence. Warmth, sympathy, friendliness and informality are appreciated most at this point in the help-seeking process. Over and over again clients talk of the social worker being a 'friend', being 'homely', or 'just like us': 'I thought they'd be uppety – they were right friendly as though it were your relation instead of a social worker' (Sainsbury 1975, 86).

Retarded mothers with young children took comfort from a similarity in language between themselves and the worker which helped them relax: 'Well, she's 'omely. She doesn't talk posh so you talk to her properly. Get any posh one you can't really talk to them, can you? (laughs) but she's just like us and you can talk to 'er' (Cohen 1971, 37).

Being treated in such a manner is a pleasant surprise to people who expected a less sympathetic response. But we should be wary of oversimplifying these concepts of 'warmth', 'friendliness', etc. Many researchers appear to assume that what constitutes a 'warm' approach is fairly obvious. Such assumptions are not always justified. Lishman (1978), when evaluating her own social work practice in a child guidance clinic, discovered that although she thought she was utilizing a warm, supportive approach not all her clients perceived her style in this way. Indeed, some clients interpreted her approach as being persecuting, rather than supportive. Lishman's findings suggest that we cannot take the terms 'warmth' and 'concern' for granted.

What are the activities social workers engage in which encourage clients to feel that someone is taking a personal interest in their plight? It often pleases a client when social workers take an interest in them outside the perceived scope of contact. For example, asking clients about their families (Sainsbury 1975), taking an interest in their hobbies and activities (Gottesfeld 1965), visiting outside officia' working hours (Sainsbury 1975; Beck and Jones 1973) – such actions do much to convince people that the social worker's interest is genuine. He or she is not just 'doing a job'. This reinforces the clients' perception of the social worker as a 'friend' rather than a 'professional'.

It is important to clients that the social worker does not appear bored, and that he or she listens attentively to what the client has to say. Things like the social worker staring out of the window while the client is talking (Reith 1975; Kline, Adrian and Spevak 1974) keeping the client waiting (Hoffman 1975) failing to apologize if the interview is interrupted by a phone call (Worby 1955) breaking appointments at the last minute (Timms 1973) – all these have caused some distress to people expecting a more personal approach. Such behaviours have been interpreted not just as ill-manners but also as a lack of concern. When such things occur social workers confirm the expectations of some clients that social workers are, in fact, no different from other officials.

Clients also value social workers who are good and patient listeners. Patients in a hospital stressed how much they valued 'informed listening' by the medical social workers (Butrym 1968). Moreover, this was felt to be important in its own right, regardless of the type or amount of practical help received later. Similarly, mothers of mentally handicapped children value a doctor's willingness to listen, even if the doctor cannot actually do anything else. As one mother explains: 'She helps you to talk and listens to what you have to say . . . she waits till you've had time to make up your own mind' (Sainsbury 1975, 87).

Clients particularly appreciate being listened to if they are in a state of crisis and have sought help elsewhere unsuccessfully. Social workers taking the time to listen when no one else would, can be interpreted by clients as acknowledging the seriousness of their problem. Thus parents of young boys with behavioural difficulties explained how this listening enhanced their self-esteem (Oxley 1977).

A patient and unhurried approach is especially appreciated by clients who compare their social work experiences with other help-seeking experiences, with professionals (Butrym 1968), officials (Jordan 1976) and their informal network of friends (Rees 1974; Sainsbury 1975) and relatives (Mayer and Timms 1970). Other professionals are often perceived as being too busy to have time to devote to clients. A mother of a young mentally handicapped child had regularly visited medical authorities and then eventually was put in contact with a social worker, of whom she commented,

> I was quite surprised they had the time to bother because they've lots of people to deal with and maybe my case, it was big to me, but it was quite trivial to them. But she was kind and could be bothered. I never knew this sort of thing existed at all (Rees 1974, 259).

Appreciation of an unhurried approach and being treated as a person is not peculiar to social work. Freidson's (1961) study of patients and their physicians illustrates how crucially important it is that the doctor is not abrupt and 'mechanical' in his dealings with the patient. Such mechanistic attributes may be adequate for purely scientific, medical purposes, but they 'leave no room for an encounter with the personal identity which the patient imputes to his own body' (Freidson 1961, 52). An overly clinical atmosphere and a rapid turnover of physicians can enhance this feeling of being on a conveyor belt, and being treated as a case.

Putting clients at ease

Some people feel stigma and shame in admitting to a formal agency that for one reason or another they have difficulty in coping with interpersonal and/or practical problems in their lives. Others, although they don't feel stigmatized themselves, anticipate that their contacts with the department will be uncomfortable. They can feel a sense of hostility towards and suspicion of social work departments, sometimes expecting to experience a punitive and judgemental authority. By no means *all* clients feel this anxiety. However, the ability to make a client feel at ease is a criterion of evaluation often mentioned by clients. Thus it is important here to examine two things:

1 which clients are likely to hold such views
2 what activities of social workers can help alleviate such feelings.

Researchers often use the notion stigma uncritically. Few studies have examined in any detail the difference between those people who feel ashamed, and those who don't. There is some evidence to suggest that stigma is felt particularly amongst clients seeking material or financial aid from an agency, although there are exceptions. In seeking such help, clients are more likely to have to 'swallow their pride'.

> I felt belittled by going there. It's just like going up and saying, 'Can you give me some money for this (holds out an ashtray)? Who am I to you that you should turn and help me (Mayer and Timms 1970, 101).

It has been suggested that the more educated clients are and the longer they have been receiving welfare, the more likely it is that they feel stigmatized (Horan and Austin 1974). Receiving financial help in the short term allows clients to believe that they have only temporarily lost their independence and this lessens feelings of shame. But elderly people who have been taught that asking help from others is a sign of weakness usually continue to stress their pride in financial independence (Rees 1978), and people who persistently regard the acceptance of financial or material help as a 'favour' rather than a 'right' to which they are entitled, often continue to feel stigma (Briar 1966). But, an American study (Horan and Austin 1974) of 50 female AFDC* recipients found that those women who knew more about Welfare Rights Organizations were less likely than others to be bothered by asking for or receiving material help. That is, they received knowledge which equipped them with values which encouraged them to discard feelings of stigma. Friends and acquaintances can also be influential in this respect. Jewish clients in America have reference group approval for accepting material help. They therefore have less qualms about taking up such help than other Americans (Rosenfeld 1964). That the support of family and friends can provide important reassurance that their reasons for seeking help are not 'blameworthy', has also been demonstrated amongst the clients of a voluntary and a local authority agency in Scotland (Rees 1978).

Which clients tend to feel suspicion or fear on referral to a social work department? Most of the studies which mention such feelings existing amongst clients fail to analyse reasons *why* this should be. For example, one-parent families' initial reactions to the use of volunteers have been shown to be apprehensive and suspicious (Humphries 1978). But the reasons why are not examined. Ten clients attending a children's department for the first time also exhibited considerable apprehension.

> I didn't know how they would react to me. I thought they might be a bit funny, not being married and going to have a kid (Reith 1975).

Once again, the origin of such fears is not examined. What is perhaps significant, is that such feelings are common amongst people with childcare difficulties. Many of these people, at least on initial contact, connect clinic or agency attendance with embarrassment, shock or some other negative

---

* Refers to Aid to Families with dependent children.

state (Burck 1978; Humphries 1978; Oxley 1977; Reith 1975). Fear of being judged a 'bad' parent and a greater fear of their children being removed by the agency have much to do with attitudes. This is particularly the case amongst clients who associate social work departments with law enforcement agencies and courts (Varon 1962).

Having established that some clients in some situations do feel shame or apprehension, what kinds of activities of the social workers can alleviate such anxieties or embarrassment? Unfortunately, many of the studies highlighting clients' appreciation of being helped to feel at ease do not then proceed to outline what it is that makes the client feel this way. Only those studies which have probed clients' reactions in more depth have provided inklings as to how the social worker manages peoples' feelings of apprehension.

The ability and willingness of the worker to anticipate and articulate what help is required has been described favourably by clients (Eisenthal and Lazare 1976). If material help is desired, a client may feel reluctance in making explicit his or her request, particularly if he or she feels ashamed of being financially dependent. Actually requesting such help can be perceived as a further humbling and demeaning of oneself (Mayer and Timms 1970). Even requesting a simple practical service can be perceived this way. As a housebound physically handicapped woman explained, 'You don't always like asking . . . (especially) when you want your hair cutting . . . when you feel so dependent' (Barker, 1975, 78). If the social worker anticipates such a request, this relieves the client of some discomfort or embarrassment. It also helps convince the client that the social worker and agency are truly 'caring'.

Only a couple of studies have examined the opinions of clients on actual receipt of material help. Clients receiving financial help from Family Welfare Association appreciated the fact that the money was handed over in an envelope and not counted out pound by pound (Mayer and Timms 1970). Being reassured by the worker that they should not feel ashamed and that they are entitled to such aid, also helps. Stressing the cost of some piece of equipment or adaptation (Blaxter 1976) or the shortage of resources (Sainsbury 1975) however, does not help ease of take up. The comments of a client illustrate the sensitivity felt when a social worker provided her with a loan but told her not to return for more. 'I don't think he realized what he'd said. He didn't take our word. He was rotten, rotten. He should never have said what he did' (Sainsbury 1975, 42–3).

The form material help takes can make a difference to clients' feelings. An American study (Stuart 1975) of 30 families on AFDC, found that clients' feelings of stigma and inadequacy were associated more with receiving cash benefits than 'in-kind' benefits in the form of subsidies, food stamps, etc. Receipt of actual cash implies greater dependency of the client on the state and thus greater shame and lower status. Receipt of 'in-kind' benefits, however, can be regarded more as a supplement as a 'helping hand' rather than a total income requirement, and this enables people to retain feelings of self-respect.

What about feelings of shame experienced by people seeking help with interpersonal problems? How is their discomfort alleviated? Part of the answer lies in the previously mentioned criteria – a friendly reception, a sympathetic ear and an unhurried approach. In addition, the importance of the social worker being *non-judgemental* in his or her responses and attitudes is often stressed. People of lower socio-economic origin seeking help with a variety of problems (Silverman 1969), young men on probation (Gottesfeld 1965), adolescents seeking counselling (Worby 1955), multi-problem families (Jackson 1973) and patients seeking psychotherapy (Orlinsky and Howard 1967) – all emphasize the desirability of this. Social workers being non-prying and non-judgemental was a source of satisfaction for several clients visiting a Family Service Unit agency in London – who had previously experienced themselves, or had heard from friends, about 'nosey' workers (Jackson 1973). Although some clients do appreciate that it is necessary for the social worker to ask some questions, too many questions too early in contact can at times only confirm a client's suspicions that he or she is being judged or cross-examined. Being reassured that anything clients say is treated confidentially and not passed on to other agencies, can also be a help (Mayer and Timms 1970). (Although it is interesting to note that 'confidentiality', does not always loom all that large in the perspective of clients – contrary to what social workers might think (Maluccio 1977).) Joking and reassuring the client that they are valued and should not feel ashamed has also helped the client (Reith 1975). Parents of young boys with behavioural problems were very sensitive to insinuations that they were 'bad parents' (Oxley 1977). The social worker's approach of 'positive reinforcement', of assuring parents that they were important to their child, and important as people in their own right was much appreciated. It brought relief to the parents who were often guilt-ridden about their child, and it gave them hope and strength for the future.

But no matter what the social worker does, some clients, particularly those with very negative perceptions of social workers, continue to feel fear and hostility. This is not surprising. No matter how 'caring' a children's department, it always potentially has the power to be coercive.

Even though clients have been helped by social workers to overcome their feelings of mistrust or apprehension, this does not necessarily change their general attitude towards the agency of department. That is, their suspicion or fear may be abandoned in relation to their particular worker, but not the agency in general. The social worker can be made into an exception. Sainsbury and Nixon's (1979) study of clients of a probation office, local authority department and a Family Service Unit found that most clients feel that their particular social workers are more humane and caring than is the norm for agency practice. A similar belief was expressed by a number of women who were former clients of a childcare agency in America (Varon 1962). Such feelings suggest that previous experience in seeking help does not necessarily make the client less anxious on the second or third time round, given that his expectation of the *agency* may not have changed.

Doing things

By 'doing things' or attempting to do things for clients, social workers confirm their concern and willingness to help. Clients frequently regard worker activity as being denotive of genuine concern. People are especially appreciative of an activist approach if they perceive it as being expended beyond the requirements of the social workers' official role in that they are involved in activities on behalf of clients not just in their capacity as employees of the social services department, but also as individuals. Indeed no clients attending the various agencies in Sainsbury and Nixon's study (1979) described a social worker's over-activity as 'officious'.* An activist approach can consist of several things. For example, it can encompass the giving of advice. Lack of advice has been taken as 'proof' of social workers' lack of concern by mothers with family problems (Cohen 1971), and also by multi-problem families (Kline *et al.* 1974). Making arrangements for people is another valued activity. Adolescents receiving intermediate treatment evaluated positively social workers who demonstrated their concern by helping to arrange the youngsters' involvement in a group and by taking them swimming (Jones 1978). Making other practical arrangements such as contacting other people on behalf of clients has been equated with concern by multi-problem families (Jackson 1973; Mayer and Timms 1970) and parents of the mentally handicapped (Hewett 1970). The following comment of a mother of young children was provoked when she felt that this effort was lacking, 'They don't put themselves out to 'elp yer, if yer know what I mean. To my opinion they never come to see how me husband were getting on wi' the children when I was in hospital for ten week' (Cohen 1971, 42).

The importance attached to 'activity' is highlighted in the following illustrations. People have expressed overall dissatisfaction with service when the social worker employed a passive approach, even when they have received the help they requested (Jackson 1973.) Although, in the following example, the researcher suggests the social worker's intention was probably to discourage the family's dependence, the family interpreted the lack of action as lack of concern.

> If we had any problems, and it needed a phone call, say, from a social worker, or something like that, he would say to my husband, 'Look, there's the phone, you phone up'. So he couldn't be bothered he just wanted to get out and leave it at that – he couldn't care less (Jackson 1973, 10).

* An activist approach is also an important criterion of evaluation in the medical field when patients assess their physicians. Active intervention in the form of naming the illness, prescribing, examining, etc. demonstrates to the patient that their doctor is 'really' working and trying to do something to help (Freidson 1961).

In other circumstances, activity and effort continue to be appreciated by many clients even though the desired outcome of contact does not materialize. The trying and the effort is regarded as being of value in itself. It gives some clients like the following a degree of psychological lift. 'I feel much brighter now there is someone trying to do something for me' (McKay, Goldberg and Fruin 1973, 488).

People who are involved in long-term contact with the social services seem particularly appreciative of workers' attempts to help. Jackson stresses how much effort is valued by multi-problem families in contact with an Islington Family Service Unit, for periods ranging from eleven months to nine years when he states, 'The effectiveness of the worker's actions seemed to have been of secondary importance − what mattered was that the worker tried on the client's behalf' (1973, 12).

Hewett's (1970) study of the parents of cerebral palsied children had similar findings. No mothers said they had requested a social worker not to call again despite the fact they were often disparaging about the lack of practical help offered. Many parents appreciated the fact that someone was interested enough in them and their child to visit. As Hewett states, 'they find this expression of society's awareness of their problem sufficient justification for such visits, even if no practical help can result' (1970, 169).

In an American study of clients' evaluation of paediatric social services (Blumberg *et al.* 1975), the social worker was judged 'helpful' by 67 per cent, even though half these respondents felt they had received insufficient concrete help. It is not clear why some people remain satisfied with effort even if no help actually materializes, but some suggestions as to why this should be are discussed in a later chapter.

As we can see, the 'social worker as a person' is a critical component in clients' evaluations. It is as important for people seeking material help as it is for those seeking other forms of help. Indeed clients seem to regard the personal approach as being a necessary prerequisite for effective service. If contacts are abrupt and impersonal, the social worker is unlikely to be thought of as a helpful person and effective service is less likely to occur. But is personal interest and concern enough?

A crucial question, which only a handful of researchers have attempted to examine, is the relationship between clients' positive evaluations of a friendly approach, and what happens later. Few studies have examined the relationship between appreciation of this approach and being 'helped'. It has been suggested that while such worker qualities as warmth and friendliness may be important initially for clients, the same qualities can lead to frustration or confusion at a later stage of contact (Maluccio 1977). The social worker's congenial approach at the beginning of contact can give clients a sense of relief and hope that they will get help. Contact with social services personnel has raised their expectations and they feel optimistic about future contact. If, in the clients' view, help does not materialize − they then feel let down. This was the feeling of some of the clients seeking help from a local authority department for the first time (Jordan 1976). One of these clients, Mrs Odhams, looked to the social worker for help with the overcrowded conditions in which she and her children were living. When such help was not forthcoming she felt considerably let down. As the researcher explains, 'For Mrs Odhams it was another disappointment made more painful by the hope originally implied in the pleasantness of the social worker's approach' (Jordan 1976, 81).

Another example of this is provided by George and Wilding (1972) in their study of motherless families. Two-thirds of the fathers were initially grateful for the warmth and sympathy provided by the social workers. However, over time, fewer and fewer fathers expressed satisfaction. Many found it frustrating and disappointing when some social workers offered vague promises of help, which never materialized. As the researchers commented, 'They [the social workers] may have felt that a vague promise was less disappointing than a downright statement that they were unable to help but some fathers were more hurt by this because they felt they were not treated as persons of any worth' (1972, 153).

Similar results have occurred in other studies (Maluccio 1977; Silverman 1969).

Contrast the experiences of these people with what happened to the families visiting a Sheffield Family Service Unit (Sainsbury 1975). These families continued to evaluate their workers as friendly, warm and concerned and remained satisfied with their contact. What can account for these differing assessments? The latter judgements were made in a situation in which the social workers employed supportive/directive help, and were willing and able to provide much of the help requested by the client (in addition to other help). The agency was informal, administratively flexible, and service was prompt. On the other hand, the judgements of the generally dissatisfied clients occurred in situations in which social workers were either unable or unwilling to provide such help. The clients then became disillusioned or lost hope.

What these findings and comments suggest is that for some clients, a warm, friendly approach is desirable, but not enough to constitute 'help'. That this approach, in some circumstances, and over time, actually may contribute to dissatisfaction has seldom been considered by researchers. Maluccio (1977) is one exception. He has suggested that some social workers' qualities are meaningful only at different times in the helping process. Although the client appreciates warmth and sympathy by the social worker early in the encounter, unless the worker displays other qualities – such as competence and knowledge – clients become dissatisfied. Silverman has made somewhat similar observations of people with interpersonal problems attending a casework agency.

> They were concerned that they were treated as people not cases, but this was not enough. The clients were not really looking for friendship, but were perhaps describing the context in which they felt helped (1969, 157).

She makes a distinction between 'helpful' and 'helping'. However sympathetic and concerned social workers may be, it does not necessarily follow that clients feel they will be able to help them. 'Helping' requires other attributes and actions than the ones we've just described. Clients are looking for more than a friend. They are searching for other things in their encounters – things related to the professional characteristics of the social worker. They believe professional competence and the ability to help are crucial if any degree of success is to be achieved.

Professional competence and the ability to help

No matter how kind and concerned the social worker, people search for more 'expert' qualities that indicate the practitioner's ability to help. These are concerned with two main functions –

1 the knowledge and experience of the social worker as perceived by the client.
2 the use of power and authority within the social worker/client relationship.

Knowledge and experience:
That the social worker is experienced is important to many clients. This desire for experience is often related to the perceived necessity of true understanding of their problem. If genuine understanding is missing, the client feels little confidence in the social worker's ability to help. However, many studies, having established that this is important to the client then fail to provide further information as to how it is a client comes to feel 'understood'.

For some clients the ability to help depends on the social workers' practical experience. There is evidence to suggest that for some clients the perceived similarity of the worker to themselves in terms of age, sex and life experiences can facilitate understanding. The importance of the age of the worker and understanding is illustrated in mainly negative comments. The following were made relating to counsellors, 'He seemed like a teenage rebel', 'He was too groovy or hip' (Beck and Jones 1973, 69).

Social workers who are regarded as being too young are not felt to have had the experience to be able to comprehend fully the client's situation particularly if it involves complex family problems. As a man seeking help with marital relationship comments of his social worker, 'He was just a young lad. He wasn't old enough to understand my problem properly' (Reith 1975, 67).

Social workers can be seen as devoid of child-rearing experiences. Glampson and Goldberg found that clients often expressed dissatisfaction with the youth of their social workers – despite the fact they were often kind and concerned. 'Well for someone like me who's older and got children, if they did have someone about my age group with children they might understand better' (1976, 9).

Single mothers in America felt they had difficulty in forming what they perceived as a valuable helping relationship, i.e. one in which they receive support and guidance, with specialists who were perceived as being of low status, or too young or too unsure of themselves (Weiss 1972). Similarly, foster parents in Britain have stated they do not always have great confidence in the advice of their childcare officer, especially if she is young (Adamson 1969).

For a minority of clients the sex of the social worker can also be significant. Particularly adolescents seeking counselling have stressed their desire that their helping person is of the same sex as themselves (Worby 1955). Moreover, the adolescent's willingness to return *and* to accept the helping person's advice is commonly related with the latter's ability to understand and desire to help.

That the social worker is not just similar in terms of age and sex, but also has experienced similar problems and overcome them was felt to be important to the multi-problem families attending the Islington Family Service Unit. 'He was just like us. He had the same problem and he'd tell us how he got out of them' (Jackson 1973, 12). The social worker talking about similar problems that he or she has had in the past has been evaluated positively by some people (Sainsbury 1975). This provides people with hope that their problems are surmountable and gives them greater confidence in the social worker's ability to understand their problems. But, interestingly, young people do not always find the social worker divulging too much of him or herself helpful (Worby 1955), although it is unclear why this should be.

In addition to this desire that the social worker has practical experience of life and its problems, some people have mentioned their appreciation of more specialized knowledge and training. Such perceptions have been expressed in negative comments. Amongst some British local authority clients there has been a sense of unease about the lack of specialization since the Seebohm reorganization. The blind seemed particularly aware of this, partly, as Glampson and Goldberg (1976) suggest, because previously they had received a special service. As one physically handicapped client commented, 'They should stick to whatever they are trained for, elderly or disabled or specifically the children, not go from one to the other' (Glampson and Goldberg 1976, 9).

One of the most commonly voiced complaints of parents of the physically and mentally handicapped is the workers' inability to help due to lack of specialized knowledge (Butler *et al.* 1977; Bedfordshire SSD 1978; Robinson 1978). Lack of knowledge about the handicap itself as well as lack of knowledge about the benefits, welfare rights and facilities available have caused much frustration amongst a number of these parents. Such feelings are expressed in the following quote from an open letter written by the parents of a mentally handicapped child.

> The social worker asked my wife is she had any problems. My wife told her that she needed three types of help: a babysitter for our retarded child, information

about getting state financial aid, referral to a church that had a special education Sunday School (if any existed). The social worker replied that she did not know about any of these things; but if we needed help or counselling we should feel free to call her. She also suggested that my wife might start a babysitting list and seemed surprised when my wife told her that taking care of Paul was a full-time job (Anonymous 1973, 113).

This desire that the social worker be professionally experienced has been confirmed in two experimental studies. In reacting to initial interviews clients' feelings that counsellors were going to be able to help increased significantly if the counsellor was believed to have had years of professional experience (Tessler 1975). Perceptions of a psychologist as being 'experienced' rather than 'inexperienced' has led clients to feel greater attraction to the therapist and to more favourable evaluations of his work (Greenberg, Goldstein and Perry 1970).

The social worker's professional experience can also be regarded as helpful in the sense that he or she is 'objective' and will not be too shocked by clients' disclosures. Lower-income clients with interpersonal problems state the importance of the worker being 'objective', as well as non-judgemental (Silverman 1969). As one client explains, 'I feel professional people shouldn't be shocked at anything. I didn't expect her to show emotion no matter what I told her' (Silverman 1969, 152).

It is felt by clients that the worker's value consists of his or her being outside their world. The social distance made it easier for the client to trust the social worker with confidence. This is felt particularly by clients with intensely personal problems, such as those who have attempted suicide (Butler, Bow and Gibbons 1978) or those who experience much marital distress (Mayer and Timms 1970). Often, people with such difficulties find it easier to talk to a professional outsider than to family or close friends. The latter, it is feared, may be too closely involved in the entanglements of the situation and thus 'biased' in their views. Another fear is that friends and relatives cannot always be trusted to be discrete and they may spread news of the client's disclosures around the neighbourhood.

That the social worker has practical and professional experience is important to the clients. Unless these attributes are present, clients feel their chances of being helped are considerably hindered. But being in possession of such knowledge and experience is one thing. How they are used in practice is another.

Power and authority
In evaluating some form of worker expertise issues to do with power and the exercise of authority are of significance in clients' assessments. Two broad preferences emerge in respect of the power relationship between client and social worker.

  1 In order to be helped, some clients expect and appreciate some element of sharing and equality in the helping relationship and do *not*

    wish the social worker to wield excessive power and authority.
2 Other clients feel that a social worker should exert authority.
    A competent social worker is an expert who will tell the client what
    to do.

The difference between these preferences can be explained by the reason
clients are in contact with the social services in the first place and by differences in clients' orientations to problem-solving. At this point we are discussing the use of power within the client/worker relationship, not the social
worker using power externally, on behalf of the client, i.e. advocacy.

Power sharing and equality
What considerations influence people's desires for a degree of equality
between client and worker in the helping relationship? Although class is to
some extent influential, it is in itself too crude a criterion to explain the variations in the ways in which clients define problems and seek help (Silverman
1969). It has been suggested that the values of clients, their previous experiences of seeking help and of dealing with people in positions of authority,
all play a part in influencing their preference for this particular helping
approach. A number of researchers, quite independently, have identified
three ways in which different people think about how to solve their
problems and the best way to relate to social services personnel.* These
orientations to problem-solving and help-seeking are not necessarily about
personality traits but illustrate adaptations to some constraints of economic
and social position (Rees 1978). They also reflect more than a client's competence or social power, but can be influenced by previous experiences in
the help-seeking system and in family life as a whole (Schwartz 1970).
    One of the groups identified, variously named the 'rational' (Silverman
1969), the 'circumspect' (Rees 1978), the 'problem-solver' (Perlman 1975)
and the 'coper' (McCaughey and Chew 1977), share a belief that the social
worker is a colleague to be consulted or a resource to be used in gaining help.
This orientation to problem-solving has occurred amongst multi-problem
families (Silverman 1969), families in poverty (Perlman 1975), clients
attending voluntary and local authority departments (Rees 1978), and
mothers of mentally retarded children dealing with the medical care system
(Schwartz 1970). Most of the people in this group have had past experience
of dealing with officials and feel fairly confident in dealing with social
workers, many are well educated, and, enjoying a certain degree of economic
security, they have a sense of control over their lives. For these clients, the
social worker is an expert and an ally to be consulted and with whom they
discuss matters in order to come to some mutual understanding and joint
decision making. The social worker may make recommendations based on
his or her professional judgement but these are open to discussion and
exploration and can be questioned by the client. Perlman provides a lucid

---

* These typologies will be discussed in more detail in Chapter 9.

summary of this when describing the group he identified as the 'problem solvers'. Such people:

> approach their personal problems and the problems of the community as matters of rational planning leading to action. In these efforts, the experts and professionals far from being feared, are to be enlisted as allies. They have a strong sense of autonomy. And while they want to cooperate with professionals they also want respect from them. They can be critical of professionals when they do not measure up (Perlman 1975, 39).

Although this general orientation to problem-solving is to be found amongst people with a variety of different problems it seems particularly prevalent amongst couples involved in fostering, and parents of the physically and mentally handicapped. A British study (Shaw and Lebens 1977) of 44 parents involved in long-term fostering found that they had mainly favourable comments to make about social workers. This was partly due to the fact that they felt they worked together as a team with the social workers in the caring for the children. Contrast this with the finding of another British Study (Jones 1975) on 90 foster homes where a decision has been made to cease fostering. That the parents involved were not given the chance to work together equally as a team with the social workers was one of the main reasons for terminating the placement. The desire to be colleagues of the social workers was not reciprocated by the social workers, who regarded the foster parents more as clients. As a result, some mothers complained of 'working in the dark' with foster children (Adamson 1969). If these social workers had treated the foster parents like partners in child rearing, and provided them with background information on the child, these placements might have been more successful.

Robinson's (1978) review of the literature on parents of physically and mentally handicapped children and their experiences with helping professionals confirms similar views (although admittedly this review is not exclusively concerned with social workers who were assessed as the most sympathetic of the helpers). Many of the parents, in Robinson's words, 'clearly feel some dissatisfaction about aspects of their relative powerlessness' (1978, 11). It is not that those people desire a completely egalitarian relationship with the workers, but they consider it important that they have a chance to express their point of view, and that their opinions are not then ignored or discounted. Being given full information about their child and being allowed the opportunity to find out more is also emphasized. As one parent explains, 'We need to be taken into the confidence of those who have professional skills not offered a few crumbs when someone else decides how much it is good for us to know' (Robinson 1978, 9). What all these clients have in common is a special appreciation of the professional and his or her 'expertise' and a willingness to act for themselves and to make their own decisions once they have the benefit of the social worker's specialist knowledge.

The social worker as expert

Many people prefer social workers to exhibit their expertise by adopting a directive approach and by exercising authority over them. Again, the client groups identified by Rees (1978), Perlman (1975), Silverman (1969) and McCaughey and Chew (1977), provides us with some information about the people most likely to appreciate this approach. Many of these people, though not all, tend to be submissive when confronted by officials in authority. They are usually poor and feel they have little control over their own lives. Past experiences with people representing authority lead them to believe that passive acceptance is the least distressing way of interacting with such people. Hence the researchers named this group 'passive' (McCaughey and Chew 1977; Rees 1978), 'the buffeted' (Perlman 1975), and the 'defeated' (Silverman 1969). These people tend to expect and accept the professional's authority and definition of the problem, as well as his or her suggestions and advice as to how their problem can be resolved. They assume a relationship of unequal knowledge and power. The social worker is the expert whom it is inappropriate to challenge. The nature of their relationship with the social worker is that of giver and receiver – the social worker giving and the client receiving advice and recommendations.

There are broadly two forms and uses of authority relating to different kinds of help which these clients value. The first of these involves the social worker giving advice and making recommendations; the second involves the social worker exercising control and discipline over the actions and behaviour of clients.

The value ascribed to the first style of intervention is reflected in the influence that the *amount* of advice (irrespective of its content) given by a social worker has on the level of client satisfaction. People rarely complain about receiving too much advice. In fact, one of the most frequent complaints about contact is that they don't receive enough (Beck and Jones 1973). Reid and Shapiro (1969) found that a direct link existed between clients' evaluations and the level of advice-giving provided by the worker. The clients in question were a number of husbands and wives with personal and relational problems seeking help from a casework agency. If the caseworker used medium to high levels of advice-giving only a small proportion of clients (less than 15 per cent) expressed dissatisfaction with lack of advice. If a low amount of advice was given, however, nearly 40 per cent of the clients expressed dissatisfaction over the lack of advice. Similar findings have emerged from studies on psychotherapy and psychiatry (Overall and Aronson 1963). However, we should be cautious about interpreting findings from research which uses criteria like 'level of advice-giving', with the implication that this can be objectively measured. Sainsbury and Nixon's (1979) study suggests otherwise. When they asked both the social workers and the clients to specify the kinds of help made available over their period of contact, they found high agreement over some forms of helping input, but quite a high degree of discrepancy in respect of the giving of advice.

Although 172 social workers reported using advice as a major helping technique, only 39 clients reported receiving it. This demonstrates that we cannot assume that clients' perceptions accord with the perceptions of others, be they practitioners or researchers.

Often clients tell the social worker their troubles and then hope the 'expert' will interpret and diagnose the problem and then explain how it can be resolved. Others are prepared to talk for a while but hope that ultimately this will lead to concrete advice and guidance from the worker (Silverman 1969). If this doesn't materialize the clients feel somewhat let down and disappointed. They experience the social worker as withholding and ineffective. For example, one woman expecting concrete advice on her marital difficulties describes her experiences at a Family Welfare Association.

> The social worker asked me what was wrong and I told her. She asked me why does my husband act like he does, and what sorts of things does he say. And I was giving her the answers, but she wasn't giving me anything back. Then she would ask me another question. She kept asking me questions, and I would be giving her the answers. I would expect someone to say, 'Well why don't you do this?' or 'Why don't you do that?' (Mayer and Timms 1970, 70).

Even if the social worker is unwilling to provide this direct guidance, clients appreciate help in arriving at some shared definition of their predicament. Low-income mothers seeking support and guidance found this help useful. As Weiss states,

> When faced by serious trouble, respondents seem quite regularly to feel some need for a temporary alliance with an *authoritative* figure who would symbolically accept their goals as his own and associate his efforts with theirs (1972, 320–1).

It is especially in this context that the status and age of the social worker becomes important.

If the social worker does provide guidance and advice, there is evidence to suggest that it is especially appreciated if it is compatible with that coming from other sources – friends, relatives, or other professionals (Mayer and Timms 1970). There are similarities here between the giving of advice by social workers, and the giving of instructions and prescriptions by doctors. Patients do not follow a doctor's instructions in a 'thoughtless vacuum'. Their assessment of the behaviour of a doctor and the value of his diagnosis and prescription can depend on the patient's social networks. As Stimson argues,

> (the patient) passes through the referral structure not only on his way to the physician, but also on his way back discussing the doctor's behaviour, diagnosis, and prescription with his fellows, with the possible consequence that he may never go back (1974, 101).

The second use of authority appreciated by some clients is concerned with the social worker exercising some control over client behaviour and actions. Sainsbury (1975) has analysed in detail this use of authority in the client/

worker relationship. He defines two aspects of this authority as used in a family agency favouring a supportive/directive approach – (a) firmness and (b) limit-setting. By 'firmness' he means such demands on clients as instructions to carry out a particular task, the exercise of moral pressure, requiring certain standards of behaviour. By 'limit-setting' he means the social worker's responsibility for the shape and content of an interview, steering discussions, resolving manipulative situations etc. The studies reviewed suggest that clients' appreciative comments are concerned with 'firmness' rather than 'limit-setting'. This does not necessarily imply that 'firmness' is more important from the clients' point of view. It may more accurately be a reflection of the difficulty people might have in talking about the less obvious aspects of social worker behaviour involved in 'limit-setting'.

What are some examples of this use of firmness? It is clear that some people feel themselves in need of limits, and believe that in the long term they are valuable and desirable. Delinquent boys have described how they prefer their social workers to be 'parental surrogates, rather than a friend' (Gottesfeld 1965). This does not imply that they want social workers to express judgemental attitudes about what they've done. But they do want their professional helpers to give guidance and to take stands for or against some aspects of their behaviour. Young people in another context, in foster care, have expressed a similar desire for firm discipline (Bush, Gordon and Le Bailley 1977). Lack of such discipline is sometimes interpreted by these children as lack of caring. People have even redefined the use of authority as a strong form of encouragement which they have found helpful (Sainsbury and Nixon 1979). As one grateful client explains:

> She's a good listener, a bit forceful – some of the people they visit are very weak: I was like that – very weak-minded. They've got to be strong. They should be able to take control of the situation. When I used to blow up at her, she would give me what-for back, but in a better manner. She got through to me (Sainsbury 1975, 81).

Some clients have no wish for demands to be made of them. They are looking to the social worker to use 'muscle' on their behalf to 'make' someone else behave or conform to some standard of behaviour. People think that the worker's authority will be far more effective than their own in bringing about some desired change in behaviour. For example, parents of children on probation consider it appropriate for probation officers to exercise control over the probationer, probably because they are fearful and uneasy about the prospect of their son or daughter returning to court (Gandy *et al.* 1975). If this help is not forthcoming, parents have been of the opinion that the probation officer has nothing unique to offer the family. As one disappointed parent commented on the treatment of his son, 'We hoped he would get the stronger handling which he needed' (Sainsbury and Nixon 1979). The desire for social workers to exercise authority over *others* is a common feature of couples involved in marital disputes (Mayer and Timms 1970), where one spouse wants the other to be 'made' to change. For some clients, then, at times the social worker is not authoritative enough for their liking.

It is important to make clear at this point that most of these clients seeking advice and some other form of authority do not wish social workers to impose this on them in an arbitrary manner. Clients' acceptance of authority and guidance and the feeling that it is helpful depends to some extent on it being blended with a degree of permissiveness. Studies have shown how people can regard social workers both as friendly visitors and authority figures (Sainsbury and Nixon 1979; Gandy *et al.* 1975). Clients' acceptance of workers' use of authority and recommendations may depend partly on how they perceive the social workers' capacity for accurate empathy (Sainsbury 1975). For example, the families attending a Sheffield Family Service Unit intermingled words like 'understanding' and 'honest' referring to social workers in the same breath as talking about appreciating firmness and authority being exercised by the same workers (Sainsbury 1975). It is also important to families that, although they are advised by a social worker, they are given a choice of action. This allows them to maintain their self-respect (Jackson 1973). The use of authority is thus only acceptable when utilized in a context that is informal, friendly and in which the client is given a choice of action.

Summary

Clients consider certain personal attributes and skills to be helpful. These include a concerned, friendly approach in which the ability to listen is equated with caring. In this respect clients distinguish between social workers as 'persons' and as 'professionals'.

The concerned, caring practitioners are only considered helpful up to a point. They may flatter to deceive. When promises or even expressions of interest are not followed up by some action, clients' initial satisfaction turns to dissatisfaction.

Clients' definitions of competence contained two ingredients. Clients gain an impression of competence if practitioners seem similar to the client, by virtue of age, sex or the way social workers refer to their own experiences.

In addition, competence is attributed to social workers who have some specialized knowledge of the problem at hand, or convey that they know how to obtain such information.

Clients distinguish between the apparent possession of competence and the way it is exercised. Clients' experience and manner of relating to people in positions of authority affects their interpretation of competence in action. People with some experience of solving problems and handling officials, such as parents with handicapped children, appreciate a relationship of some equality in which the social work develops as a mutual task. Other people, such as almost anyone who feels both ashamed and powerless at a point in time, appreciate social workers who demonstrate competence by taking action on their behalf.

Such skills and behaviour are not always sufficient in themselves to bring contact to a satisfactory conclusion. Clients also take into account the types of services and the ways of providing them. Some examination of these considerations is the concern of the following chapter.

4

Different Clients, Different Outcomes

We know the importance clients attach to their encounters with social workers in the process of seeking help. But what are the outcomes they experience? This chapter explores people's opinions of the services made available to them. We want to discover whether social service help contributed in any way to the alleviation of clients' distress. More particularly, we want to elicit which types of help are found useful by which clients with what problems − hence the division of this chapter into six sections dealing with different client groups − (i) the elderly, (ii) the mentally and physically handicapped, (iii) those involved in residential childcare and fostering, (iv) those with interpersonal/mental health problems, (v) multi-problem families, and (vi) probationers and prisoners.

The elderly

Considering that the elderly comprise such a large proportion of social work clients, it is perhaps surprising that there are relatively few studies concerned with eliciting their viewpoint of service. However, completed studies suggest that the elderly are the group who expect least from social workers. Either they have no idea of what to expect, as was the case of over half of the frail elderly and physically handicapped people attending a local authority department, (Glampson and Goldberg 1976) or they have very limited and narrow views of the help they hope to receive (Goldberg et al. 1970). Their expectations are sometimes influenced by certain ideals, a striving for independence and an unwillingness to accept charity (Glampson and Goldberg 1976). As an elderly man over 81 years of age explains, 'I didn't expect anything for nothing. I expected to pay for it. I'm very independent' (Glampson and Goldberg 1976, 8).

When the elderly do articulate their expectations, they consist primarily of practical help in the form of aids, adaptations, outings etc. Very few seem to expect *other* forms of social work help. When they receive this practical help the elderly express much satisfaction. Domiciliary and material help, such as meals on wheels, carpets, etc. are found valuable. Home helps are also found very helpful, although a few clients in one study said they would much appreciate if the home help would come at a regular day and regular time each week (Hillingdon SSD 1974). Aids and adaptations are also appreciated. But while the elderly regard a delay in the provision of adaptations as reasonable, *aids* are expected to be provided in a much shorter space of time (Hillingdon SSD 1974).

However, many elderly clients, at the same time as talking about receiving practical help emphasize how much they also value the security and the social support which can be provided by a social worker (Goldberg 1970 Glampson and Goldberg 1976, Hillingdon SSD 1974). The value of just having a chat is emphasized. Many of the elderly are lonely, and they greatly appreciate having someone to talk to, as the following comment of a 72 year old widow illustrates:

> It's helped me a lot to know that someone's trying to put you in touch with people for company. I'd be on my own here day after day. I think loneliness is the thing with sick people. They do give me a little hope, and come to see me now and again (Glampson and Goldberg 1976, 8).

As well as relief of loneliness, regular visiting by social workers gives the elderly a degree of security and reassurance that someone is available to help them. As one elderly man explains, 'It's good to feel someone is looking after me' (Hillingdon SSD 1974). Having a telephone installed can also provide this security as it enables help to be contacted easily. (Hillingdon SSD 1974)

Perhaps the value of such 'intangible' help to the elderly is sometimes underestimated by helping professionals. In an American study (Keith 1973), a number of elderly people and helping professionals were asked to rank a list of service priorities. Despite the fact that the researchers provided the list and it consisted overwhelmingly of services of a practical and tangible nature, one of the services ranked highest by the elderly (fourth) − reassurance phonecalls − was one of the very few of a more 'intangible' nature. The importance attributed to this service was that it provided the elderly with the comforting knowledge that help would be available should they need it, and that they were not being forgotten. (Interestingly, this service was ranked thirteenth in the professionals' list of priorities.) A visiting programme to older people in hospitals and nursing homes, as well as in their own homes, was the service ranked third by the elderly. This again testifies to their desire for more 'intangible' aspects of help, in addition to services of a more practical nature.

Those elderly people who manage to visit a Day Centre through the week express great satisfaction (Hammersmith SSD 1979) because it combats their loneliness, cheers them up, gets them out of the house and helps give them confidence. However, the comments of some of the elderly indicate that Day Centres would be more attractive places if separate provision was made for psychogeriatric cases (Hammersmith SSD 1979).

Overall, elderly clients express a very high degree of satisfaction with their social service contacts. They make few complaints and they are less likely than other clients to hold views at variance with their social worker that during their contact 'things could have been done better' (Barker 1974). If they do make complaints they tend to be about irregular or infrequent visits which again highlights their need for more informal help (Glampson and Goldberg 1976). Their lack of criticism is partly due to their low expectations of help. But it has also something to do with their idea that if they criticize the *service*, it will somehow reflect on the *social worker*, towards whom they usually feel well disposed. In addition to this, an element of fear may exist. They may be anxious that a critical evaluation might have a deleterious effect on the provision of some future service. Given their age, many old people are likely to be increasingly dependent on these services in the coming years (Goldberg *et al.* 1970). They do not want to jeopardize their chances of receiving help in the future by being over-critical in the present.

The mentally and physically handicapped

Compared with the elderly, there have been relatively more consumer studies carried out amongst the mentally and physically handicapped. The results suggest far more varying degrees of satisfaction with the services available, ranging from high satisfaction to some considerable degree of criticism. Because of the nature of their difficulties, many families of mentally and/or physically handicapped people tend to have contact with the social services over a longer period of time than many other groups. Their perceptions of what kind of help is valuable or most appropriate change over time. Thus when they evaluate services they describe what help is found helpful at a particular time in the handicapped person's development. Many of these people's opinions are retrospective, and some respondents are asked about their experiences with the social services as far back as 18 years ago. Therefore their comments have to be interpreted within the context of social service change and availability (Bedfordshire SSD 1978).

   Parents of a handicapped child emphasize how greatly distressed they feel on discovering that their child is not 'normal' (Bedfordshire SSD 1978). For example, parents of children with Down's Syndrome emphasize the need for continued support in these initial stages (Gilmore and Oates 1977). This period obviously causes much trauma, yet supportive help does not always seem to be made available. At this time, for example, 41 per cent of 314 parents of handicapped children in a recent survey in Bedfordshire (Bedfordshire SSD 1978) said they had received *no* help of any sort during this period of shock. Moreover this remained their view after being given examples of types of help that might have been offered. Given the chance, however, these parents can articulate clearly what they would have found helpful during this period. They stressed the importance of having more opportunities for contact with people who have a real knowledge of the handicap. Contact with other parents with similar problems is also considered important (Bedfordshire SSD 1978). Moreover, these two forms of help are often given priority over help from a social worker (Bedfordshire SSD 1978). Parents feel that continued support is necessary when the child is still very young, but has not yet attended school. They would like more opportunity than they seem to be given, to discuss their child's handicap prior to his or her going to school. Particularly if the child is mentally handicapped they are concerned with the arrangements for his or her future education (Bedfordshire SSD 1978; Taylor 1978).

Emotional stress is not confined just to the initial stages. Butler found that almost half of the 255 mothers of mentally and physically handicapped children in his study had received treatment during the last month of the research for at least one of six 'neurotic' symptoms. This suggests a high rate of mental stress. Having someone to talk to temporarily gives to these parents an emotional outlet which alleviates their anxiety and depression. As the mother of a mentally handicapped child states, 'It's given me a chance to talk, otherwise it would build up inside me having a child like K' (Glampson and Goldberg 1976, 8). More often than not, however, there are criticisms that parents are not given enough opportunities to do this. Indeed some families have had no contact with the social services for eight to nine years (Bayley 1973). Many parents feel they need more frequent and regular contacts with the social services.

> I need more frequent visiting. I see someone about once a year. You need someone to talk over the problems and the same person. A person like Johnny [mentally handicapped child] needs continuity (Glampson and Goldberg 1976, 10).

As the above comment suggests, several parents believe that the value of the emotional support they receive from these visits depends much on the actual person doing the visiting. Thus, not only continuity in service is important, but also continuity in the personnel providing the service. Parents say it is far from helpful to see a new face each time they are visited. A rapid turnover of social workers precludes any depth of relationship with the family, or any realistic understanding of their needs (Bedfordshire SSD 1978).

Although many parents express the need for more emotional support, on the whole their primary needs are for practical information and support. As Bayley (1973) has stated, the day to day grind involved in the caring of handicapped people cannot be over-emphasized. Yet it is precisely in the 'practicalities of the daily routine' that social work help is often judged by parents as being irrelevant, inappropriate or just non-existent. Families of handicapped children in the East Midlands who received visits from mental welfare officers found that there was little that the officials could do to help the parent manage in the home, 'Well, he doesn't have much to say. He just wants to know if there's anything he can do in any way to help, which he can't and that's about all that goes on . . .' (Hewett 1970, 165). There is much criticism that social workers know even less about the handicap and the available benefits and facilities than do the parents. For example, 10 per cent of 255 families in Avon, complained about social workers' insufficient knowledge of benefits and the lack of information passed on to parents (Butler 1977). If it *is* passed on, it is often regarded as being too late. Many parents in the recent Bedfordshire study (Bedfordshire SSD 1978) expressed dissatisfaction that information about sources of help and available benefits was 'gleaned haphazardly' from a variety of sources.

It is particularly frustrating for people if they seek practical help and advice, but are given 'casework' by the social worker. For example, a young disabled family man seeking help with a problem he defined in practical terms said of the social worker,

> I don't really know what was going on. I just wanted these forms filled in. She kept on talking about the disease – what I felt about it – what the wife felt about it. Coming to terms with it. All I want to come to terms with is these forms (Blaxter 1976, 123).

The disabled argue that sometimes social workers are too anxious to talk, and inadequate when it comes to getting things done. A disabled client who wanted a hoist explains,

> He just comes and talks but he's not doing anything for us. There's nobody to turn to at all. My husband did ask the social worker but all he said was, 'I have no idea at all' (Robinson 1975, 13).

This criticism was voiced despite the fact that the social worker was thought to be 'an awfully nice man'.

If practical help, aids and adaptations are produced fairly quickly the physically handicapped and their families feel satisfied. When there are never-ending delays however, clients can be strongly critical of too much bureaucracy and red tape (Butler 1977). Faced with such delays, some people have given up and gone ahead and carried out alterations in the house often at considerable expense to themselves (Bedfordshire SSD 1978). Sometimes the aids and equipment are thought to be unsuitable or inappropriate but are regarded as being better than nothing, e.g. the physically handicapped have complained that standard hospital beds supplied on discharge are too high and never come in double bed form (Robinson 1978). Proving eligibility for such material help can cause additional distress. Nevertheless, 122 parents (nearly half of the sample) of the handicapped in Bedfordshire felt there was some type of financial help which should have been available to them but was not, e.g. financial help with transport to hospital and schools, a clothing allowance particularly for parents of cerebral palsy and educationally sub-normal children (Bedfordshire SSD 1978).

Practical help which is regular and reliable is valued. For example, home helps, when available, are greatly valued by the disabled (Hillingdon SSD 1974) and by families with a mentally handicapped member (Seed 1980). Training centres for the mentally handicapped (Bayley 1973; Bedfordshire SSD 1978) are also appreciated. One of the resources most valued by parents in particular are day care facilities. Indeed, such day care provision is regarded by some parents as being *more* essential than residential provision (Bedfordshire SSB 1978). Such help enables the family to cope more easily with problems at home. Also it meets the parents' desire for temporary relief rather than permanent relinquishment of their responsibilities for caring for the handicapped person (Seed 1980).

Training and day care centres are also appreciated by the handicapped person (Hammersmith SSD 1979; Wandsworth SSD 1977; Wigan SSD 1979). They provide these people with social contact, get them out of the house and enable them to meet other people. It should be noted, however, that younger physically handicapped people have expressed dissatisfaction with sharing centres with elderly people. As one person said after visiting a day centre for the elderly and physically handicapped for the first few times, 'I vowed that I would never go again, so many people were sick and old. The next time I went, I met someone I knew, so it was alright then' (Hammersmith SSD 1979). In the only study in which the mentally handicapped themselves have been asked about a training centre, most said they enjoyed attending and particularly enjoyed the creative activities (Wandsworth SSD 1977). However, about one-third of the sample of 54 expressed real dislike of some of the employment activities at the centre. They particularly disliked industrial contract work which involved boring and finicky work with pins and hooks. Most dissatisfaction was expressed by the young, moderately handicapped female trainees. It would seem important to find out why they are least happy with their attendance at a centre.

The literature on the handicapped indicates a need for both timely emotional *and* practical help. It is the lack of practical help which causes clients most distress and which results in most dissatisfaction. However, there is evidence to suggest that the level of service made available to the handicapped and their families is not uniform. The level of service may depend on the exact nature and degree of the handicap. On examining 255 families in Avon, (Butler 1977) found that the handicapped in the most severely impaired group were more likely than those in the middle range of handicap to have received help recently. This result was replicated in a study (Taylor 1978) of a rural area in which, once again, it was people with a less severe handicap who were more likely to experience an inadequate level of service, if indeed they received any service at all.

But we should be cautious about relating level of service to client satisfaction. Although those in the middle range of impairment were less often satisfied with the social services than were those with a more severe handicap, the greater level of contact received by the latter families did not necessarily result in client satisfaction. Similarly, lack of practical help need not imply dissatisfaction. Ignorance of available services, or resignation to the fact that no help is going to be forthcoming is significant here. The following comment of a parent of a handicapped child illustrates these attitudes well,

> You can cope on your own and any difficulties you come up against, you call on your doctor, and that's more or less it. We've never felt there's been any particular need to get in touch with them. We've never felt there's been anything they could

do. I heard that when he finished at Norfolk Park at 16 (the special care unit) that they just stay at home and that was it (Bayley 1973, 358).

Low expectations mean few 'demands' and a high likelihood of expressions of satisfaction. For example, in the study (Taylor 1978) in which most satisfaction was expressed, some of the physically handicapped clients were apparently happy with 'service' when it merely consisted of the provision of disabled car stickers! But there is some evidence to suggest that expectations are changing. Younger people (particularly the physically handicapped) now have higher expectations of service than do more elderly people − with the result that they are more demanding and critical of the services offered (Glampson and Goldberg 1976).

Residential child care and fostering

This is an area of social work in which the answer to the question, 'Who is the client?' is far from simple. In residential child care, there can be two clients involved − the parents and the children. In fostering there are three parties involved − the children, the natural parents and the foster parents. These people's perceptions and evaluations do not necessarily tally.

The children

Children are among the most powerless of people. Their views are rarely sought. Important decisions affecting their lives are frequently made without consulting them. In recent years a few studies have actually included children's views in the evaluation of some forms of social service provision, more specifically, of residential care and fostering.

Three main themes consistently emerge from the children's comments on residential care. These reflect the children's concern with having some freedom within the home, with having an opportunity to have a say in how their lives are run and with experiencing some preparation for the outside world. Lack of freedom in residential homes is often mentioned (Page and Clark 1977). Regimentation is disliked: the children always having to be clean, bedrooms being shut in the daytime, reading of children's letters by staff, set times to eat and to go to bed, set number of baths allowed in a week. These are generally resented and are unpopular. Such restrictions are just as disliked by children in recent years as they were in 1965 (Holman 1965; Page and Clark 1977). However, one follow-up study (Bandcroft 1970) of 25 boys who had been in residential care found that they did appreciate a consistent ordered daily routine. What accounts for this discrepancy? This study took place in a fairly atypical residential care situation while the other studies were based mainly in the more typical British local authority homes. What distinguished the former situation was that central to the organization of the home was the power of the residents to effect changes which influenced its daily programme. The boys' approval of its regime was influenced by the fact that they themselves had played some part in its organization.

This leads us on to the next common theme apparent in children's evaluations of residential care – and that is the lack of opportunity to participate in arranging their own affairs and the general lack of consultation with them with regard to their future. We have noted previously how much children in homes are concerned with having a say in what happens to them in the future. They are also concerned that what they have to say is taken into account in any decisions made (Chambers 1978; Page and Clark 1977). In addition to this desire for more consultation, children have described how they would like to be given more responsibility in the running of the homes (Chambers 1978; Page and Clark 1977). This is related to their desire for more preparation for the outside world. Many children experience worry and anxiety because they recognize their lack of social skills. They dislike not being able to handle money, not being able to cook, and not being allowed to buy their own clothes. As one child explains, 'They do everything for you. I don't really know how to look after myself. I don't know how to cook and I don't know what kind of job I'll be able to do' (Page and Clark 1977, 52). The consequences of this for their departure from the home can be traumatic. This is made all the more so by the general lack of preparation for leaving the home and the absence of any kind of organized aftercare service. This is a period which produces the greatest stress for children yet the homes can do little to help. Adults who had been in care in their youth have described how dramatic leaving home can be (Bandcroft 1970; Mulvey 1978). The young adults found themselves with nobody to go back to for Christmas or at weekends, and nobody with whom they could exchange letters. Thirteen to sixteen young adults in a London study (Mulvey 1978) said they would have welcomed some assistance from the social services, either psychological or practical within six months of discharge from care. Many had lacked advice during this period, and had felt the need for a confidant. In addition, many had suffered serious financial difficulties.

Despite the above criticisms of the organization of the homes, many children express appreciation of the staff within the homes (Page and Clark 1977). They like warm relationships with staff, and dislike formality, coldness, and inconsistency of care when, for example, there is a high turnover of residential staff and also of social workers (Bandcroft 1970; Page and Clark 1977). Related to this, one of the most hurtful things about care from the children's point of view is 'chopping and changing' from home to home (Page and Clark 1977). This seems particularly important for those children with no links, or only tenuous contact with their families, like the following child, 'It's the coming and going that hurts. The first time you move to another place it hurts bad so you build up a shell but one day the shell cracks' (Page and Clark 1977, 29). Despite the children's recognition of the staffs' genuine concern for them, the latter are not perceived as substitutes for 'parents'. Rather they are regarded by the children as being nice people paid to do a job of work, 'professional' people towards whom they feel respect and affection, but not love (Holman 1965; Page and Clark 1977). Partly as a consequence of this, the children sometimes feel at a loss as to whom they can turn when they need to talk. At times they feel that too many people are involved in their welfare, and this compounds the difficulty in knowing to whom to go for help (Page and Clark 1977). For example, many children feel they are in the middle of a tug of war between residential and field social worker, and that they sometimes receive conflicting advice from the various people involved in their welfare (Page and Clark 1977).

How do children assess residential care versus fostering? There is little in the literature that can inform us on this point. What sparse evidence there is, however, suggests that children's evaluations of residential care versus fostering may be changing. When Holman (1965) carried out a study of 20 children in 1965, he found that they felt more secure in foster homes than in children's homes. Holman made the interesting suggestion that the children's expectations influenced this judgement. It was not so much that a foster home provided more security as such, but that it was more likely to give the child 'an expectancy of permanent tenure'. Here, the context was of crucial importance. The mid 1960s witnessed an expansion of fostering. Children were not expected to stay permanently in a home because it was the accepted policy of the children's department to foster out all the children they could. As Holman says, 'this cannot be hidden from the children, they expect to be fostered and wonder what is wrong if they are not' (1965, 22). This expectation, then, may have had much to do with the children's feelings of insecurity, and their relative unhappiness with residential care.

A more recent study (Page and Clark 1977) suggests a change in views. In this study, children from all over the country and from a variety of residential settings, were unanimous in describing foster care as undesirable, moreover,

> this was said to be the general opinion of children living in residential homes many of whom, like themselves, had experienced fostering and its breakdown on a number of occasions (Page and Clark 1977, 44).

The impact of a fostering breakdown can be very hurtful for children. They talk of the lack of preparation for going to live in a foster home. 'Matching' the child with someone in the family of similar age is *not* generally regarded as a good idea as more often than not this leads to jealousy and resentments. After one or more foster breakdowns the children became adverse to the idea, and residential care becomes more attractive due to its permanency and relative security. However, it should be said that during the course of the study period, some of these children changed their minds about fostering, and became happily fostered themselves.

Children's feelings of discomfort with fostering are related to their relationship with their own family. An American study (Bush, Gordon and Le Bailley 1977) of 125 children found that if a child sees his own family regularly and believes it possible to return home, he is less likely to want to stay in a foster placement. This suggests that it is not so much foster care as opposed to institutional care that should be the concern of research. It would be valuable to ask which type of institution and which type of foster care are valued by which children in what circumstances rather than to pose the simplistic question which type of care is better? Social workers' claims to be professionally competent depend on their knowing such things.

Taking into account children's opinions of their care may have more important implications than some professionals realize. An American experimental study (Bush, Gordon and Le Bailley 1977) divided the sample of 125 children into two groups. One group of children had had a pre-placement visit to their current foster home, a choice of living there or in another specified placement or had chosen to live in their present placement. The second group of children lacked one or more of these conditions. It was found that, when the two groups' level of satisfaction with their placement was measured, the first group was significantly more satisfied with their placement than was the second group. The authors suggest that

> Even when a placement had been deemed fit by concerned citizens, a social worker, or a court, if the child finds the placement uncomfortable and unsupportive the placement will not be very successful (Bush, Gordon and Le Bailley 1977, 500)

The natural parents
There are fewer studies on the natural parents' views than on those of the children. This has something to do with difficulties in tracing natural parents, particularly when the child is in long-term care. Two studies on parents' evaluations of residential care are concerned with children in care for a relatively short period of time. But they are concerned with two different forms of residential care. One is based on voluntary care in two local authorities in Scotland (Aldgate 1978), the other is based on involuntary care in a residential home in San Francisco for young boys with behavioural difficulties (Oxley 1977). One of the main distinguishing features of the American home is the active participation by parents while their children are in care. Despite the differences in these two caring regimes, there emerged some similarity in parents' evaluations.

For those parents whose children are in care for a short term only, contact with the children is essential. It is crucial to these parents that they have ease of access to their children when they wish. It was of immense value to the Scottish parents that the children's homes had flexible visiting times which fitted in with their domestic arrangements. This was in contrast to their experiences with foster homes. Visiting was regarded as being important because it helped retain the parent/child relationship, reassured the parents that their child was being well looked after and made them feel they had a valued and trusted role to play in the care of their child. Both boys and parents in the American study in which visiting times were more rigid, desired greater flexibility and choice in determining the schedule of appointments. Indeed, the parents felt the need for visiting varied over time. Some felt that regular appointments were essential early on in the 'treatment' process, while in the middle period appointments were more on an as needed basis, and that towards the end when the boy was due to return home more frequent appointments could take place. It was also important to the parents in both these studies that they were made to feel they had a part to play in their child's care. The American parents wanted more contact with the staff and more information from them about their child. They did not want to feel excluded from their child's life. They were particularly sensitive about this when their child first entered the home. As one parent describes graphically,

> They showed me where he was going to be – the house he was going to live in. I put his duffel bag on the floor and then left. That was it. I never met the people he was going to live with. Never saw the lady who washed his clothes or helped take care of things. Indirectly she was taking my place, but I never saw her. This was a painful experience to me (Oxley 1977, 612–13).

When 'family nights' were introduced to this setting, the parents evaluated this very favourably. Similar informal arrangements were considered to be most important to the parents of children in local authority care and helped them recover from the initial trauma of their children being placed in care.

> They said for me just to let them know I was coming and I could see them any time. When I go, I can see them by themselves, sometimes I put them to bed. You don't feel in the way. They make you feel as if you were wanted (Aldgate 1978, 30).

Social workers being kind and sympathetic and communicating to parents that they are important to their children is particularly appreciated by those people who are very sensitive to insinuations that they are 'bad' parents.

In one study natural parents were asked whether they preferred residential or foster care. The views of the 60 natural parents in the Scottish study (Aldgate 1978) suggested that foster homes were regarded less favourably than residential care. A variety of reasons were given by the parents for this preference. Children's homes were regarded as being more part of other social services provided by the local authority. They did not place parents in direct competition with foster parents. This was a relief to some of the natural parents who felt inferior to foster parents in terms of emotional capabilities and the ability to provide for the material needs of the children. In general, the natural parents felt that children's homes were less threatening than foster parents. The homes had the advantage of easy and flexible contact with children. That houseparents' attitudes tended to be more encouraging to natural parents than were foster parents was another factor in the former's favour. (In a five year study of foster parents, it was found that child care officers were understanding and tolerant of the natural parents but the foster care parents were sometimes inclined to moralize. This moralizing sometimes filtered into arrangements over visits by natural parents to their children in foster homes.) The homes were also seen as providing more opportunity for brothers and sisters to be kept together and having more consistent standards of material care. In addition the 'professionalism' of houseparents was perceived by parents as lessening the chance of the residential staff stealing the affection of the children. As one parent explains, 'they get looked after but the people in charge are just doing a job. That's how it should be' (Aldgate 1978, 31). In general, children's homes were perceived by parents as being the most conducive to family cohesion. This is extremely important when residential care is regarded as being 'a short-term measure to facilitate rehabilitation' (Aldgate 1978, 32).

When children *are* fostered, how do natural parents assess their experiences with the social services? One study dealing with this question (Jenkins and Norman 1975) was based on the experiences and evaluations of 160 mothers over a five-year period between 1966 and 1971. A variety of specialized fostering agencies were involved and they differed in encouraging the natural mothers to visit their children in the foster home. Three-quarters of the mothers reported having at least one problem or difficulty in making these visits. About half felt that the agencies could have made the visiting easier e.g. by placing the children in homes closer to where the mothers lived, and by making visiting times more flexible and convenient. In addition, although over one-quarter of the mothers reported lacking the money to visit their children, only 4 per cent of the mothers felt that it was a function of the fostering agencies to help in this respect.

How did the placement of the children affect the mothers? More than half (51 per cent) of the mothers felt that the fostering placement had affected their situation. Two-thirds of this number said it helped, and one-third that it had aggravated the situation. Those who found it helpful mostly talked about the relief in knowing that their children were being cared for when they themselves could no longer cope. In addition, several found counselling by agency workers was 'useful'. But in what way these sessions were found 'useful' was not analysed by the researchers. Those mothers who were dissatisfied with the placements often felt a sense of frustration and powerlessness. The fostering agencies were thought to be keeping the children from the parents, as well as withholding information from them. What accounted for these differences in evaluations? The study could not answer this question – but the researchers stressed the need for a deeper analysis of the mothers and their situations. They were also sensitive to the possibility that agency policy and services and the attitudes of agency personnel may have been of equal importance in accounting for the divergent evaluations. For example, the dissatisfied mothers may have encountered positive and negative reactions on the part of the agency staff. Furthermore:

> it may be that the foster care system itself tends to differentiate in placement and that clients in the two different groups were in fact receiving a different level of

service, that their children were placed in different kinds of agencies, and that the responses of mothers were valid reactions to the nature and quality of services offered (Jenkins and Norman 1975, 73).

This study illustrates well both the *value* of ascertaining clients' opinions, and at the same time the *limitations* of studying these opinions in isolation. To facilitate interpretation and understanding, clients' opinions *must* be placed in context. To be able to weigh the meanings and merits of clients' evaluations, we have to know what services and attitudes were encountered by the clients.

Foster parents

Foster parents are the third party in the triangle of people involved in child care. How helpful do they find their contacts with social services departments? There seems to be conflicting evidence here. Some 68 per cent of the foster and adoptive parents in a Southampton study (Glampson and Goldberg 1976) made complaints about contact, a higher percentage than any other group. Most of the 44 foster parents in another British study (Shaw and Lebens 1977), however, had generally good experiences with social workers and the social services, some parents being very generous in their praise. Perhaps this difference in opinion can be partially accounted for by the clients in the latter study drawing a clear distinction between the *social workers* and the *social work department*. There tended to be much more criticism of the latter. As the researchers explain,

> It was not easy to disentangle the contributions of law, departmental policy, local authority financial restrictions or of the individual social worker in many such complaints and County Hall serves as a highly visible scapegoat in the face of frustration (Shaw and Lebens 1977, 13–14).

What is the cause of such criticism? A Portsmouth study (Jones 1975), which was specifically concerned with 90 parents who ceased fostering, found that 59 per cent of mothers felt that they had insufficient preparation prior to receiving the child. Whereas the social workers felt that during the visit they had both assessed the parents *and* prepared them, the parents perceived the visit only in terms of assessment. This suggests that more preparation would be useful from the parents' point of view. This may be particularly important for these people who expect fostering to satisfy their own family needs, e.g. that it would be good for the wife, for the husband, or some other family-orientated reason. The higher the expectations, the greater the chance that these people will be disappointed or disillusioned later on.

Another criticism of the department is its lack of awareness of the impact some of its actions can have on the rest of the family (e.g. sending cards to foster child, but not to other children in the family). Foster parents resent feeling that they are being exploited. They do not want to feel that they are just a departmental 'resource'.

A 'substantial minority' of the foster families in Portsmouth did not find the visits of the social workers helpful – they did not visit the family when required and failed to provide some advice and information. Over half of these families gave as their main reason for ceasing to foster as being 'internal' e.g. insufficient support from the department of social services, or not getting the type of child requested, not being treated as colleagues of the social workers. Social workers have been found helpful by some parents, however, in giving moral support and advice (Jones 1975). But frequent changes of social worker are regarded as unhelpful (Shaw and Lebens 1977). Parents see no point in getting to know someone who is going to move on within a short time. There is little else that can be added to this brief review of foster parents' evaluations. This seems to be a little-explored area of social work which does not appear to have attracted the attention of researchers.

People seeking help with interpersonal mental health problems

There exists more detailed information on clients seeking help with inter-personal problems than on many of the other client groups. * Their prob-lems range from marital conflict, difficulties in relationships with other family members, particularly children, to feelings of anxiety and depression arising from more general social relations and problems. These clients have encountered a variety of agencies and helping approaches. They have sought help from local authority social service departments, family welfare agencies, specialized counselling agencies, mental health clinics and child guidance clinics. Within these agencies they have experienced psycho-therapy, task-centred casework, open-ended casework, as well as less explicitly defined approaches. Despite these diverse experiences, clients have often made remarkably similar comments in relation to the services they have found helpful or unhelpful.

Unlike problems involving the elderly or the handicapped, where the origin and nature of the problem is usually fairly obvious, mental health and interpersonal difficulties can involve many conflicting definitions of what the problem is, what is causing it and how it might be 'solved'. These conflicts of definition occur both among the clients involved (for example between spouses in marital disputes) as well as between client and social worker. To understand fully the reactions of some clients to the services encountered, it is necessary first of all to examine how their problems are defined. Lack of agreement between client and social worker over the nature of the problem can be one of the most important factors related to outcome (Beck and Jones 1973; Maluccio 1977). What are some of the causes of this lack of agreement? Clients commonly define their problem and its cause as

* This is because many research studies have been carried out in specialized counselling agencies.

being external to themselves. The problem is seen as being rooted in another person and in his or her behaviour. For example, 25 per cent of a sample of 2,460 people interviewed in America could not take the responsibility of having caused a personal problem (Gurin, Veroff and Feld 1960). Only 23 per cent of the sample believed that they themselves were at least partially responsible for their problem.

This belief does not seem to be peculiar to one particular section of the population. People with generally secure incomes and of higher than average education also frequently perceived the major cause of the problem as being situated in the attitudes and behaviour of others (Reid and Shyne 1969). This belief convinces many clients that it is appropriate for service to be directed towards the 'other' person rather than themselves. For example, a number of clients attending a Family Welfare Association 'took for granted that the only way to improve the situation was to bring about changes in the offender's behaviour' (Mayer and Timms 1970). This belief is particularly prevalent amongst parents seeking help with child-centred problems (Burck 1978; Lishman 1978).

If the social worker refuses to share this definition and instead tries to focus on the individual concerned as part of the 'treatment', some people feel highly dissatisfied. For example, ten parents attending a child guidance clinic (whose policy was to include the whole family in the treatment of a child) felt that a focus on themselves was inappropriate (Burck 1978). A similar belief was linked with dissatisfaction amongst a number of parents attending another child guidance clinic (Lishman 1978). Indeed in this latter study, the policy of focusing on the whole family resulted in the parents feeling that they were being blamed and persecuted for their child's behaviour. Other people simply feel puzzled over the social worker's approach. A couple attending a Family Welfare Agency due to concern about the behaviour of their sixteen-year-old daughter, Penny, eventually dropped out of contact after four interviews. Mrs Skinner reported,

> When we came out of there the fourth time, my husband said, 'What do you think of it?', and I said, 'I don't know what to think of it'. Then my husband said, 'He just don't give you any idea of what he's going to do or anything. He just keeps on saying come back and have more talks and he says he's going to have more talks and more talks. Well, while he's doing that we're not getting anywhere. Penny's the problem, not us (Mayer and Timms 1970, 71).

People who do believe that some of the social work attention should be directed at them are far less dissatisfied. It is these clients who are more likely to make a favourable assessment of their social work contact (Gurin, Veroff and Feld 1960). More than any other group, they claim they have been helped by professionals personally to change, to feel comforted and generally more happy.

Assuming there is some common definition of the problem between client and social work, what does the client feel is helpful? Many of these clients arrive at an agency deeply distressed, some even suicidal. Of immense importance to them at this stage is the emotional relief of having someone to talk to and on whom they can unburden their troubles (Gibbons *et al.* 1979). For example, the ability of the worker to relieve the tension of clients attending a children's department is greatly valued, even if no other help is forthcoming at a later date (Reith 1975/6).

This emotional relief is related to several factors. That the social worker is kind, patient and concerned is often crucial for the client feeling that he or she can talk freely. One woman who suffered from deep depression explained,

> I let everything out. You know it does not help if you let it build up inside you. When you have someone listening patiently showing that they care – it helps you to go on especially when you have the feeling that everything is lost (Maluccio 1977, 149).

This illustrates the appreciation of relief when feelings and emotions have been bottled up for a long time – a common finding in the literature (Beck and Jones 1973; Mayer and Timms 1970; Reith 1975/6). People are especially grateful to find someone on whom they can unburden themselves if they have lacked confidants in the past (Butrym 1968; Mayer and Timms 1970). Relief is often due to the fact that the confidant (the social worker) is an *outsider* i.e. someone who is dissociated from the emotional entanglements of the client's situation (Butler, Bow and Gibbons 1978; Mayer and Timms 1970).

For example, a woman who had attempted suicide after hearing from abroad that her husband wanted a divorce, felt that having an outsider to talk to was essential: 'When most depressed I could talk to her, get it off my chest . . . could not do this with family or close friends; an outsider was important' (Butler, Bow and Gibbons 1978, 395). Other people's relief is related to their being reassured. For example, parents are immensely relieved on being told that their child is normal, not abnormal (Burck 1978). This emotional unburdening has various consequences. It temporarily lifts clients' depression even if their circumstances remain the same (Mayer and Timms 1970; Silverman 1969). It can improve feelings of dissatisfaction, helplessness, of being alone or overwhelmed and confused by events (Sacks, Bradley and Beck 1970). Parents have described how ventilating their feelings of inadequacy or anger about their children removed much of the hostility or tension from the parent/child interaction (Sacks, Bradley and Beck 1970). The following quote illustrates how relief can also provide people with more confidence to do things for themselves and to improve relations with others (Mayer and Timms 1970; Maluccio 1977).

> The counselling was worthwhile. It felt good . . . because it was the first time in years I could talk to someone about what's on my mind . . . she helped me to gain confidence. I began to get out more with people, to get along easier . . . I still have a long way to go . . . but I speak out more for my rights (Maluccio 1977).

It is clear that relatively 'simple' changes in feelings and emotions are evaluated favourably by clients. Just how valuable such emotional relief is in the long term, however, is a debatable point and one not examined in great detail by researchers. Sacks *et al.* have argued that the value of such changes depends not on their magnitude but on 'the leverage they provided for coping with immediately pressing problems' (1970, 85). Other researchers have suggested that emotional relief is only a temporary respite and that, unless other forms of help materialize, clients (particularly those in long-term 'treatment') become dissatisfied. This option has been substantiated by the few studies which have examined clients' evaluations of service at different points in time (Maluccio 1977; Silverman 1969). These studies strongly suggest that talking is perceived as being valuable by clients mainly due to the emotional relief they experience – and that is all. Few clients perceive any other real benefits in 'just talking' (Maluccio 1977; Mayer and Timms 1970; Reith 1975/6; Silverman 1969). They experience relief, but then want something more. A few do appreciate the opportunity of talking which can provide them with a new perspective on, and insight into, themselves. What little evidence there is suggests that these clients tend to be more educated than the majority of clients (Silverman 1969), or else have had previous experience of this form of help, i.e. they had already acquired the 'talking set' for help (Burck 1978).

The vast majority of clients, however, from *all* socioeconomic backgrounds (not just from the lower socioeconomic classes as is commonly believed) are waiting for their talking to lead to something, to some other form of help that usually involves some concrete activity on the part of the social worker (Maluccio 1977). Thus many clients who find their worker passive and introspective, employing techniques of exploration, do not feel they are getting any help. We have already noted how large numbers of clients with emotional/interpersonal problems value highly the social worker adopting a directive approach. This is because they expect and desire advice, recommendations, and active prescription. The 17 clients attending an American casework agency varied in their expectations of how much effort they *themselves* would need to expend, but all expected that the social worker could 'fix things', and that there were concrete and specific ways of helping. As one mother explained:

> I got tired of talking. It was the same routine every time; she asked how I was, how my daughter was. It would have helped if she had just told me what to do about my daughter. She had more experience with this kind of child (Silverman 1969, 179).

Clients complaining of receiving 'just talk' from the social worker and not enough action is a very common finding in the literature. If, however, 'help' (as defined by the client) does eventually materialize, clients feel much happier. For example, social workers' interpretations of problem behaviour can give individuals some sense of enlightenment. Mayer and Timms (1970) describe how some social workers, who were in contact with both partners in a marital dispute, acted as 'go-betweens' and occasionally offered interpretations to one about the other. As one satisfied client explains,

> The social worker sort of pointed out things to my husband which he should see and understand in me, and she did the same to me about my husband. For example, she said to me 'your husband is having a hard time. He has had to put up with your mother for quite a long time. He's had your mother in the home and that in itself is quite a difficulty. A man can't possibly feel at home when there's someone watching every move he makes and word he speaks.' You see, my husband is a bit self-conscious anyway – he's inclined to feel a bit inferior and it doesn't help if someone stares at him. He was tense all the time and Miss C. said that it had to come out somewhere in the end (Mayer and Timms 1970, 87).

Given the distinction made between 'talking' and 'helping' (Silverman 1969), how does this aid our understanding of clients' reactions to particular 'treatment' approaches? We believe that it partially explains the increasing evidence from experimental and exploratory research which suggests that people with interpersonal problems evaluate more favourably a task-centred than an open-ended casework approach. Some experimental studies (Gibbons *et al.* 1979; Reid and Shyne 1969) have discovered that a higher proportion of those clients receiving task-centred casework as opposed to open-ended casework, express satisfaction with service. Furthermore, those receiving task-centred casework are more likely to express liking for the caseworker, more likely to perceive improvement in their problem, such as reduced conflict and increased communication with others, and more likely to experience a general amelioration of difficulties in personal and social relationships (Reid and Shyne 1969). There are several reasons for individuals' preference for this approach. Firstly, research suggests that task-centred casework uses more of the directive and active approach valued by clients than does open-ended casework (Reid and Shyne 1969). It is perhaps not surprising that clients prefer the 'components of service' of the former method. Secondly, one of the distinguishing features of task-centred casework is the attempt of the social worker and the client to come to some common agreement on what the problem is and what can be done about it. After exploration and discussion of expectations and methods of helping, the formulation of a clearly defined target problem and task is arrived at. When this occurs, people feel good that they have a plan of action for the future (Butler, Bow and Gibbons 1978). It gives many of them a sense of relief and hope for the future. For example, clients just recovering from attempted suicide have described how encouragement from the social worker to plan and take immediate action to overcome their distress provided them with the courage to feel that they could 'master the confusion of the crisis' (Butler, Bow and Gibbons 1978, 395). The third typical feature of task-centred casework is the time limit set on the service period. This was found helpful by people recovering from suicide attempts as 'the planning of termination right from the start helped the process of coming of terms with it' (Butler, Bow and Gibbons 1978, 407). When the time of termination of contact arrives, however, client's reactions vary. Some people don't mind, while others have mixed feelings,

> I was very apprehensive about the ending of social work contact but pleased that it did have a definite end because I was becoming quite dependent. If it had gone on much longer I think I would have wanted social work help for ever (Butler, Bow and Gibbons 1978, 407).

The dissatisfaction of the minority of clients (especially wives involved in marital disputes) who dislike the brevity of service, may perhaps be qualified. Reid and Shyne (1969) note that there is no relation between client's dissatisfaction with the *brevity* of service and clients' evaluations of the *helpfulness* of service. About half of those complaining feel they have been 'helped considerably', about the same proportion as those who do *not* complain about the termination of contact. Reid and Shyne speculated that those who expressed dissatisfaction did so partly because they found the service helpful and wanted more.

The research on people with interpersonal and intrapersonal difficulties illustrates many of the complexities involved in clients' evaluations. The nature of the help encountered by clients varies from agency to agency. The outcomes experienced depend on the definitions employed by clients and by their professional helpers of problems and the appropriate problem-solving activities. The perceived value of help that is offered depends on the particular stage of the help-seeking process. All these considerations underline the importance of relating clients' evaluations to context. Without specifying what kind of help offered at which point in the 'treatment' process is found valuable by which particular clients – our understanding of what 'works' in social work is undermined.

Multi-problem families

Most multi-problem families are poor. Many are unemployed and experience housing and financial difficulties. These problems are often exacerbated when the family has only one parent. Such material problems rarely exist in isolation. As a result, many of these people have problems with child care and interfamilial relationships, and they are often in a state of depression and anxiety. What do these disadvantaged and often powerless people expect of the social services and how do they evaluate the help they receive?

When these families are asked what they hope to receive from the social services, they usually mention material and practical help. Few seem to expect other forms of help. The striking feature about these people is that their satisfaction is strongly related to their receiving the help that they expect and want, although it may not be as much help as they would like, or in the precise form desired. The kinds of help families with multi-problems most appreciate fall into two main categories: (1) financial, material and practical aid, e.g. money, clothing, furniture, housing, home-helps and

(2) practical help in the form of the social worker negotiating and making arrangements on behalf of the client, e.g. advocacy.
(1) The provision of financial, material and practical resources usually results in client satisfaction. Clients are especially appreciative if their material needs are met and dealt with early on in the help-seeking process (Mayer and Timms 1970; Sainsbury, 1975). Of the families attending a Sheffield Family Service Unit, Sainsbury (1975, 121–2) comments, 'A client's acceptance of an agency as helpful relates to the immediate meeting of needs in the manner presented'. These families expressed much satisfaction with service because it was the practice of the social workers in the Family Service Unit to meet the needs of the client in the way they were presented, as soon as possible, and irrespective of other kinds of help offered later. The importance of the social worker accepting the client's definition of the presenting problem has been stressed elsewhere. For example, Perlman has argued that

> except for people who are clearly disoriented, we lack the diagnostic skills to determine certainly on first contact, which statements represent 'real' needs and which distort or conceal 'the problem'. From a pragmatic point of view, unless the social agency begins by confronting the problem as perceived by the consumer, the latter is likely to show his lack of confidence by voting with his feet and terminating the relationship (1975, 21).

Others have argued convincingly that the early provision of the help requested by clients is a quick and effective way of winning the client's confidence in the caseworker's intent (Baird 1976; Parkinson 1970). It has also been suggested that the prompt meeting of their initial material needs is seen by clients as being *symbolic* of further help forthcoming in the future (Sainsbury 1975).

If, on the other hand, the resources are not forthcoming, this can be a main cause of client dissatisfaction. This dissatisfaction is particularly prevalent when there is a discrepancy between clients' requests and a lack of resources to meet them. This is especially true when the desired resources are jobs, homes and adequate incomes. For example, George and Wilding (1972) found that fathers of motherless families assessed the social services as failing to provide any meaningful help. The fathers' primary criticism was the lack of available resources, e.g. home helps and day care facilities, combined sometimes with perceived inefficiency on the part of the social worker.

> They sent me to the home helps. But although they saw me, I never heard anything from them. They said they would write to me. I am still waiting [two years later] (George and Wilding 1972, 154).

Such feelings of disappointment or anger can be heightened if the client believes that other people in similar circumstances to themselves have received more help (Jackson 1973; Mayer and Timms 1970). In other words, here 'evaluation' is the making of judgements relative to, or in comparison with, the treatment of others.

This last observation re-emphasizes that the reasons for clients' satisfaction are sometimes more complicated than simply receiving or not receiving the desired resources. Sometimes the help provided by the social services is evaluated in relation to that coming from other sources. If the social work agency can provide resources that are not available for instance from friends and neighbours, clients are especially appreciative. For example, Mayer and Timms (1970) note how some clients value getting help which their 'informal network' cannot provide. Usually, this is because friends and relatives are in a similar predicament – as was the case of one woman, 'My sisters couldn't help me . . . they got families of their own to keep' (Mayer and Timms 1970, 42).

George and Wilding's study (1972) of motherless families provides another example of the relativity of clients' judgements. The fathers were asked which source of help they valued most. Significantly, 60.1 per cent mentioned that coming from relatives, 18.9 per cent from friends and neighbours, and only 6.9 per cent from the personal social services. Help from the social services was insignificant in comparison with that from elsewhere. The criteria used by the fathers in establishing the usefulness of various forms of help were stability, reliability and scarcity. The few fathers who did rate social services help highly received day nursery care and home help facilities – resources which obviously could not be provided by friends.

Other people experience feelings of frustration, even resentment, despite the fact that they do, in the end, get what they wanted from social workers. Such feelings are related to their perceived powerlessness *vis-à-vis* the social worker. This conception of social worker power is different from that previously mentioned. It is not to do with the worker's use of authority in the form of giving advice and recommendations to the clients. It is the power that is 'inherent' in the worker in that he or she holds the key to the desired resources. This perceived imbalance of power in the relationship between clients and their social workers results in some people believing that they have to resort to various 'tactics' in order to get the help they seek. The adoption of such tactics can be unpleasant for the client. For example, several clients have expressed dislike at having to prove their eligibility for financial help, particularly if this involves certain ingratiating techniques like having to appear 'deserving' (George and Wilding 1972; Mayer and Timms 1970). It was a source of irony and embitterment to the fathers of motherless families that if they had coped less well then they did, i.e. neglected their children, they would have been more likely to receive help (George and Wilding 1972). In fact, some of these fathers had been advised by officials to adopt such techniques. As one father explained,

> [One headmistress] asked if I was getting any help. She said I was looking after them too well. She said I should let them look dirty and ragged so that people would take notice of the fact and say I needed help, and then I could ask for help. Yes, she meant I should do that (George and Wilding 1972, 155).

Other clients, particularly those families with child care problems, many of whom are involuntary 'captive' clients, hold to a more explicit view that their relationship with the social services department is essentially that of bargain (Cohen 1971). The worker has the desired material goods; the client has to bargain for them. How successfully this bargaining works affects subsequent expressions of satisfaction. In order to get the desired services, these people agree to allow the social worker 'in' on the private affairs of the family. If this exchange occurs, all is well. If the help fails to materialize – the clients feel 'cheated', in that they have kept their side of the bargain, but the workers have broken theirs (Cohen 1971). These families' dissatisfaction is most prevalent when the social worker fails to provide resources and instead attempts 'casework'. For example, single-parent families were greatly frustrated when they asked for material help but received only casework treatment (George and Wilding 1972). Faced with scarce resources, perhaps this is all that social workers feel they can do. Casework becomes a substitute for 'real' help (Perlman 1975). Alternatively, it may be that the social worker believes that people are best helped by talking through problems and discussing feelings (Silverman 1969).

(2) The second form of tangible help which is much appreciated by multi-problem families is the use of power by the social worker on the clients' behalf. Such advocacy is regarded by some people as the most useful form of help they can get from the social services (Glampson and Goldberg 1976; Jackson 1973; Rubenstein and Bloch 1978). We must remember that many of these families are in danger of being evicted or (in Britain) having their electricity or gas cut off. They also often have difficulty in dealing with the various authorities, particularly social security. In these circumstances, the families are very grateful if social workers take their side and contact other agencies on their behalf, pointing clients in the right direction for help and guiding them through the maze of welfare rights entitlements. A social worker who prevents an eviction or the electricity being cut off, who disarms a creditor or negotiates more money for the client is highly valued. Providing support in threatening situations, e.g. accompanying them to juvenile courts, is also valued (Jackson 1973).

The following comments illustrate such appreciation. The first person was in difficulty with creditors, and the second needed help in dealing with a Housing Department.

> When I told her someone from the electric company had been around to see me, she got straight on the phone and said, 'I told you not to bother Mrs Wood. We're going to pay the bill for her, but its going to take another couple of weeks.' She really told them off and I thought, she's on my side . . . I liked to think, she's got some go in her (Mayer and Timms 1970, 108).

> It was someone to turn to when I was in a difficult position. He [the worker] rang up the Housing Department and spoke for me. That was a great help. For me to go on my own was worrying. He took the heaviest of it off me (Jackson 1973, 14).

In the clients' view these are substantial deeds. Among families attending the Family Service Unit in Sheffield they are 'ones in which the notions of "successful" and "good" were most frequently employed by clients to describe both the work and the worker' (Sainsbury 1975, 445). Here appreciation of social workers' advocacy is directly related to the clients' belief that social workers can do more than just ordinary friends. They are friends with power and it is this power which constitutes their usefulness (Jackson 1973). A client, Mrs Wilson, explains this advantage in dealing with other officials.

> It sounds better saying 'Mrs . . . from the FSU' than what a friend of mine would, picking up the phone and saying, 'I'm a friend of Mrs Wilson' They'd turn round and tell her they hadn't got time, and put the phone down (Jackson 1973, 12).

Nowhere is there any evidence of clients complaining about the social worker's use of advocacy. There are only complaints that sometimes the social worker's efforts come to nothing. This usually occurs when clients over-estimate the power invested in the social worker *vis-à-vis* other agencies.

More detailed study is required of client appreciation of advocacy. Few of the studies examine in any depth which particular 'advocate' activities of the social worker are valued, why such activities are rated highly and whether such advocacy results in any permanent change in these people's lives.

Probationers and prisoners

Probationers and prisoners differ from other clients in that all their contacts with the social services take place in a context in which some responsibility for control is explicit. A probation officer is directly responsible for a probationer's supervision. In prisons, the position of the prison welfare officers is more ambivalent.* Although the prison welfare officers might not regard themselves as being control agents, they are often concerned to enable prisoners to accommodate to their situation. Furthermore, a minority of prisoners make little distinction between the officers and the rest of the prison 'screws'. For example, some short-term prisoners when asked their opinions as to the function of the prison welfare officer, answered that they believed his job was to assist in the custodial aims of the institution (Holborn 1975).

The context in which these people and social workers meet is fascinating. Yet, little is known about what probationers and prisoners think of the social services made available to them. The existing literature on their views, is on the whole, sparse and fragmented. The studies tend to examine only certain

---

* The status and role of prison welfare officers varies from country to country. For example, in Scotland prison welfare is the responsibility of the local authority social work departments. In some states in Australia, some prison welfare is carried out by parole officers but this service, as in England is administered separately from other social work-related services.

factors involved in the social work service and fail to analyse a more combined approach. Thus there is research on such isolated factors as the probationers' or prisoners' attitudes to their probation or prison welfare officer (Beker 1965; Gandy *et al*. 1975; Jones 1978); on their evaluations of certain methods of working (Gottesfeld 1965); on their assessments of the degree of effectiveness of service. No study has encompassed all these aspects, or attempted to explore the links that may exist between them, i.e. what attitudes of social workers combined with which methods of helping to contribute towards a desired outcome. Despite the unsatisfactory nature of much of the research some common trends in probationers' and prisoners' thinking emerge.

The evidence suggests that probationers' and prisoners' expectations of social service are of a relatively clear and limited nature. (That is, if they have any expectations at all; it has been found (Sainsbury and Nixon 1979) that a large percentage of these clients have no expectations or knowledge of social · work.) This contrasts with the confused expectations commonly found among clients attending local authority agencies for the first time (Sainsbury and Nixon 1979). For example, 62 per cent of a sample of 120 prisoners in three British prisons, were able to be fairly specific about what they felt a prison welfare officer was there to do (Holborn 1975). Nearly all mentioned 'immediate' problems, these problems usually involving practical difficulties (often domestic) outside the prison. The majority of prisoners in a study of a Scottish prison (Harris 1978) confirmed this view when they stressed that the problems with which they could expect help from a prison welfare officer, were essentially of a practical nature. The expectations of probationers (and sometimes also of their families) have been shown to be comparatively low and are again related to pressing immediate problems such as help with children's behaviour, with housing, material/ financial help and with the prevention of criminal behaviour (Holborn 1975; Sainsbury and Nixon 1979; Shaw 1974). Given these expectations, it is not surprising that these clients frequently define 'help' in material and practical terms.

A phrase probationers and prisoners could use to describe good social work would be 'Action Speaks Louder Than Words'. It is primarily on the criterion of social workers' activity that their judgements on the usefulness of social work are based. For example, probationers appreciate the social worker taking an active interest in their hobbies and interests, as well as encouraging them to participate in sports or getting help with educational or occupational skills (Gottesfeld 1965; Jones 1978). Probationers *and* their parents value the social worker being involved in making practical arrangements for the youth, to receive, for example, employment, school, financial or medical assistance (Gandy *et al*. 1975).

The social worker adopting an advocate role on behalf of the probationer or his family is especially appreciated, particularly when the parents are relatively poor and have to cope with a family single handed (Gandy *et al*.

1975). For example, parents in Canada have reported improvement in their child when probation officers acted both as mediators between the family and the school, as well as advocates for the probationers (Gandy *et al*. 1975). Sainsbury and Nixon (1979) confirmed this finding in Britain when they discovered this 'negotiating' role of the probation officer was the second most helpful form of help rated by the probationers. Unfortunately, *why* this was found helpful and *how* it had contributed to improvement was not examined. Interestingly, the Canadian probation officers were willing to take on this advocate role and regard it as helpful. However, the probation officers in the British study ranked 'negotiation' *lower* than the clients when ranking the relative helpfulness of particular inputs of social work. They also *underestimated* the extent to which clients felt helped by such worker activity.

A similar discrepancy emerged in the value ascribed to the provision of financial and material help. On the other hand, officers ranked advice and insight very *high* on their list, and considerably *overestimated* their helpfulness to clients. But to many probationers, particularly youths, talk is simply talk (Gottesfeld 1965). The verbalization of emotions and feelings is not seen as having value. (Also some are concerned about the question of the confidentiality of what they tell the professional.) This is not to say that some discussion is not found helpful. 'Encouragement' has been highly evaluated by both probationers and officers in Britain (Sainsbury and Nixon 1979). What clients see as constituting encouragement is not clear. The authors suggest that action in the form of the probation worker's use of authority over the probationer is redefined by the latter as 'encouragement'.

Prisoners' desire for action is understandable. Enclosed in an institution, they are powerless to deal with worrying problems outside. These problems are mainly related to practical or interpersonal difficulties involving the family or others close to the prisoner, e.g. the paying of bills, business or tax worries, family welfare, marital relationships (Harris 1978; Holborn 1975; Shaw 1974). Other practical and interpersonal problems are related to the prisoner himself, e.g. post-release problems on discharge and parole, problems of prison life itself (Shaw 1974). These problems are reflected in the kinds of requests made to prison welfare officers. For example, the majority of requests made by 120 prisoners in one study of three prisons were for the prison welfare officers to take *active* steps to preserve the prisoner's links with the outside world (Holborn 1975). One quarter of these men wanted the prison welfare officer to act as a 'go-between' between themselves and people outside, communicating messages, settling debts etc., many hoping the prison welfare officer would act as their negotiator with people outside the prison. About a fifth of the men also wanted help in negotiating *within* the prison system to enable them to get, for example, special letters or visits. Very few of the men in these three prisons, then, wanted 'talking' help as opposed to 'doing' help. This was confirmed amongst the men in another two prisons, one open and the other closed, in which the researchers found that, on the whole, action was preferred to discussion (Shaw 1974). The only time when talk and general support was felt to be desirable was after release from prison. Those prisoners who did use or planned to use aftercare service appreciated having someone available to fall back on in times of crisis. In addition, a minority of men have expressed considerable satisfaction at being given the chance to have more time to talk to the prison welfare officer in the prison, the content of their discussions being fairly traditional casework (Shaw 1974). One prisoner said to the researcher, 'I used to feel inferiority about speaking, he's helped me with that. I wouldn't be able to talk to you now otherwise' (Shaw 1974, 69). Nevertheless, even the men who found discussion helpful added that talking alone was not enough, 'Just talking doesn't do any good – you've got to know something is being done as well' (Holborn 1975, 116).

As a consequence of their desire that the social workers act as advocates and negotiators, or as one man said, 'your arms and legs on the outside', the men's satisfaction very much depends on whether they do or do not get the help requested (Glaser 1964; Holborn 1975; Shaw 1974). As the social work staff are most often the persons to whom requests are directed, this is not surprising (Holborn 1975). When the social workers can solve the problem as requested, they are judged as being effective. For example, one man was very worried because his girlfriend had stopped writing to him.

> I hoped the welfare officer would talk things over with her and sort things out . . . she thought I was going to stay in here for ever. He got me a welfare visit and explained to her that I would be out as quick as I could (Holborn 1975, 90).

Thus, if for one reason or another, the social worker is slow or fails to produce immediate solutions to problems, the prisoner can feel considerable dissatisfaction,

> He's elusive you can't reach him, he's hardly ever on the wing. He keeps coming up with excuses all the time. He talks but doesn't do anything. I asked him for train times 2 weeks before I went on home leave . . . in the end I got them off the PO instead (Shaw 1974, 52).

It is also essential to inmates that their requests are dealt with relatively quickly and are not put to the side and forgotten. As Holborn states,

> When many prisoners are frustrated by their impotence to deal with things themselves it is easy to understand why speed and reliability on the part of prison welfare officers were rated so highly (1975, 93).

While problem solving is the main criterion of evaluation, other considerations affect inmates' judgements. Prisoners' evaluations can also be affected by their perception of the prison welfare officers' power to act. Men with favourable attitudes towards prison welfare talk sympathetically about officers who have to struggle hard to help under the very difficult circumstances of the prison's rules and regulations. Other men with far more negative views of prison welfare considerably overestimate the power of the

social worker to carry out some of their requests. In these latter circumstances some men label the social workers as 'useless', 'promise merchants'
or just 'idle' (Shaw 1974). Contextual considerations undoubtedly affect
evaluations. This point and its implications shall be discussed more fully in
the following chapter.

In examining inmates' opinions, note should be taken of the overall significance of prison welfare officers to prisoners. All the prison studies reviewed
found that a large number of men had no contact with the social worker.
Compared with other prison staff, such as work supervisors, prison welfare
officers have little influence on the men. From inmates' points of view welfare staff do not occupy a central place in prison life for inmates.

Summary

In identifying which people, with which problems, find which kinds of
help valuable, we are testifying to the *particular* nature of clients' evaluations. Their verdicts are particular to their problem, to the particular stage
of help-seeking, to their problem-solving orientation, to the service offerings
they encounter. At the same time, their evaluations are *general*, i.e. their
responses have much in common. People want help in the form of information and advice. They want help that is supportive and directive. They want
and appreciate help that is tangible, material. They rate highly advocacy and
negotiation. The reasons why these services are so highly valued are not
hard to find. Many clients are poor; many are deprived in terms of housing, jobs, education, and many are powerless. It is not surprising that they
are most interested in help that is concrete, immediate, and directive. This
is the help they feel is most likely to alleviate some difficulties, at least
temporarily.

Yet clients' evaluations are not simply related to the receiving or not
receiving of such help. The previous two chapters are replete with evidence
to suggest the relativity of clients' verdicts. They are relative to context, to
knowledge of services available, to expectations, to help received in past
encounters, to help received from other sources, to perceptions of the 'pleasantness' of the social worker. These issues need to be taken up and explored
further, which the following chapter attempts to do.

5
The Meaning and Merits of Clients' View

Throughout the two previous chapters, we have constantly referred to the context in which clients make judgements about their experiences with the social services. Wherever possible we have clarified which clients, seeking what kind of help find what social worker attitudes or services helpful and at what point in the help-seeking process. In addition, at particular points in the analysis we have attempted to establish links between clients' evaluations and their expectations, values, previous help-seeking experiences and problem-solving orientations. When appropriate, methodological considerations have also been discussed. The importance of such contextual matters requires re-emphasis. The concern of this chapter is to place clients' evaluations and the general trend of research findings in a *broader* context than that previously discussed – a context that is sociopolitical in nature and implications.

As we have seen, some clients' comments on services are very critical in tone. It is perhaps a strange, but not uncommon finding, that people are often far more articulate about the events and experiences which cause them anger and dissatisfaction, than they are about those that lead to satisfaction. Despite the critical tone of many clients' comments, the overwhelming majority of studies report a considerable degree of overall client satisfaction with help-seeking contacts. Does this imply that the social services can be relatively happy that they are providing relevant and useful social services? Can we assume that client satisfaction necessarily equates with clients' feelings that they have been helped? On what exactly do clients base their *overall* evaluations of social services? In an attempt to answer these and related questions, three relevant issues are discussed,

1 the meaning of 'satisfaction' as a criterion of client evaluation in social work,
2 the methodology of consumer research studies and its bearing on the general research findings,
3 the distinction between 'helpful people' and 'helpful services': the relationship between evaluations of these and expressions of satisfaction, and the implications of this in broad sociopolitical terms.

Discussion of the above considerations will enable us to come to some conclusion about the meaning and merits of the research findings on clients' evaluations.

The meaning of 'client satisfaction'

Expressions of client satisfaction with service must be as comforting to social workers as the comments of dissatisfaction are disturbing. Without question, many people feel satisfied and helped by their contact with the social services. At the same time, however, some people express much dissatisfaction. 'Satisfaction' is a commonly used criterion of client evaluation. But many researchers fail to take into account that human 'satisfaction' is a complex notion. It is a notion which is related to a wide variety of factors – such as lifestyles and experiences, expectations and values. Yet the influence of such factors on client evaluations of social work is often overlooked – and the concept of 'satisfaction' is often oversimplified. Runciman's (1966) notions of 'relative deprivation' and 'reference groups' illustrate the complexity of the concept. As he explains,

> The related notions of 'relative deprivation' and 'reference group' both derive from a familiar truism: that people's attitudes, aspirations and grievances largely depend on the frame of reference within which they are conceived. Examples readily suggest themselves from everyday experience. A person's satisfactions, even at the most trivial level, are conditioned by his expectations, and the proverbial way to make oneself conscious of one's advantages is to contrast one's situation with that of others worse off than oneself. The frame of reference can work in either of two ways: on the one hand, a man who has been led to expect, shall we say, promotion in his job will be more aggrieved if he fails to achieve it than a man whose ambitions have not been similarily heightened. On the other hand, a man taken to hospital after some minor mishap will feel a good deal less sorry for himself if he is put in a bed next to the victim of a serious accident who has been permanently maimed (Runciman 1966, 9).

A similar analysis of human satisfaction/dissatisfaction was made in Coates and Silburn's study (1970) of a district in Nottingham. The study area was centrally situated but rundown and scheduled for comprehensive redevelopment. The standard of housing was described by the researchers as very poor. Few of the houses had bathrooms, most had outside toilets, decaying brickwork, rot, damp and overcrowding. Such conditions, however, did not lead residents to make overt expressions of dissatisfaction. The researchers comment:

> Human beings are almost infinitely adaptable, and provided that they are ill treated consistently, they are apt to regard ill treatment as 'natural'. If the lavatory leaks a little, and has always leaked a little, one comes to regard the leak as 'normal'. If the roof blows off such a lavatory of course one will expect to be annoyed. But all the myriad petty discomforts can too easily be borne with remarkably little complaint. Damp, cold, rot, decrepitude are as 'natural' in St Ann's as is the smoky atmosphere: for all most people know, they have been sent by Providence and must be endured. Indeed, since Providence has never sent anything else, what other response would be possible? Only exceptional damp, unusual cold, excessive rot, and decrepitude to the point of collapse, are felt to be legitimate subjects of discussion (Coates and Silburn 1970, 81–2).

A situation which outsiders might find intolerable, was bearable to these inhabitants. They compared their living conditions with those of people like themselves who inhabited the same area, and with what they themselves have experienced in the past.

This is precisely the attitude of people residing in another working-class district, this time in Sunderland. The local authority wanted to move these residents to a large self-contained estate, and then to demolish their old homes (Dennis 1970). But many of these people wished to remain in the old houses, despite their lack of basic amenities. These people did not compare themselves with the 'national average', against which they were relatively deprived, 'but with standards of their own past against which they are relatively well off'. Thus the following comments from some of the residents,

> I've only got one plug for the TV, the frigerator and the vacuum. I use the vacuum off the light in the other rooms. Can't complain: I've used them all these years! (Dennis 1970, 220).

> I haven't got any facilities! It doesn't take much to heat a kettle or pan, man! I have to be satisfied, I have to manage without it! (Dennis 1970, 220)

These findings on human satisfaction/dissatisfaction are important to this review for three reasons:

1 many people in contact with the social services come from areas not unlike these districts,
2 people's low expectations of what to expect from life are reflected in what they expect from a social service department and their evaluation of it,
3 people's lifestyle also has implications for how they perceive satisfactory service. What others regard as a 'basic necessity' for living, they regard as a luxury.

This 'normalization' process often occurs among people who have experienced material and practical difficulties over a prolonged period. For example, Goldberg has said that old people with notoriously low expectations and high levels of satisfaction, − who have experienced great deprivation − 'had to be resigned to their decreasing mobility, growing isolation and restriction of their life space and may prefer to leave things as they are' (1970, 116). However, similar processes can occur amongst people with more intangible problems. For example, Clare Creer who has studied the problems families encounter when they have a schizophrenic relative living in their home, has the following to say about the families' reactions to their situation:

> Another problem is that relatives may become so used to an unhappy state of affairs that they cease to regard their situation as anything remarkable or worthy of complaint. This is not to say that their distress is relieved but rather that they come to regard their distress as a normal state of mind. They cease to expect anything better from life and therefore no longer seek solutions to their difficulties

... living constantly with disturbed behaviour may eventually alter relatives' ideas about what is 'normal'. This is not to say their ability to tolerate such behaviour increases. They may continue to feel depressed or anxious but without attributing this to the patient. Thus they do not see themselves as having a need and are not likely to be very demanding of services. If they do ask for help, they will probably easily be put off or fall out of contact (1975, 6).

This 'normalization' of distress has its parallel in medicine. A study (Freidson 1960) of patients' views of medical practice noted the difficulties that medicine can sometimes have in reaching and treating those illnesses which are most elusive to all — those the patient has accepted as part of his existence. Freidson elaborates:

> Indeed, those symptoms tend not even to be defined as symptoms by the patient, but as idiosyncracies or annoying but tolerable facts of life. Chronic indigestion, persistent colds, headaches, backaches, and nervousness are often accepted by the patient in this fashion, particularly after their significance has been shrugged off or deprecated by a physician or two in the past (1960, 84).

The above examples emphasize the importance of lifestyles and past experiences in affecting expectations, and in turn influencing peoples' judgements. They also forge a link between clients' evaluations of social services and other aspects of their lives. This underlines our previous statement that clients' evaluations do not occur in a vacuum. Clients usually evaluate social services in comparison with something else, i.e. evaluation is relative — we have plenty of examples of this in the preceding chapters. We have seen how clients' opinions of contact can be related to previous positive or negative help-seeking experiences with other officials (Mayer and Timms 1970; Rees 1974; Sainsbury 1975); professionals (Butrym 1968); to previous helpseeking experiences in the same agency (Mayer and Timms 1970); to perceptions that others are getting more help than they are (Mayer and Timms 1970); to the perceived adequacy/inadequacy of their informal network of friends and relatives (George and Wilding 1972); to lack of any help received in the past and lack of information about available services (Butrym, 1968; Handler 1973); to their orientations towards problem definition and solution (McCaughey and Chew 1977; Perlman 1975; Rees 1978; Silverman 1969). Several studies have illustrated that it can be factors such as these rather than the service itself, which are responsible for client satisfaction (Sainsbury and Nixon 1979). Furthermore, what clients refer to when they say they are satisfied varies over time. Evaluation need not be constant. Some attributes of the social worker can be evaluated highly early on in contact but may lead to dissatisfaction later on if other qualities are not exhibited (Maluccio 1977). Contact with the social services can heighten people's expectations, this in turn affecting evaluations. For example, the pleasant demeanour of the social worker (Jordan 1976), or increased knowledge of available services (Goldberg *et al.* 1970), can raise clients' awareness of possible improvements in their living situation with the result they are likely to be more demanding or critical of services. It goes without saying, that all the above factors must be taken into account for any meaningful evaluation of social work. Only then will studies do justice to the complex concept 'client evaluation'. Otherwise, we can never be sure whether the high rate of client satisfaction is related more to factors like lack of knowledge or limited expectations, than to the actual helpfulness of social service contact.

Methodology

How far are research methods sensitive to the above considerations? How aware are researchers of the problem involved in eliciting and interpreting clients' evaluations? Is there any relationship between research methods and the level of client satisfaction? These are difficult but important questions. The following analysis attempts to answer some of them.

Many of the research studies adopt an overly simple view when studying client evaluations. This can sometimes result in distortion of clients' assessments. For example, some studies use structured interviews. One of the drawbacks of this method is that the data collected are often that which the researchers, but not necessarily the clients, think is relevant; that is, the researchers, sometimes aided by professionals, devise the questionnaire which may exclude considerations which are important from the client's perspective. The chances of this occurring are increased when it is the researchers who provide the criteria to which the clients have to respond. For example, Rubenstein and Bloch (1978) in an otherwise interesting study, wanted to explore clients' opinions about their relationship with the worker. However, the clients were not given a free rein in their evaluations, but had to rate the social worker on three criteria provided by the researchers – worker's fairness, worker's honesty and the clients' feelings of ease with the worker. From the client's perspective these may not be necessarily the most important aspects of their relationship with the social worker. Thus, the assumptions which lie behind apparently straightforward questions may not be shared by the client. As Cohen suggests, 'a question which invites evaluation of a service may have different meanings for different consumers' (1971, 42). The consumer's evaluation may be concerned with only a part of what the researcher or social worker defines as a service. For example, social casework may not be regarded by the client as the service, but only as an 'interference one has to tolerate in order to receive the service' (Cohen 1971, 42), i.e. tangible goods. This emphasizes how important it is for the researcher to elicit what the consumer sees as the boundaries of service. This is best achieved in guided interviews which give clients the opportunity to express opinions and also to clarify ambiguous or unclear statements which may be included in a structured questionnaire.

Other studies provide fixed response rates to questions, obliging respondents to limit their answers to specified categories. Thus the client may be asked to evaluate service as being 'satisfactory' or 'not satisfactory'. Apart from oversimplifying the concept as we have discussed in the previous pages, this approach provides no information as to what it is exactly that clients find satisfactory or otherwise, or what the reasons are behind their opinions. In more detail, other researchers provide different fixed response ratings to certain aspects of service. Thus, the client has to relate the helpfulness of service as 'good', 'fair', 'poor', 'bad', etc. Nowhere, however, is there any recognition that we have to know what these ratings mean. If a service is rated as 'good' we have to know, 'good' compared to what? (Giordano 1977). This type of research curtails clients' freedom to answer completely and precisely. Any analysis of such 'results' will leave too many unanswered questions. But we must also be cautious about studies which go beyond simple ratings of 'satisfactory', 'unsatisfactory', 'good/poor', 'helpful/ unhelpful', and attempt to study clients' assessments of progress and change during social work contact. This is a useful device which adds an important dimension to clients' evaluations. It illustrates an awareness that a client may be satisfied with contact, but perceive little or no change in his or her circumstance. But difficulties arise when researchers assume that it is the social work contact that is responsible for client change or improvement. For example, family situations do not stay the same, but may either worsen or improve because of factors totally unrelated to social work intervention or the original referral problem. A couple of studies have suggested that clients are more ready than social workers to attribute the reasons for problem improvement or deterioration to factors *outside* social work services (Maluccio 1977; Sacks, Bradley and Beck 1970). The following quote illustrates the client-worker disagreement over the effect of one such outside influence.

Client	Worker
Mrs Gates: I felt real good when they made me a supervisor after being there less than a year. This made me want to go on and live my life even though we had decided to get a divorce.	The promotion was a mixed blessing for Barbara. It demonstrated that people thought highly of her, but it also put more pressure on her to perform at a time when much of her energy was going into coping with the divorce.

(Maluccio 1977, 151)

This example underlines the necessity of inquiring of clients not only whether their situation has improved but also both what constituted and what was responsible for the improvement. Researchers too often assume that 'improvement' is related to social workers' interventions.

Yet another oversimplifying feature of some studies is the generalized nature of many of the research questions. Depending on the types of questions asked, different responses can be elicited (Morris, Cooper and Byles 1973). Global questions of satisfaction typically result in vague, stereotyped answers involving little criticism. Specific questions and probing interviewing techniques reveal clients' responses which tend to be more precise, discriminating and critical in tone. Glampson and Goldberg's study (1976) of clients attending Southampton Social Services Department found that in response to a summary question about satisfaction, most people (73 per cent) replied positively. However, when the researchers analysed this further, and looked at other components of satisfaction they found that 40 per cent of the clients had something to complain about. Somewhat similarly, while considering the types of question posed to the clients attending Family Agencies in Canada, Rondeau (1976) observed that the more precise and personal the question, the lower was client evaluation of results. Positive evaluations were highest in response to questions of a general nature.

A question such as 'Did you profit from your sessions with the social worker?' elicits generally high assessments by clients. But a more detailed question, 'Did the sessions with the social worker help you understand yourself better?' tends to reveal far less positive evaluations. Similar research observations have been made with regard to patients' evaluations of health services (Robinson 1978). Thus those studies utilizing fairly rigid and fixed response research techniques combined with overly general questions produce results indicating the highest levels of client satisfaction.

We are not implying that open-ended, face-to-face interviews are always the best method of collecting clients' assessments. In the hands of a skilled (trained) interviewer they may be adequate.* But for various reasons, such as compliance bias, negativism, 'leading' probes and body language, interviews tend to allow idiosyncratic interpretations of questions to be given to different respondents. We will develop these reservations by examining the power of the interviewer and the timing of research. How aware are researchers of these considerations?

Some studies are carried out by independent researchers who take great pains to assure clients that their replies will be treated confidentially and that the study is quite independent from the service-providing agency or department. Not all studies exhibit such sensitivity. Some believe that an introductory letter from the Department or Agency assuring confidentiality, will dispel clients' fears or reluctances (Hillingdon SSD 1974). Furthermore, a few studies appear to foresee no methodological problems in representatives of the agency administering a questionnaire or completing an interview schedule with a client (McCoy *et al.* 1975; Powell, Shaw and O'Neal 1971). Occasionally, it is even the particular service providers encountered by the clients who are responsible for the execution of the research (Giordano 1977). (In some respects there is nothing wrong with

* In this respect Professor Wyatt Jones pointed out to us that social workers are often notoriously poor survey interviewers because they keep 'treating' the respondent.

this if the 'practitioner' as researcher is sensitive to the considerations mentioned above: what do respondents mean by their answers, what aspects of the researcher's methods of enquiry affect people's responses?)

However, there can be several problems involved in these latter approaches. Firstly, they completely disregard the power relationship between client and social worker or the social work agency. Clients may be extremely reluctant to criticize services if they remain in contact, or expect future contact with the agency. They may feel that they would be jeopardizing their chances of receiving help in the future if they are too critical of service received in the past. For example, parents dealing with an adoption agency sometimes feel dissatisfied and frustrated over certain aspects of their contact. This occurs when the adoption procedure is not fully explained to them. However these parents are often reticent about asking too many questions of the social worker, or openly expressing hostility. As one parent explains, ' . . . we did feel so entirely in their [the Agency's] hands and nervous about antagonizing them in any way – after all, they had the babies!' (Timms 1973). This comment is particularly interesting considering it comes from a couple who are themselves professional people, and who are therefore presumably used to dealing with people in positions of authority.

A perceived imbalance in power can also have the effect of some clients considering it completely *inappropriate* for them to evaluate a social worker or a social work agency. We would expect that clients with a 'passive' orientation to those in authority, and who perceive the social worker as a professional expert would be most likely to adopt this view. Lack of knowledge combined with lack of confidence convinces such clients that they are not in a position to voice criticism of the social services, even if they feel dissatisfaction. For example, one woman seeking help from a counselling agency was asked about the helpfulness of contact with her social worker. She replied:

Mrs A: 'No – *me* tell a social workers she's incompetent?'
P.R.: 'Why do you say this with such a shock in your voice?'
Mrs A: 'Well, she's just there to help people and maybe she feels that just listening is helpful and I didn't, and I didn't feel that I wanted to tell her differently.'

(Silverman 1969, 136).

This woman obviously considers it inappropriate for a lay-person to evaluate a 'professional'. She voiced her dissatisfaction to Silverman, partly due to the intensive semi-structured interviewing techniques from the counselling agency. One wonders how open this woman would have been if workers from the agency had been responsible for conducting the interviews.

The location of interviews or questionnaires may also affect clients' responses. Some take place in the home, others in the agency; some are sent by mail and others even completed over the telephone. But just how important the setting is, is hard to say.

More important for results, however, is the *timing* of the research interviews. Almost all the studies reviewed are retrospective in nature. Indeed some studies require clients to think back to social services experiences which may have occurred *years* beforehand. This retrospection has several implications for the reliability of research results. It is frequently difficult for clients to recall aspects of their behaviour which took place even a few weeks previously (McKinlay 1972). This difficulty is exacerbated when the aspects of behaviour have to do with attitudes, expectations, assessments – given that it is very much harder to remember the beliefs held at a particular point of time than actions. Sainsbury (1975) states how the retrospective nature of his study made it difficult to interpret clients' expectations at referral which, as we have seen, can be a decisive factor in influencing clients' opinions. Sainsbury found it impossible to be sure whether the apparent realistic initial expectations of many of the families attending the Family Service Unit indicated good work by referral agents or 'a subsequent tidying up of memories'. Clients may realign their recollections depending on their subsequent experiences. It has also been suggested that *after* service, people sometimes overlook matters that trouble them during actual contact (McKinlay and Mitchell 1975). Also people using a service only occasionally may be able to tolerate inefficiences or irritations without becoming too dissatisfied (McKinlay and Mitchell 1975). The timing of the research is also significant from another perspective. As we have seen from the preceding analysis, very few studies exhibit an awareness that clients' appreciation of different services can change over time. What a client finds helpful at one point in time may not be valued later on. For instance, Sacks *et al.* (1976) has noted that people can have rapid changes in perspective when their problem has to do with marriage breakup. Their rating of progress can fluctuate – sometimes it is based on relatively temporary changes, such as shifts in feelings, or sometimes it is based on more lasting changes. In accounting for discrepancies in social worker/client assessments of progress, Sacks suggests that small differences in the *timing* of the evaluation assessments may be significant. Together all these factors relating to the timing of research interviews makes it difficult to interpret the 'meaning' of results, and once again suggest caution in accepting some research conclusions about client satisfaction.

Helpful people and useful outcomes

The last, but not least important, of the three main considerations to be taken into account when assessing the meaning and merits of clients' views is concerned with the distinction between 'helpful people' and 'helpful services' or, to put it another way, 'useful outcomes'. It is perhaps worth repeating that this analytical distinction is one that we, as researchers, have made in an attempt to separate out clients' evaluative criteria which relate to the social worker as a person, and those which seem to stand independent of the person providing the service. Nevertheless, it is a differentiation which is not always made by clients themselves. Some clients react to the social worker and the social service as one. Others perceive, in varying degrees, some difference between 'helper' and 'help', and respond to each aspect separately. The interesting question to ask is, what is the relative significance of each of these components for clients' overall evaluations?

The most common response of clients implies that few make a clear distinction between the social worker and the social service (McKay, Goldberg and Fruin 1973), or between the social worker's personality and his social work skills (Sainsbury and Nixon 1979). Many clients respond to the social worker rather than to the agency or department, or regard the two as inseparable. The few researchers who have attempted to examine the relationship between clients' perceptions of the social worker and their evaluation of results, find that generally these two factors are closely associated. For example, Rondeau's study (1976) of Family Agencies in Montreal found a tendency among clients with a positive perception of the social worker to feel well satisfied and to evaluate outcomes favourably (though the latter being less marked than the level of satisfaction). On the other hand, the majority of clients who held a negative perception of the social worker felt little satisfaction and had a low opinion of the results attained from contact.

The material from the preceding analysis illustrates the large part played by the social worker in influencing clients' response to social work contacts. Given the nature of the client/social worker relationship, and the attendant difficulty in distinguishing the help from the person providing it, it may be that clients are very reluctant to be critical of social work contacts. If clients perceive their social work contact essentially as an interpersonal relationship with the social worker, they may feel extremely uncomfortable if asked to express any dissatisfaction with service. As Cohen explains, 'If the service is presented by someone regarded as likeable and well meaning the clients may feel disloyal or unfair to him if they criticize the service he represents' (1971, 41). Furthermore, those clients who believe that social workers are doing them a *favour*, rather than providing a service which is theirs by *right*, may feel similarly (Cohen 1971). This reluctance may be similar to that felt by patients when they evaluate doctors. It is interesting to note that an even higher rate of patient satisfaction exists with physicians and medical care, than that of clients with social workers (McKinlay and Mitchell 1975). This is probably also related to the previously mentioned idea that some clients feel it is inappropriate for them to pass judgement on people whom they regard as 'experts'.

Factors such as these can account for some research results which even researchers have found 'puzzling', and which have led them to be suspicious of their own studies' conclusions. Several researchers have recognized the danger of a 'halo effect' affecting the validity of their research conclusions indicating high satisfaction. This 'halo effect' has been defined as 'a general orientation of goodwill toward the service-providers concerned rather than a reliable picture of people's real life, day-to-day encounters with the services' (Robinson 1978, 7). This suspicion is aroused when researchers have examined client satisfaction and its relation to 'help', 'progress', or 'improvement', in fact to outcome in general. Barker's study (1974) of 32 clients of a social services department revealed a high level of client satisfaction yet one third of the respondents failed to receive the help requested. Goyne and Ladoux's study (1973) of patients attending a mental health clinic also revealed high client satisfaction. However, although 78 per cent of the clients expressed satisfaction, the problem still existed for 68 per cent at the end of the treatment, and a third said that they sought help elsewhere after their contact with the clinic had finished. Most clients attending a Neighbourhood Counselling Clinic appeared to be satisfied with the service, yet once again, a considerable number estimated that their problem had in fact not markedly improved and some even felt their problem had worsened (Hoffman 1975). Although as the researcher states, some of the problems, mainly of an interpersonal nature, could not have been ameliorated and a slowdown of the deterioration was perhaps all that the services could be expected to achieve, the fact remains that over one-third of the clients found no alleviation of problems. Similar discrepancies occurred when clients received task-centred casework in a medical social services department (Reid and Epstein 1972). 'Of the eight clients whose assessment of task achievement at best was partial, seven rated service as "helped substantially", or "could not have gotten along without it" ' (p. 251).* These results thus raise considerable doubt on any question of 'satisfaction' with 'help'. We cannot assume that clients' expressions of satisfaction always imply that they feel helped or that the service has been useful. Neither can we assume that client dissatisfaction implies lack of help. Several studies have illustrated clients' discontent, despite the fact that they received the help requested (Jackson 1973; Mayer and Timms 1970).

Although the above discrepancy between 'satisfaction' and 'help' is quite a common finding in the literature, only one researcher seems to have attempted to analyse the effects and implications of this in any detailed way. Jordan (1976) became interested when he discovered that 12 of the 15 clients in his study attending an English Social Services Department for the first time had feelings of incongruence in their experiences of social work contact. More specially, some felt a lack of congruity between the interpersonal quality of the encounter and the experience of what was actually achieved. Despite disappointing outcomes of contact, all but two of the respondents commented favourably on the personal quality of the social worker. The clients then developed an explanation to account for this

---

* The authors speculated, 'Possibly these clients . . . were reacting in part to the helping *efforts* expended by an interested and concerned caseworker, a factor that may also have influenced the clients' evaluations of particular aspects of service' (p. 252).

dichotomy. This involved the client placing the social worker, as an individual, in a particular working context. The clients talked of the social workers being under considerable pressure of work, of being too busy, of having too demanding caseloads or of trying to cope with a situation in which material resources were scarce. This belief sometimes occurred when social workers explained the need to ration resources with reference to the amount of help the client has already been offered. Over time, the clients come to regard the social workers as being as much victims of the situation as themselves. The social workers were perceived as being relatively powerless to help given the limitations of their work situation. Several other researchers have noted similar forces at work in other situations. Robinson (1978) in his review of studies relating to the opinions of parents of the mentally and/or physically handicapped with regard to helping professionals, found that most studies suggested generally appreciative views. He adds, however, that

> Even when they [the professionals] are seen as acting in ways that would normally justify criticism, there seems to be a common tendency to explain this away in terms of factors like overwork, staff shortages, or lack of resources, rather than to blame the professional personally (Robinson 1978, 12).

A number of clients attending voluntary and statutory agencies also made comments about the impact of the organization upon the work of social workers (Sainsbury and Nixon 1979). Some saw the agency as a hindrance to the natural helpfulness of the social worker. 'It's not the fault of the welfare workers – they feel frustrated by the attitudes of their own managers' (Sainsbury and Nixon 1979, 11).

In the very different setting of prison welfare, Shaw (1974) has somewhat similar things to say. She discovered a link between the men's level of satisfaction with social work in prison and their perception of the welfare officers being restricted or under pressure. Some 28.7 per cent of the men made favourable comments about the prison social workers, which often included sympathetic remarks about the latters' job being difficult given the circumstances.

> They do their best within the limits they can, but their hands are tied – a lot of blokes won't see this. They are kind of handicapped in what they can do – they come up against a brick wall' (Shaw 1974, 51).

Another 46 per cent of the men had mixed attitudes, again many of them feeling that 'they [the p.w.o.'s] can only do so much'. However, 25.4 per cent of the men were very direct in their criticisms, calling the prison social workers 'promise merchants', Shaw explains,

> the blame was placed by these men entirely on the welfare officers, whom they saw as unwilling to put themselves out for the inmates. Unlike those with more favourable attitudes, these men expected attention and help on demand, and immediate satisfaction. The fact that the welfare officers were under great pressure of work, that the demands made of them were often unreasonable, would appear to pass unnoticed by those men (1974, 52).

A tentative suggestion of Shaw's is that younger men and those with less experience of prison tended to be more demanding and critical of the welfare staff. On the other hand, the prisoners in the experimental group, who experienced extended contact with the welfare officers, tended to have more favourable attitudes towards the welfare officer and his job than the control group. Those in the experimental group tended to be more appreciative of the difficulties under which the welfare officers worked. Thus, while the ability of the prison social worker to solve the men's problems was one main criterion of clients' satisfaction, it is clear that the men's reactions were also influenced by factors outside their receiving or not receiving the desired help.

If clients perceive social workers as sympathetic and pleasant people, whose power to help is often limited, any dissatisfaction they may feel can be qualified to some extent. Such perceptions have a 'cooling out' function which can have a dampening effect on clients' frustrations or disappointments. This may partially explain the appreciation expressed by clients in many other studies of the *efforts* of social workers to help them – whether or not the desired help actually materializes – the 'He's doing all he can' idea.

It was Goffman (1952) who first introduced to the study of human interaction the term 'cooling the mark out'. The phrase describes a process which operates whenever people become disengaged from their involvements, that is when they adjust to impossible situations and are forced to revise their self-concepts in the face of failure. Adams and McDonald (1968) have used this concept in their analysis of poor people attending child psychiatry clinics. They were particularly interested in the general lack of orientation of child psychiatry clinics in the 1960s towards the poor and the socially delinquent. The clinics' belief that such people were 'untreatable' or 'unmotivated' resulted in their lack of involvement in psychotherapeutic treatment. In describing how poor people and their families give up on being suitable or adequate patients, the authors quote Goffman –

> The psychotherapist is, in this source, the society's cooler. His job is to pacify and re-orient the disorganized person; his job is to send the patient back to an old world or a new one, and to send him back in a condition which he can no longer cause trouble or he can no longer make a fuss (Goffman 1952, 451).

Thus people sometimes devise explanations which help them cope with their 'failure' to get the help they feel they need. It has been argued that this occurs amongst clients seeking help from the social services (Jordan 1976). But this process can apply equally to social workers as to clients. The social workers' pleasant approach acts as a consolation to both practitioners and clients in the face of lack of resources. Providing social casework or counselling may be a response to frustrations felt by both clients and workers. As Silverman explains:

> Offering counselling is one means by which the worker copes with the consumer's anger and disappointment. Simultaneously it provides the worker with an oppor-

tunity to handle his own sense of helplessness by 'doing something' that he hopes will be of use to the client (Perlman 1975, 52n).

Perlman (1975) has also suggested that counselling can be offered as a substitute for resources that are not available and can become a 'lightning-rod for the ensuing frustrations'.

The main point to be made is that when evaluating social work, clients frequently refer to aspects of 'process' – attributes of the social worker and his style or method of working, as well as to 'outcome' – the result of the social work intervention. Both are important to the client. However, what can sometimes happen is that the certain perceived qualities or actions associated with the social worker serve to confuse the clients' overall reaction to the service. Clients' perceptions of social workers as kind, pleasant and helpful people doing a thankless job in difficult circumstances, and the very nature of the client/social worker relationship can obscure the fact that 'help' is not always forthcoming. This is perhaps the reason why so many clients express satisfaction despite their experiencing poor outcomes. For any of these reasons they may feel it would be unfair to criticize too heavily the efforts of helping professionals whose intentions are generally good. Here is another consideration then, that can have important consequences, for client evaluations. It is one which, although little researched, has important social economic and political implications.

Social workers are not paid to be liked. They are paid to provide useful services to people who need them. Yet their very pleasantness can act as a smokescreen which obscures the fact that these services are not always forthcoming. Furthermore, the smokescreen serves to cloud the fact that social workers are powerless to effect changes when many clients' difficulties are rooted in structural problems of unemployment and poverty. Taking 'the heat' out of ensuing frustrations and anxieties, or in the words of one social worker helping people 'survive' their current social and economic difficulties – implies social workers are playing an implicitly political role.

Summary

Many clients are unqualified in their praise for the work of social workers. But client evaluation is a complicated, confusing and often seemingly contradictory phenomenon which requires sensitive and detailed analysis. As such, we should be cautious about accepting too readily all the results of consumer studies in social work.

Rather than trying to come to any conclusions about levels of satisfaction, we have been concerned with degrees of success in social work – identifying the specific criteria valued by clients in particular situations. We can draw some general conclusions about the type of social work preferred, the forms of help most appreciated and the overall effect social work intervention has had on some people's lives. We have seen how important it is to the client that the social worker be seen as a 'person' and a 'friend'. We have noted how clients from all backgrounds seem generally oriented towards help that is concrete, directive and supportive. This is not to deny that some clients have felt helped by other forms of help, but on the whole the former kinds of help are the most appreciated. Finally, specific examples have been given about how people have felt their problems have been relieved, or not relieved, through contact with the social work services.

There exists much material that provides an interesting insight into specific aspects of clients' experiences, but in our view evaluation requires a study in depth of what kinds of social work activities at what point in the help-seeking process have been found helpful by clients with which particular problems. Only a few recent studies have met such a requirement.

We have also emphasized the importance of examining the context in which these evaluations occur. As the major theme of this book unfolds, we shall argue that evaluations – be they clients', managers' or social workers' – have political as well as social and economic implications. Those who carry out their own research, or who assess others' work, should spell out these implications and say how they affect any interpretation of results.

Part III
Workers Weigh their Practice

Introduction

The verdicts of the 'neglected' client have been examined. But how do social workers evaluate their own activities? This section has three main aims: to explore practitioners' perceptions of 'success', how they think this is best achieved, and the constraints affecting their evaluations of practice.

Our study of social workers' evaluations was hampered by a lack of research material. In our judgement, the research into social work has provided a fuller picture of the evaluative criteria used by clients, than that used by practising social workers. It seems that it is the practitioner rather than the client who is 'neglected' in research into the evaluation of social work. As a result, our analysis of social workers' perceptions is somewhat sparse and fragmented compared with the material on the clients. It is based on three sources.

1 On studies in which the main aim of the research has been to examine how social workers make judgements about their effectiveness. Only a handful of studies have been concerned with this.
2 On studies in which social workers' evaluations are a peripheral concern, but in which workers do make statements about 'success' and how this might be achieved. The bulk of the material in the following three chapters is based on this source.
3 On a couple of pieces of work in which the evaluation of social work students is the central research focus.

Social workers' evaluations are just as complex as clients'. Practitioners work in a variety of agency settings. These agencies' social workers differ in their approaches to solving problems. Even within the same agency – social workers are different; some are experienced, some fresh to social work; some are trained, others untrained; some employ traditional casework techniques, others prefer other methods of work. Some link their professionally based notions of success with criteria concerning the circumstances of client groups. Some begin to be explicit about the ideological basis of their attitudes and practice. Others continue to behave as though ideological stances do not affect practice, not even implicitly. It is not surprising that practitioners have different ideas about what are valuable and helpful activities, as well as different ideas about how the success of their interventions can be measured.

Social workers also vary in their ability and willingness to talk about 'evaluation' and 'success' in social work. This does not necessarily imply that they are unwilling to conceptualize and reflect on their work, but even in the course of their supervision they often have some difficulty in doing this (Silverman 1969; DHSS 1978). Perhaps this is because their training does not include any examination of the material contained in this book, or perhaps their training does not include any familiarity with methods of research. Recognition that in the context of social work the use of the term 'success' can be ambiguous may be another reason for this difficulty. For example, a number of practitioners from a Sheffield Family Service Unit (Sainsbury 1975) felt that the use of the word 'success' carried anxieties concerning the achievement of short-term expedients without regard to longer-term feelings and needs. Another study, (DHSS 1978) based on in-depth interviews with 360 social work staff in various local authority teams, also found that most workers were very diffident about claiming success in their work with clients.

In exploring further social workers' evaluations, the following chapters deal with three related issues. Chapter 6 outlines the activities and ingredients of social work interventions valued by social workers. It discusses those elements in the helping process which are felt to be necessary for a successful outcome. Chapter 7 examines the criteria of outcome which have been used by practising social workers when measuring the 'success' of their interventions. Chapter 8 discusses the dilemmas involved when practitioners attempt to evaluate their work. Both Chapters 7 and 8 include references to the constraints affecting social workers' verdicts.

6

Valued Images and Activities

> Occupations vary in the extent to which effort brings tangible results. Casework is obviously different in that respect from chopping logs or growing wheat, but it is certainly not unique among occupations. Since the day's work cannot be measured in cords or bushels, the worker may search for intangible 'proof' that his or her effort has been worthwhile (Greenaway 1976).

The above quote describes how the nature of social work can impede its evaluation in terms of outcome. Yet, whether or not a social worker thinks in terms of 'success' and 'outcome', at the end of a working day he or she could make some kind of assessment of what has been achieved in particular cases. Ideally, such on-going evaluation should be made in order to justify future intervention and influence its direction. However, given social workers' difficulty in talking about 'results', and the absence of clear criteria by which any 'results' are measured, many practitioners find it easier to talk about the 'doing' of social work and the ingredients in the helping process that are viewed as essential if improvement is to occur.

In describing these things, social workers are sometimes doing more than relating valued images and activities. It is often hard to separate their feelings of personal satisfaction, of competence, and of achievement from the activities and relationships they are involved in with clients. The following chapter elaborates on the two main aspects of the helping relationship which are highlighted by workers as being important:

1 Worker attributes and activities
2 Client qualities and responses

Worker attributes and activities

Charles Levy (1974) is one of the main exponents of the idea that because results in social work are so difficult to measure and interpret, the criteria of competence should be related to the input of the worker. He clarified this point,

> All the social worker can certify to is what he possesses to put into the practice situation and what he decides or agrees that he will put into that situation – not what it will lead to (p. 378).

What appears to be relevant to the issue of professional competence is what the practitioner has to offer by way of knowledge and skill/and whether and how he goes about offering it (p. 379).

In this view, attributes of the worker, and the activities he or she engages in are of great importance. But the above statement implies that defining these 'inputs' further should not be too difficult. Our evidence suggests it is not as easy as it sounds.

Worker attributes

There appears to be a widely accepted assumption that everyone knows what a competent social worker looks like. There is much talk of professional standards, of 'good' and 'bad' practice, of levels of competence. Yet this talk obscures confusion and uncertainty as to what these terms might mean. How are these notions defined? What do 'good' and 'bad' mean? Are these temporary judgements, or generalizations which apply until confounded? When attempts are made to define such terms, management, social work educators and practitioners alike run into difficulty. For example, one of the Directors of Social Work we interviewed, on being asked how he knew if someone was a 'good' social worker, replied:

> Oh well now – I think that's a ridiculous question. I think one would have to be terribly stupid altogether if you couldn't tell the difference between a good worker and a bad one.

Yet the same director later admitted having difficulty in expanding on his statement.

The same confusion and lack of clarity surround tutors' assessments of social work students – one of the contexts in which evaluation in social work is most visible and explicit. Brandon and Davis explain,

> By examining the circumstances surrounding a small number of students who either failed or nearly failed to qualify as social workers, questions are posed, not only about social work education, but about the theoretical structures underlying social work and the context in which it is practised (1979, 296).

Brandon and Davis asked tutors from six social work courses in England to give examples and reasons for 'marginal' students who were in doubt of passing their course. Some of the tutors showed surprise when the researchers asked them why they thought a student's fieldwork was satisfactory or not, an attitude which suggested to Brandon and Davis 'that they were adopting an impressionistic or non-conceptual approach to assessment' (1979, 335). Some other tutors, however, were aware of the importance of providing 'proof' to back up such judgements. The tutors' replies reflected the difficulties involved in making decisions about practice competence or incompetence. These, in turn, were almost certainly associated with the ambiguities and disagreements over what constitute appropriate skills in social work.

Most social workers are also unclear about how to discuss or define what 'standards' might be or how to distinguish between good and bad practice. As one researcher remarked 'the question of quality of work, as distinct from simply making a service available, seemed fraught with difficulty' (DHSS 1978). Most of the 360 local authority workers interviewed in the Parsloe/ Stevenson (DHSS 1978) project (unpublished material) were very unclear about how to discuss or define what 'standards' might be, or how to distinguish between good and bad practice. Although there seemed to be agreement that there existed in the various agencies and departments included in the study an unspoken expectation that standards were to be maintained, nobody was terribly clear as to what these standards might be. (Moreover, the social workers felt they knew little or nothing about the standards of their colleagues.) Other workers felt they did have some idea of what might constitute good standards. These ideas were gleaned from a variety of sources – from training, from informal discussions with colleagues, from theory, from the organizations in which they worked. The most articulate responses from social workers on these issues were gleaned from Sainsbury's study (1975) of a Sheffield Family Service Unit. Most of the workers in the Unit had similar notions about the components of 'good casework'. The most frequently mentioned were sensitivity to clients' perceptions of themselves, their situations and their caseworkers and achieving this even though the relationships were not close; making constructive use of a relationship; ethical and moral integrity; patience and acceptance of client's feelings without assuming total moral relativity, unforced understanding and respect; caring without making emotional demands on clients; and accountability of workers jointly to their clients, their agencies and their profession.

Although workers are willing to agree that professional training encourages them to look at standards of work and gives them ideas about good and bad practice, professionalization in itself is felt to be no guarantee of competence, i.e. there is no necessary link between qualifications and quality. As one local authority worker said, 'It is perfectly possible to have brilliant academic qualifications and still be a lousy social worker' (DHSS 1978, unpublished material). There seems to be a general agreement, amongst British local authority practitioners at least, that good social work training may enhance whatever talent is already there, but without that extra 'something', it will not produce a good social worker.

Concern with standards varies with circumstances. For example, there is evidence to suggest that when social workers feel themselves to be bombarded by cases (DHSS 1978, unpublished material) they express less concern with standards. But when caseloads are not so demanding, concern with standards seems to increase. In those circumstances, practitioners feel they have more time to contemplate their work. The context in which social work is practised also seems significant. Social workers working in a hospital setting seem aware of the need for 'excellence' (DHSS 1978, unpublished material). Surrounded by other professionals some say that they cannot afford to be vague about their role. Working in a hospital 'sharpens' their ideas about what they should or should not be doing as well as how to do it. Thus one hospital worker explained,

> In this kind of setting one is more likely to be aware of the need for something called excellence. Here you are constantly aware of having a different point of view — you are having to justify what you say and what you do (DHSS 1978, unpublished material).

The level of standards may also be related to the level of interest shown in specific areas of social work both at basic grade and senior level. In the Parsloe/Stevenson study (DHSS 1978 unpublished material) interest in the mentally ill and handicapped was said to be low, and standards in this area of social work were said to reflect such an attitude. On the other hand, interest in the field of adoption and child care was high, and standards were felt to be good in these fields. Much of the work in these latter areas was subject to rigorous scrutiny from senior staff, since they were more often interested and experienced in these particular fields.

The relation between standards and levels of interest and expertise seems related to the unease, at least in Britain, about the lack of specialization since Seebohm, felt by a number of social workers (Glampson and Goldberg 1976). For example, concern has been expressed about the standard of service to such people as the blind. The 1975 Neill, Warburton and McGinness's study (1976) of Southampton social workers' reactions to Seebohm reorganization found continuing confusion and uncertainty about lack of specialization. For many workers, their feelings of competence and effectiveness were bound up with how knowledgeable and experienced they were in a given field. The following social worker's reaction is fairly typical,

> As far as I am aware, Seebohm talked of generic social work departments, which I consider a very good thing, but I have reservations about 'every good' social worker being generic. Although there is some enjoyment in variety, lack of knowledge and experience inevitably leads to a feeling of impotence and to less efficient service (Neill, Warburton and McGuiness 1976).

However interesting the above findings, none of the studies mentioned were explicitly concerned with connecting notions of competence and quality with outcome. Only Sainsbury's study (1975) of workers in a Sheffield Family Service Unit asked the question 'What makes a good and successful caseworker?' The workers' replies indicated diversity of opinion. Seven of the eleven workers made a distinction between 'good' social work and 'successful' social work. Whereas the notion of 'success' was seen to be related to outcome, the notion of 'good' social work was related to the worker's input of feelings and beliefs. In this view, good social work did not necessarily imply change in the client. However, two of these workers suggested 'good' social work was a prerequisite of success. But the other four workers felt no distinction could be made between 'good' and 'successful' social work. These two notions were regarded as being interchangeable. Success for these workers was dependent on, and rooted in, good social work. For example, a client's success 'may depend on the worker being a good person, or a good parent-figure' (Sainsbury 1975, 106).

Lack of clarity and lack of agreement as to what worker qualities and behaviour comprise professional social work skills partly explains managers', educators' and practitioners' difficulty in talking about the quality of worker 'input'. Another consideration is that researchers have not been concerned with asking practitioners which of their qualities have contributed to the success or failure of a particular intervention. In the past, there has been a tendency to 'blame the victim' when interventions failed, i.e. some researchers examined characteristics and qualities of the client (e.g., whether he or she was 'motivated' or not) in an attempt to explain, or predict, which clients were more likely to achieve successful outcomes and which are more likely to have negative outcomes. Characteristics and qualities of the social worker, often escaped analysis. Sainsbury's (1975) analysis, however exploratory and tentative, exhibits awareness of the complex issues that are involved in social workers' evaluative perceptions. His concern to elicit what constitutes worker qualities, and whether or not they are related to success, is rare.

Worker activities
Social workers are more articulate when they describe the activities they believe they should be involved in, and which are necessary for success to be achieved. As clients' views vary, so do social workers'. In describing these activities, we get closer to practitioners' definitions of the meaning of 'help' in social work.

The provision of tangible help (material/financial)
Three broad views emerged from practitioners' evaluations of this type of help.

1 some workers perceive little or no value in the provision of such tangible help.
2 other workers do provide such help, but with reservations. It is provided under certain conditions and is usually used as part of a general casework plan.
3 other workers give material aid as freely as possible with few reservations. They regard such provision as an integral part of social work and as necessary for satisfactory outcomes in particular cases.

1 This first view is held primarily by those workers who adopt an 'expert orientation' to social work, i.e. they believe themselves to be the 'experts' and know better than the client what are the latter's best interests. In particular, these workers seem to be of the 'orthodox expert orientation' as described by Whittington (1977), in that they hold to a psychodynamic theory in social work. Essentially, this theory espouses that clients' problems stem from inadequacies in themselves and their relationships. Environmental

factors are very much a secondary consideration. Even though a client may believe that his problem is essentially a practical one, such a social worker often feels that this is only the 'presenting' problem and that it is necessary to get down to the 'real' problem underneath, i.e. the problem primarily based in the characteristics of the client. Thus, the mere mention of debt is not seen as a problem in itself, but is seen as being indicative of, for example, a client's inability to manage his or her resources. As the *cause* of the problem is perceived as being personal rather than environmental, the only kind of help that will be effective, will be of this kind. Although Mayer and Timms (1970) interviewed only a very small number of social workers in their study, they provided a neat illustration of this way of thinking in a worker concerned with 'insight therapy'.

The following was said of a young mother of two, whose husband was in prison, and who was in financial difficulty over a large electricity bill. The electricity bill, in the worker's view, 'was a terrific projection of all her resentment against her husband's being taken away and going to prison' (Mayer and Timms 1970, 128). Moreover, her demands of the agency 'were symbolic of the fact that society owed her something – because society had taken her husband away' (1970, 128). Practical aid was thought to be of very little help to this woman, who was persuaded to see what her need for the payment of the bill really 'meant'.

Silverman's (1969) study of a variety of mental health agencies in the USA provides a good example of linking perceived need, objectives, help and outcome. The main concern of the child guidance clinic, the adult outpatient clinic, the family agency and the multi-service centre involved in the study, was casework counselling. The social workers in these agencies utilized a psychodynamic approach to their work. Their perceived purpose was to help clients learn more about themselves so that they, the clients, could sort out their own problems or learn how to deal with them more effectively. Changing or ameliorating the clients' 'reality' problems was not perceived as being very helpful. Silverman's study was concerned mainly with 'failed' contacts between clients and social workers. As it transpired, through successive meetings and sessions with clients, these social workers became more and more pessimistic about their ability to help clients. This was due to the caseworkers' view that the clients were too preoccupied with problems in their current realities to spend time examining themselves and working out how they could help themselves. Eventually, there reached a stage when many of the workers 'gave up' their desired approach, and shifted to a supportive role and talked less about feelings and more about the reality problems faced by clients. But the workers were never happy to 'resort' to talking about these reality problems and providing tangible help. One worker described the change she made with a client:

> I felt at one point that it wasn't quite that she was manipulating me, but that I was using a technique. This is at the point when I felt I had failed in trying to explore the area of loss and realized that I had to shift and talk with her on the 'phone for a

long time about a recipe for sweet potatoes. In other words what I was trying to get into is to show some interest in things she was interested in – things she could do (Silverman 1969, 147).

The workers allowed themselves only reluctantly to provide support and concrete service. Significantly, the very point at which these workers, in their own view, 'gave up' their ability to help and instead provided tangible resources (thereby classing these cases as failures) was the time when many of the *clients* began to make appreciative remarks about help received. The workers, from their perspective, did not perceive that this latter stage in the helping process was found helpful by the clients. In the formers' view, the contacts largely resulted in failure. *

This reluctance to provide tangible help appears to be particularly prevalent amongst some psychiatric social workers and some probation officers. For example, literature reviews and observation of psychiatric social work practice has revealed that the provision of practical and material help is regarded by trained workers as the province of untrained workers (Sheppard 1966). Straight supportive and practical help is often felt to be an inferior way of working compared to face to face casework. That 'good casework is associated with insight, limited casework with the giving of money' has also been claimed regarding the work of probation officers (Parkinson 1970). It should be acknowledged, however, that the above observations were based on work carried out in the 1960s, and are probably a bit dated.

2 The most common feeling amongst workers with a less exclusive view of social work, is one of ambivalence towards the provision of tangible help. Generally they are agreed that in certain situations and with certain client groups, the provision of material aid contributes to 'success'. There is no doubt that many British local authority workers (DHSS 1978), as well as some agency workers in America (Rubenstein and Bloch 1978), spend a considerable amount of time in their day to day practice, making arrangements to obtain material or financial aid for their clients. But there is evidence to suggest that although they are involved in providing this help, many are unhappy in doing so, particularly when it involves money. For example, the social workers in an American agency (Rubenstein and Bloch, 1978), who perceived the problems of unmarried mothers as stemming both from psychological and from environmental factors, expressed some dissatisfaction at the high proportion of time and energy devoted to the provision of tangible services. The prevalent feeling amongst these workers, and amongst British local authority workers, is that such activities are not 'real' social work and are hence of a relatively low value.

Given the ambivalent attitude towards the value of this help, what criteria do social workers use when they decide that such help is desirable and

---

* It should be said, however, that the social workers in this study seemed to have an exceptionally narrow and limited idea of what constituted help.

appropriate? The following material reveals that practitioners' opinions of the 'helpfulness' of tangible aid and their willingness to use it, depend on such considerations as the actual form of the aid (i.e. whether financial or material), on the wish to establish a good relationship with the client, and on whether or not most clients are felt to be 'deserving' of such help. Rees argues strongly that decisions about material aid depended on social workers' ideologically based commitments. Practitioners were unlikely to put themselves out by giving financial aid in cases which they found ideologically unpalatable (Rees 1978).

Heywood and Allen's study (1971) of social workers in four children's departments in England and Wales, found that practitioners' view of the helpfulness of tangible aid varied depending on whether it was in cash or in kind. Many of these social workers believed that actually dealing in *cash* 'confused their role and had no positive contribution to make to their casework' (Heywood and Allen 1971, 72). A similar finding was made in the Parsloe/Stevenson study (1978), in which a number of social workers working in local authorities felt that financial help confused work objectives and distorted social work practice. For example, if financial aid is given in the form of a loan, social workers can sometimes find themselves in the position of having to retrieve money from clients. This is felt to be time-consuming. More importantly, however, it is felt that this interferes with and adversely affects the client-worker relationship.

Although casework and relief-giving are felt to be incompatible by these workers, casework and the provision of tangible help 'in kind' are acceptable. *Material aid*, in the form of the second-hand clothing and furniture was provided fairly freely and willingly in the children's departments. The provision of this material aid was said to be important in contributing to mutual trust between worker and client. This point of view was *not* mentioned with regard to the giving of money. Moreover, little if any consideration was given to the therapeutic effect of financial aid on depressed clients. Parsloe and Stevenson (1978) found that social workers very rarely complain about restrictions on the provision of financial help, yet make known loudly their complaints about the lack of other non-financial resources. Perhaps this is indicative, in Britain, of a similarity in attitude between the workers in today's local authority teams and those in the previous children's departments.

Another justification for the use of practical help is that the provision of such aid is a useful way of developing and fostering a good working relationship with the client. This is thought to be necessary for any degree of success to be achieved. For example, Sheppard (1966) talks of the value of giving 'tangible evidence of our love' immediately and generously to people who have mental health problems, or behaviour problems which upset the community. By giving people help with money, housing, clothing, food as well as taking them out for meals, working for them etc., social workers demonstrate their care and concern.

In a similar vein Sainsbury (1975) describes how workers in a Family Service Unit felt it was important to meet at once the needs of clients in the mode in which they were presented (usually material) with the least possible delay and irrespective of other kinds of help offered at a later date. By doing this they entered the clients' trust and provided them both with feelings of hope and with a symbol of the practitioners' willingness to help with other problems later. Parkinson (1970) talks of the use of material and financial help to make probationers feel valued, and to help break down their isolation. He openly admits that such help is a way of showing his concern which involves 'buying' probationers' cooperation and friendship.* Rees (1978) identifies clients' and social workers' appreciation of money given as a loan as a means of establishing some element of reciprocity in relationships. What all these practitioners have in common is a belief that there exists a link between material and emotional problems, and that people have multiple needs. The provision of tangible help can alleviate some of these material problems and so improve the chances of other forms of help being successful.

Not all social workers who provide material and financial assistance believe that such a resource is in itself sufficient. Rather this help can be used merely as a 'carrot' to entice or persuade clients to agree to attending casework sessions, i.e. it is used as a tool to enable the worker to get down to the 'real' social work. Handler (1974) has described how the provision of help with housing, the promise of rehousing or finding a solution to other housing needs, was used by the workers in three London children's departments to work with a family and gain its confidence. Some of these workers felt it was a good idea occasionally to make people anxious about money, the possibility of losing their home, or more seriously, their children. They would then be in a good position to 'bargain' with clients and persuade them to accept certain forms of help. For example, an unmarried mother in Handler's study (1974) had three children in care due to bad housing and poverty. She was very resentful and had resisted casework. When she was rehoused, she wanted her children returned, began to 'cooperate' with the child care officer and eventually accepted casework help. The child care officer readily admitted that the department had got through to this woman because she knew she had 'to play the game if she wanted her children returned' (Handler 1974, 71). It is impossible to say how widespread is such use of practical help. (Certainly, the child care worker in the late 1960s was legally unable to give money without it being tied to certain conditions, e.g. to the prevention of family breakdown, or the rehabilitation or restoration of the child to his own home.) Also in America, such practice was written into legislation, at least in the AFDC Programme (Handler and Hollingsworth 1971).

---

* Although he believes these methods would have been abhorred by professionals in the 1960s, Parkinson believes an increasing number of probation officers are employing such techniques.

We have seen that attitudes to the giving of practical help can be influenced by the nature of that tangible help, and by the worker's special interest in working with particular clients and in a particular way. On occasions it is 'appropriate' for the worker to give tangible aid, on other occasions it is 'inappropriate'.

However much it may be abhorred or denied by many social workers, there is evidence that they believe some clients are more 'deserving' than others. For example, when the child care officers in Heywood and Allen's study (1971) were asked when they considered it 'appropriate' to offer financial and material aid, they gave the following sorts of answers: when there was absolutely no alternative, e.g., where there were large families with no alternative accommodation, handicapped members in the family; or when families were in immediate danger of disintegration; if the families had been 'really trying' to help themselves, e.g. when parents were 'good managers' but had inadequate incomes. Some workers would provide financial help only in cases where there was a possibility of the family responding to the help and being able to cope better. Financial help was considered 'inappropriate' when workers thought a family was 'uncooperative' and did not make a consistent effort to pay their debts; where help could be got from other sources, where it was thought the father's irresponsible spending of money was the main problem; where the client tried to manipulate the caseworker or when the clients had not benefited from previous financial aid. A minority of the workers in one department also considered it inappropriate if the family gambled, drank or squandered money. Clearly such beliefs were influenced not only by professional judgements as to what would 'work' but also by personal decisions that some clients were more deserving than others. This finding is similar to that of Rees's study (1978) of two social work agencies in Scotland, one a voluntary casework agency and the other a local authority department – each concerned with people with a variety of problems. Here, too, the decision of a social worker to provide tangible assistance largely depended on whether clients were perceived as being 'deserving' or 'undeserving'. For example, in 'audition' type contacts between client and worker, in which the client made some request for material help, social workers were pleased to provide a relatively simple service to people who had maintained and valued their independence and were unlikely to make other demands. On the other hand, clients who 'moaned and expected you to work miracles' or who gave the impression that the agency was 'just a place for handouts' were regarded as being less 'worthy' of practical help. Decisions to provide practical help depended on social workers perceiving in the clients evidence of deserving 'moral character'. However, as Rees points out, such perceptions depend on social workers' reaction to the clients in relation to a particular context of work at a specific point in time. Due to the lack of available resources, practitioners have to be selective in deciding who does get tangible help, and who doesn't. This partially explains why moral calculations influence social workers' decisions.

3   Some social workers believe in freely providing material aid and regard it as an integral part of their definition of 'help'. These workers seem to fit Smith and Harris's (1972) ideal type of the social worker who holds to an ideology of '*relief*'. This points particularly (but not necessarily exclusively) to the economic situation of the client as the root of his problem. Thus the amelioration of poverty and an improvement in living conditions is regarded as being the main objective of social work practice. In these circumstances, practical help is crucial to any chances of achieving success. From the evidence in the literature, it is impossible to say to what extent this view is adhered to in practice. The existing evidence suggests that in British local authority departments anyway, only a very few social workers single out this form of help as being of greater importance than help with relationship or emotional problems (DHSS 1978).* Of the detailed studies on social workers' perceptions and evaluations we have encountered, not one has dealt with an agency in which this ideology is dominant.

Yet, there are indications that this ideology is held by some social workers in certain circumstances, i.e. in relation to particular client groups. It has been shown, for example, that the needs of the elderly and physically handicapped are often perceived in a stereotyped way by social workers (Rawlings 1978). These people are usually felt to have predominantly practical needs for which practical assistance is believed to be the most appropriate form of help. Even qualified workers can be of the opinion that the problems of the elderly are mainly 'straight-forward'. One study carried out in the Social Services Department of a large northern industrial city in Britain compared and contrasted clients' and social workers' definitions of help (Barker 1974). The clients in this study were mainly physically handicapped and elderly. Although the 17 social workers interviewed saw themselves as offering help in a variety of ways, usually the help provided involved practical service in the form of material aid and domiciliary help. The majority of these social workers felt satisfied with what they had been able to do, tangible aid being regarded as the integral part of the caring service for the clients. In this respect, stereotyped views of the needs of certain sections of the population also play their part in social workers' decisions on whether or not tangible help is necessary or desirable.

Non-material help
This section encompasses, for want of a better word, the more 'intangible' aspects of the helping process. The nature of these 'intangible' activities varies. In recent years, at least on a theoretical level, more and different methods and styles of working have emerged, e.g., task-centred casework, group therapy, contract working etc. Yet it remains difficult to discern whether social workers ever employ the different methods which are elabo-

---

* However, this ideology is central to radical social work which may soon be gaining ground in practice, especially in view of the current political drift to the right.

rated in the literature. When they are asked to describe the help they provide, their descriptions of intangible help are often on a very general level, e.g., 'being supportive' or 'developing a relationship'. This help may or may not be linked to any more specific objectives. But it is rare to find practitioners talking in detail about what 'non-material' help looks like and how it contributes to a successful outcome. Our analysis is based on the very small number of studies which attempted to explore these questions further.

Although the studies were concerned with a variety of social work settings two broad common denominators appear to exist amongst the different practitioners working in these settings. The two social work activities regarded as being 'helpful' can be subsumed under the general categories of 'caring' and 'talking'.

(1) 'Caring'

Most social workers feel it is important that clients feel that they are truly concerned and interested in them or their problems. This is not always easy if workers have heavy caseloads and are under considerable pressure of work. The ways in which this concern is conveyed to clients vary. For example, some social workers, whose approach is supportive/directive, use practical help as a tool for indicating their care and regard, thus building up a relationship of trust, confidence and support for their clients (Sainsbury 1975). Other social workers attempt to show their concern in other ways. The social workers in Silverman's study (1969) of casework counselling agencies, describe how in the very early stages of contact with clients, they played down information gathering. As the important thing was to engage clients in a meaningful encounter, they attempted to give clients hope for the future, presenting themselves as someone who could be of help, talking about things the clients wanted to talk about and just listening to what they had to say. In the early stages of the helping process it was also deemed important that workers appear non-judgemental and 'objective', and willing to hear anything the clients had to say. For example, one worker said of a woman, who eventually admitted . . . 'I think that the only reason she could finally say this, was because she could sense in me that I wasn't afraid to hear this' (Silverman 1969, 182).

Such activities enable workers to form a relationship which they feel is necessary for any success or improvement.

Such social worker concern for showing acceptance, interest, warmth, support and a willingness to listen to clients, has been illustrated in other studies. Yet, apart from the descriptions in the previous paragraph, there are few clues as to how practitioners believe they convey such interest, warmth, and support, or at which point in the helping process each is felt to be most important. Joyce Lishman's (1978) retrospective evaluation of her own practice in a child guidance clinic provides a reminder that these things are not as obvious as they may seem. On interviewing her ex-clients, whom she felt she had provided with 'support' and 'encouragement', she discovered that a number perceived such help as 'persecution'. Unfortunately, we are left high and dry as to the reasons for this. Lishman could only speculate. Notions of 'interest' and 'concern' cannot be taken for granted.

(2) 'Talking'

Another activity felt to be necessary for 'help' is encouraging clients to talk and articulate their problems and feelings. Those social workers who identify themselves as caseworkers or counsellors regard 'talk' as a central aspect of 'help'. For example, getting clients to talk about their difficulties was regarded as necessary by the 'insight therapy' workers in a London Family Welfare Association (Mayer and Timms 1970). Talking was also regarded as being the main problem-solving activity by the caseworkers in a Catholic Family Service Association (Maluccio 1977).*

Silverman's study (1969) yet again, provides the most lucid and informative account of the reasons *why* such an activity is central to the notion of help, and *how* it is linked with objectives. The psychodynamically oriented workers in the agencies she studied shared very clear ideas about what they should be doing, and how they should be doing it. In the psychodynamic tradition, they believed people could only be helped by verbalizing feelings and emotions. The initial purpose of talking was to enable clients to express their feelings. Thus, of one woman, a worker explained, 'I started treatment with her with the idea of working – of talking about the loss of her son. I tried to get her to talk about those losses' (Silverman 1969, 143). The second, and later, purpose of talking was for the client eventually to make a connection between past experiences, her feelings about herself and her current problems. Such an explicit description by social workers of the purpose, method and goal of 'talking' is rare. These workers' explicitness probably resulted from a very similar and well clarified perspective derived mainly from Freudian theory on problems and their resolution. Such clarity about methods and purpose is far from common.

Advocacy and advice

Social workers' views on the importance of advocacy and advice differ. Many social workers are ambivalent about providing such a service. This ambivalence occurs despite the fact that social workers do advise on how to get help from other agencies and often do contact these agencies on the clients behalf (Beck and Jones 1973; DHSS 1978; Rubenstein and Bloch 1978). As well as negotiating with other resource-giving agencies and professionals, social workers also participate in case conferences and in court proceedings (Jackson 1973). But in Britain, few local authority workers perceive themselves as 'welfare rights' advocates, and indeed few accompany clients to appeal tribunals (DHSS 1978). Such work is generally regarded as being a 'necessary evil' of local authority work. For example, Parsloe and Stevenson

---

* But many of the clients wondered what such an activity had to do with their problem and did not share the workers' view that verbal communication was a key component of the client-worker engagement.

found 'relatively few social workers saw such tasks as central to their work, though many acknowledged that they spent considerable amount of time on them' (1978, 260).

Hospital social workers in particular are very reluctant to become involved in activity of this kind although it is unclear why this is so (DHSS 1978). Some social workers, perhaps those who have great respect for people's 'independence' abhor being involved in giving direct advice and being involved in negotiation on behalf of the client. As one indignant probation officer, on the suggestion that he should tell a woman to apply for a separation order, stated, 'We don't *tell* people to do things like that – we'd arrange things if they asked us but we don't *tell* them what to do' (Rodgers and Dixon 1960). Sainsbury and Nixon's newest (and as yet unpublished) study (1979) also found that the social workers in a FSU agency, a local authority department and in a probation office, all ranked 'negotiation' lower in a scale of helpful activities than did clients (although 'advice giving' was ranked somewhat higher). Social workers in other agencies and in other countries have expressed similar views. Although the American social workers working with unmarried mothers described how they counselled and advised their clients, accompanying them to other agencies and carrying out negotiations on their behalf, they expressed some dissatisfaction about the high proportion of time and energy devoted to such activities (Rubenstein and Bloch 1978). In a more casework-oriented agency, dealing with people who have emotional and relationship problems, the workers described any advocate activities 'somewhat apologetically' (Maluccio 1977, 98). They expressed not only uncertainty about the value of such activities, but also concern about how to reconcile them with their image of professional counselling. It seems that the more counselling and casework-oriented are the social workers, the less value they perceive in the giving of advice or advocacy. From such a perspective, it is inappropriate for clients to bring their problems to an agency, and then sit back, waiting for workers to direct them. It is up to clients to solve their own problems as far as possible. In this way a naive, apolitical view of client independence and self-determination is thus upheld.

Activities involving advocacy and advice-giving constitute a considerable part of many social workers' day to day work. Yet in the studies examined, analysis of the general ambivalence of social workers to these forms of help is largely non-existent. It seems important to find out why this help is often provided reluctantly, and is often felt to be 'inappropriate'. This need seems especially urgent in view of the fact that (as we have seen previously) it is precisely such activities that are often desired and appreciated by social work clients.

In analysing the worker activities valued by practitioners, it becomes increasingly apparent that it's their particular *ideological* commitment which influences priorities and certain ways of doing things. By ideology we are referring to a system of beliefs and values, sometimes explicitly acknowledged but frequently implicit, which incorporate assumptions about how society works and thus guide people to view the functions of state institutions, such as social welfare, in particular ways. For example, a social worker who takes for granted that society is basically just and fair will tend to encourage individuals to fit into the existing pattern of things (Philp 1979). By contrast, the social worker who views society as unjust and unfair is more likely to attempt to challenge and change certain routine ways of responding, to try to ensure that even short-term humanitarian objectives represent at best 'unfinished business' and should be linked to activities which will affect long-term political prospects (Cohen 1975).

The attachment to particular ideologies involves usually a 'preparedness to act', some definite 'social ambitions' and an 'investment of emotional capital' which is difficult to shift (Hunt 1978, 13–16). In these respects, an unmasking of social workers' ideologies is crucial if one wishes to understand why practitioners have particular perceptions of social problems and why they act with urgency in some cases, with a sense of unhurried routine in others and with indifference to some demands. Silverman gives a simple summary of the importance of ideologically based commitments in social work practice:

> This ideological outlook structures and justifies for them the worker's practice in terms of the kind of information they seek from the client, and the kinds of activities they will involve themselves with (Silverman 1969, 51).

Ideological considerations determine the social workers' attitude towards, for example, the usefulness of practical help, the appropriateness of counselling, the desirability of advocacy and negotiation. It is ideological considerations which affect the social workers' belief that some clients are more 'deserving' of certain kinds of help than others. Without reference to 'ideology', evaluation of help and helping methods is meaningless.

Client qualities and responses

Considerations of ideology also affect practitioners' perceptions of people they are most likely and able to help. That is, some social workers' beliefs that a successful outcome can be achieved, depend not only on the provision of valued help, but also on an appropriate response from the client. The evidence for this emerges almost exclusively from studies of social casework agencies.[*]

Three studies illustrate how practitioners' evaluations can be influenced by the perceived quality and response of the client. The first is that of Borgatta, Fanshel and Meyer (1960), carried out in the Family and

---

[*] Part of the reasons for this could be methodological. Two of the studies on such agencies have involved intensive semi-structured interviewing of social workers. It is largely through this method that interesting material has emerged which might otherwise have been untapped.

Children's Service in Pittsburgh in 1960. Its main interest was in social workers' perceptions of clients. Sixty staff and 331 clients were included in the study, the client sample consisting of persons coming to the agency with personal or family problems for which casework help would seem to be appropriate. An interview schedule was conducted by the social workers with the clients, in which 40 items of information were collected, such as background characteristics, judgements about the client's background and problem, personality ratings and outcome variables. It appeared that the workers judged clients mainly on what was termed 'personality ratings'. These 'personality ratings' seemed to be connected with the social workers' judgement of the potential promise of a favourable outcome. Some examples will clarify this. Of the female adult clients and unmarried mothers, it was discovered that there existed clusters of ratings. Thus at the negatively evaluated pole would be clients who seemed apathetic and discouraged, unable to cope with problems, lacking in confidence, energy and morale. At the other end, the positively evaluated pole, would be clients who displayed characteristics of personal competence, energy and effectiveness in inter-personal functioning. Those clients perceived to be at the negative pole of the dimension were rated as unpromising for casework help, while those at the positive end were rated as potentially promising. Thus unmarried mothers who were regarded as being poorly organized, unintelligent and ingratiating were regarded as likely to get little success from casework inter-views, while the converse, well organized, bright, attractive and relatively independent girls, were rated by the workers as being far more likely to improve with help. Of the adult males, at the negative pole were those defined as stubborn, defeatist and ineffectual in relationships; at the positive were those rated as outgoing, friendly, and confident. Once again, the potentiality of promising help from casework was markedly associated with the client's position on this positive—negative continuum.

These 'personality ratings' seemed to be significant for the *potentiality* of 'success' or 'help' from casework. This is interesting – but leaves many questions unanswered, e.g. how the workers might define 'stubbornness' and what kinds of behaviour denoted its presence? These results were based on only one interview done at one point in time with a fixed questionnaire. The workers' perceptions were confined to *predefined* categories in the ques-tionnaire, (although the questionnaire was pre-tested and based on what the social workers themselves thought should be included). As such these ratings and predictions themselves tell us little about *why* certain criteria are favoured or not favoured as the case may be.

Nevertheless, these findings are somewhat similar to those of two more recent studies carried out in 1969 and 1977. All of the social workers in an American agency (Silverman 1969) (who held a psychodynamic perspective of social casework) stipulated that what mattered most was the *client's capa-city* to use the available existing services, i.e. clients had to have the capacity to recognize the psychological or emotional aspects of their problems, to relate to the worker, to be able and willing to discuss their problems and to identify them as emanating, at least partly, from within themselves. In a similar instance, social workers in a Catholic Family Service Agency (Maluccio 1977) valued clients who were motivated and eager to change, and who were capable of emotional involvement and insight. Clients who tended to be more rigid, resistive, defensive and distant, were viewed more negatively.

Clearly social workers have preferred and non-preferred clients. The important point to be made, however, is that these workers did not simply like to work with the 'preferred' client. Unless the client displayed desirable qualities and responses, the workers felt only very limited achievement, if any, would occur. The possibility of a 'self-fulfilling prophecy' is clearly evident.

For example, it was precisely because clients did *not* exhibit the above characteristics, either in the initial interview or in the subsequent sessions, that the social workers in the first agency did not think contact was achieving very much. In the social workers' view, these cases were classed as 'failures' largely because it was felt the clients had approached the agency with little forethought and were not ready to get involved in a manner the workers thought appropriate. Such clients were regarded as lacking in a basic motivation for change. For example, one worker said of a female client after the initial interview: 'I was not sure she would get involved. She was unable to relate to another person because of her absorption with herself, her pregnancy and her marital situation. She couldn't go forward or backward' (Silverman 1969, 131). Despite this initial pessimism, the workers attempted to 'educate' these people to 'play the role of the client', i.e. behave and act in a manner deemed appropriate by the workers. When the workers failed to recruit the client to play this role, they felt disappointed and let down.

Similarly, the sense of achievement and competence of the workers in the second study (Maluccio 1977), was related to clients' responses. As Maluccio states, 'the preferred client seems to evoke a sense of competence and fulfilment in the worker while the non-preferred client provokes feelings of self-doubt, inadequacy and frustration' (1977, 174). Maluccio illustrates this conclusion. In the first quote the worker is talking about a 'preferred' client who had, in her view, made considerable progress within a few months:

> She was a satisfying woman to work with . . . there were frustrations, especially since she was so self-critical and she took things too little at a time . . . but she is a warm, responsive, 'with-it' person. She is highly motivated . . . she tries so hard and she gives you such a nice feeling . . . she always gives you feedback, lets you know how she appreciates what you're doing — makes you feel that you're accomplishing something worthwhile (Maluccio 1977, 110).

Another worker describes an unsatisfactory case with a woman with marital problems:

I tried to be supportive with her but she turned me off. She expected simple, concrete answers for her complex problem with her husband – she wouldn't let me get close to her . . . I wanted to reach out to share my feelings but this backfired. I felt even more frustrated and inadequate . . . there were many complaints and unreasonable demands from her. I tried to get her to see what she was doing but didn't get far. I felt angry, but it was difficult to tell her since I didn't want to hurt her feelings (Maluccio 1977, 110).

These studies suggest that the onus is on clients to prove themselves good candidates for the role of client. This can result in the blame for failure being placed on the client. This is somewhat similar to the findings of research in psychotherapy. One such study (Strupp, Fox and Lessler 1969) explicitly stated that for patients to be accepted for individual psychotherapy they must meet the criterion of 'good' patient. This is regarded as being altogether 'valid' and 'economical'. The above studies suggest there are two main reasons for this. Firstly, the 'preferred' clients' responses must fit into the model of 'help' held by the worker. If the most helpful activity is felt to be verbalizing feelings and emotions, then clients who are articulate and willing to talk are most likely to achieve 'success'. Secondly, the clients' responses affect the workers' feelings and needs for human involvement in social work contacts. Segal (1978) talks of 'need fulfilment' in social work both societal and professional. He suggests that professionals have personal needs which are part of the reason for continuing to offer service, even in the absence of proof of its effectiveness. Segal outlines three professional needs: the continued use of the professionals' skills, the altruistic need to help others and the need for 'self-fulfilment' in the therapeutic endeavour. In turn, this self-fulfilment can be related to the workers' belief in their own competence and value as helpers. Amongst some workers, the degree to which such professional needs are met varies depending on the client. In summarizing, Segal states,

'Self-fulfilment' seems to be tied to the intellectual manipulation of varying conceptions of psychotherapy. Such 'self-fulfilment' is often absent in work with the unmotivated client or the psychotic patient and may account for the relatively low percentage of trained workers involved with these types of clients (1978, 11).

Summary

In exploring the valued images and activities of social workers, we have been examining the vital ingredients of a successful social work intervention. These ingredients consist of both worker and client qualities and actions. Social workers' ideas about which particular qualities and actions are important and valuable, vary. They vary depending on the ideology of the social worker, on the type of social work being practised and on the nature of the client's difficulties. In describing such attributes and behaviours, some social workers are illustrating the means by which a desirable outcome can be achieved. But others sometimes seem to be more than simply describing the 'ingredients' of success. They are describing 'success' itself. Maluccio has suggested that it is the interaction between the qualities of the client and the needs of the worker which affect the outcome of their encounter. As he explains, 'In some cases, a client and worker made such a good connection that the worker feels satisfied and effective, in others, the connection is missing or incomplete and the worker feels frustrated or ineffective' (1977, 144). That is, the means appear to become the ends. Sainsbury's observation rings true.

> The end products of social work (whether for a caseworker, neighbourhood worker, welfare rights activist, or houseparent) become increasingly difficult to state, the more he emphasizes the quality of the process by which they are to be achieved (1975, 104–5).

But what are the 'end products' of social work and what are the constraints that affect realization? These are the questions posed in Chapter 7.

7

Constraints Controlling Outcomes

What is the 'result' of a person's contact with the social services? What outcome criteria do social workers use to measure the success of an intervention? As might be expected, the literature reveals differences in ideas about good and bad or desirable and undesirable outcomes – if indeed the ideas are articulated at all. Comments on outcomes are often couched in very general terms and rarely discussed in detail.

What, then are the outcome criteria used by practising social workers? Four broad outcome criteria were identified: (1) Client change; (2) Bureaucratic obligations; (3) Social/moral control of the client; and (4) Client satisfaction. This list is not exhaustive. No doubt other, perhaps more subtle criteria are utilized in practice. But until further research is carried out on just this issue, our knowledge remains limited.

Client change

Client change or adjustment is regarded by many workers as a desirable outcome, and has been used as a measure of success in a variety of social work settings. Usually, this is change as observed by the worker, but occasionally clients' views on change have explicitly been stated as being valuable. The term 'client change' is very broad and needs further exploration.

Silverman's study of 13 professionally qualified social workers in a variety of mental health agencies in Boston provides one of the best accounts of the nature of desired change (Silverman 1969). The following example is, however, perhaps fairly extreme in that the social workers adopt a fairly 'pure' or 'narrow' interpretation of what they do, based mainly on Freudian theory. However, elements in this view can be found in other social work settings in which a broader view of casework prevails.

In the psychodynamic or psychotherapeutic approach to social work, environmental factors tend to be rated as a very secondary influence on people's problems. One worker from a mental health counselling agency stated:

> Usually there is extensive emotional or economic deprivation in an unhappy childhood. I think that the childhood deprivations and primarily what happened in the family with an overlay of the social influences on them are what causes problems (Silverman 1969, 51).

This belief in the causes of client problems structures the social worker's approach to his work, and his definition of a desirable outcome. What is seen as being desirable is not so much changing the situation of the client but changing the client to *believe* or *think* differently. Basically, a successful case is one in which the client learns more about his present predicament in relation to his past. The presumption is that people who can make links between their feelings and behaviour can work out their *own* solutions to their problems. If clients do not achieve this insight, then their cases may be regarded as a 'failure' by the worker. An example of this can be given by the social worker of a Mrs J. seeking help with bereavement. Clearly in the eyes of the worker this case was a failure because the client was felt to be 'denying' and 'resisting'.

> I have never seen a patient in whom denial was so clear a mechanism as in this woman and a very specific example of it was – specifically right after we would talk about one of these losses she would immediately revert back to talking about her physical symptoms so that she really did not want to open up that area at all, and this became increasingly clear to me as time went by. I don't know what the change was – I think it was partly a change in her and partly a greater awareness within myself of the extent of denial (Silverman 1969, 171).

This may be an extreme example. Certainly the researcher herself commented that the social workers in this study had a very limited view of their clients and of social work, and that clients' reactions were sometimes seen in 'very simplistic terms'.

Not only this 'pure' psychodynamic approach evaluates changes in clients' perceptions and behaviour as being the main outcome criteria. Changes in clients' perceptions of what their problem *is*, as well as its main causes have been a major criterion of evaluation utilized by social workers in other areas of social work (Sacks, Bradley and Beck 1970). This change in perception often involves clients changing their own definitions to that of their social workers. For example, a study in which clients attended an agency with a parent/child problem showed that, although the parent/child relationship was uppermost in the parents' mind, the workers tended to view the problem as largely stemming from the marital relationship (Sacks, Bradley and Beck 1970). By and large, however, the parents did not perceive the situation this way. 'Success' for these workers largely consisted of clients' shifting in their perception of the cause of the child's problem, i.e. in recognizing that they themselves contributed to the behaviour of their child, and accepting the workers' definition of the causes of the problem. In more recent studies similar views of success in the sphere of child guidance have again been demonstrated as being at least one stage of success (Lishman 1978). The achievement of 'insight' has also been cited by workers in social casework agencies in England dealing with low-income families (Sainsbury 1975) and by workers dealing with marital problems in an agency in America (Sacks, Bradley and Beck 1970).

Changes in *attitudes* of clients have also been regarded as a criterion of success in other settings – although it is not really clear in the literature whether or not 'insight' and 'attitude' are to be considered synonymous. Again, these changes have generally involved clients adjusting their attitudes to those deemed appropriate by their workers. For example, social workers in prison welfare have defined one criterion of success in terms of the prisoners' attitudes toward them (Shaw 1974). If the prisoners perceived the interviews with the caseworker as being valuable, were willing to communicate with their caseworkers and were generally satisfied with their relationship, some measure of success was thought to have been attained. Changes in List 'D' boys' attitudes to their peers and the development of a sense of responsibility have been regarded by other social workers as important criteria to take into account in any decision to recommend release or probation (Rushforth 1976). Attitudinal changes of a similar nature have also been deemed good amongst high-risk offenders on probation in three English cities – although additional criteria relating to more situational factors were also taken into account in this study (Home Office 1974).

Changes in the *feelings* and *emotions* of clients are other outcome criteria used by workers, e.g. when clients feel less angry, less depressed or less helpless. However, the degree of importance workers attach to feeling changes is not always clear. In one study in which workers were dealing with couples with marital problems, the workers felt that a change in client feelings was not enough (Sacks, Bradley and Beck 1970). Of the couples where only one partner wished to separate, the workers acknowledged the feeling changes of the deserted party, e.g. relief at ventilating hurt feelings. However, it was felt that such feeling changes had little bearing on the fundamentals of the marital relationship and hence could not be considered as reflections of progress. This study suggests that the value of such changes is largely to be viewed in the short term, rather than the long term, i.e. as one stage on the way to a 'successful' outcome.

Many of these perceptual and attitudinal changes mentioned above have resulted in change in clients' *behaviour*. Clients becoming more confident, mature, and independent and thus more capable in dealing with their own problems have been taken as a measure of success among workers dealing with unmarried mothers (Rubenstein and Bloch 1978). Couples with marital and family problems (Maluccio 1977), low-income families (Sainsbury 1975), clients with mental health problems (Silverman 1969) and clients in penal institutions of one sort or another (Home Office 1974; Rushforth 1976; Shaw 1974). Clients are thus seen as having improved relations with family, friends (or fellow prisoners) and generally better able to cope with day to day living.

The majority of these 'client changes' then have involved perceptual, attitudinal and behavioural changes in clients. It is rare to find discussions in the literature as to the exact nature of these changes. Neither is it clear who is felt to be the best judge of these changes, i.e. whether it should be the client or the worker. It is also difficult to assess the relative importance of this criterion. It raises the question of whether an ultimately successful outcome can exist, or whether such changes are just stages of success in a never-ending search for improvement.

Agency obligations and statutory duties

The carrying out of agency functions and statutory obligations can in itself constitute an important criterion of success for social workers. These functions may include such activities as establishing a client's eligibility for certain kinds of tangible help, or carrying out regular interviews and meetings with a client because it has been prescribed, e.g. by a juvenile court – in general operating bureaucratic or statutory duties. The literature does not suggest that bureaucratic criteria are the only ones used by social workers. What it does suggest is that the use of bureaucratic criteria varies depending on time and circumstances.* For example, two studies, (one involving a variety of mental health agencies (Silverman 1969) and the other, a public welfare agency (Blau 1960) found that bureaucratic criteria gave least satisfaction to newly qualified workers in the field for the first time. Inexperienced workers go into the field with positive feelings towards clients and their needs, and 'idealistic' notions of how they will be able to help these clients. However, through time, the 'reality shock' hits them and they find themselves faced with a large caseload, restricted resources and bureaucratic restraints within which they have to carry out their work. In the study on the agencies primarily concerned with casework counselling, for example, the workers discovered that, due to limited resources, the agencies had to restrict access to their service, despite the 'needs' of the clients. Some of the workers in these agencies were highly critical of the agency's need to restrict its intake to certain kinds of clients, i.e. those who it was thought would be able to benefit most from the 'treatment' available. But the majority of the workers, although frustrated and upset about this at the beginning, came to accept the administrative needs of the agency and the limitations on what they do.†

In the other study, the agency was concerned with a combination of welfare assistance and social casework. Again it was the newcomers who most frequently voiced complaints about the clash between the needs of the

---

* Evidence of this criterion influencing the social workers' evaluations of outcome emerged in only a few of the studies reviewed. However, in these studies, the emphasis has been on a methodology employing fairly intensive and semi-structured interviews with workers. By employing such a methodology, the researcher can gain access to information that might not otherwise emerge from more structured studies. It may be, then, that in practice the utilization of this criterion is more common than the literature suggests.

† The researcher states that it is unclear what made the difference between these two groups of workers.

clients and the agency's requirements. They also frequently criticized the old-timers for growing 'callous' and 'inflexible' in the course of having become adapted to the bureaucratic organization. They found compliance with the regulations a great cause of dissatisfaction, and some workers subsequently left the agency. However, those caseworkers who did remain with the agency for a few years gradually came to accept the limitations of official procedures, and eventually incorporated them into their own thinking − '*because doing so was a prerequisite for deriving satisfaction from the job and performing it adequately*' (Blau 1960, 232, our italics). The implication of this is that the utilization of bureaucratic criteria by social workers as a measure of 'success' may increase their perceptions of their own competence. This will be discussed in more detail in the next chapter.

The social or moral control of the client

In some of the studies reviewed the social workers viewed a desirable outcome as one in which the client is socially or morally controlled. As we shall see, this control may be either explicit or implicit. The idea of 'controlling' people is most likely to be an anathema to many social workers. Nevertheless, elements of its existence appear from time to time − particularly in the social work field dealing with offenders of some kind, whether in or out of institutions. For example, amongst a variety of outcomes designated as 'successful' in the field of Community Service Orders,* one team explicitly stated that the scheme would be a success 'if clients manage to keep out of trouble and become more responsible' (Pease 1974). In another study of Community Service Orders 'success' was achieved if the offender managed to keep out of trouble while in the scheme, and fulfilled all the contracted hours (Parsloe and O'Boyle 1980). In some List 'D' schools in Scotland, staff who were more 'control' orientated than 'treatment' orientated looked for the following signs in a boy's behaviour that would indicate 'success': that he behaved generally well in school, and kept out of trouble while home on leave, i.e. that he generally conformed to moral and social control (Rushforth 1976). For juvenile delinquents out of institutions, and on probation, similar beliefs appear. A Canadian study of children on probation (the boys mainly for offences against property and the girls on 'moral' offences) examined volunteer probation officers' views of 'improvement'. It became clear that most 'improvement' seen by the volunteers was related to the probationers' social control and respect for authority. Indeed, most court volunteers identified social control as a major objective of probation. Of course, other objectives were mentioned, but social control was regarded as being the most important.

In all the above instances, the social control of the client is of a very explicit nature, in many cases being officially part of the practitioners' work.

* Refers to work carried out by order of a court but under supervision and usually used as an alternative to imprisonment.

But the desirability of some form of social control is not confined solely to services with offenders. For example, Handler (1974) in his study of a child care office in London, talks of a 'bargaining' type relationship between clients and workers. In order to get the desired 'goods', e.g. clothing, furniture or whatever, the clients felt they had to cooperate with the approach of the child care officers. An unmarried mother with three children in care because of poverty and bad housing wanted to be rehoused so she could have her children returned. She began to take the advice of the child care officer and generally cooperated. As the child care officer stated, the woman was 'more willing to accept authority' and was 'working with us rather than against us' (Handler 1974, 71).

What all these workers have in common, then, is the idea that 'success' implies some element of moral and social control in the behaviour of the client whether it be explicit or implicit. In the former sense this view has similar elements to the idea of 'success' held by some researchers when 'evaluating' the effect of social work with probationers and prisoners. Success or failure is regarded as depending mainly on whether or not the person re-offends, and thus breaks 'out of control' once again. In the latter form of control there are perhaps traces of the old idea of the 'moral reform' of the poor.

Client satisfaction

The final main outcome criterion identified is concerned with client satisfaction and the meeting of needs as defined by the client. Recent studies, in particular, have exhibited a willingness on the part of social workers to use clients' evaluations as one measure of success. For example, Lishman (1978) used parents' evaluations as one of her main criteria of success and failure. Rees (1978), on questioning a number of local authority and voluntary agency social workers, found that success was described mostly in terms of clients' happiness. As one social worker explained, ' "Success" would be seeing her happy because if she were happier it would do a tremendous amount for this family' (Rees 1978, 43).

In the new field of Community Service Orders, success has also been defined in terms of client satisfaction. Pease (1974) found that many of the people running the schemes talked of the success of the programmes as dependent on whether or not the clients (who might otherwise be in prison) regarded their experience as positive. This was matched against the negative experiences of prison. Moreover, in at least one area, further offences committed were not regarded as failure so long as the client perceived his community service experience in positive terms. Thus a worker said of one man, who had previous convictions and a history of disastrous personal relationships, but who was working on a CSO with the elderly and the young,

> I consider this to be satisfactory because there is no doubt that he enjoyed what he was doing. It was of real value to his own community and he put more into it than was asked of him (Pease 1974).

It seems then, that some social workers are content if their clients are happy. This appears to be true even if the workers perceive their clients to have greater needs than those defined by the clients. For example, this was evident in the case of one social worker involved with a client who was terminally ill. All the client wanted was convalescence, but the worker felt that he had greater needs, such as more facilities and additional help. Nevertheless, the worker concluded, 'I find very much that the client, you know, was very satisfied with very little . . . and I felt I was going over the mark to go on and offer him more' (Whittington 1977, 83).

In some circumstances the social worker complies reluctantly with the way clients present problems. However, yet again, we are left in the dark as to what these circumstances might be. We also know little about what can account for the difference between those workers who are content to use this criterion as a gauge of achievement or success, and those who are not. Furthermore, the situation is complicated when the question 'who is the client?' is asked. A decision of a medical social worker to agree to the wishes of an elderly client to help him return home to live, may conflict with the wishes of his relatives who may wish him to be placed in residential care. The notion 'client satisfaction' is a complicated criterion. The question of which person's needs or wishes are given priority in a situation in which several people are involved, as in the above case, remains to be studied let alone answered.

Summary

This short chapter testifies to our lack of knowledge of the outcome criteria used by practising social workers. The brevity may also be indicative either of the difficulty or of the reluctance or of the dilemmas involved in talking about 'outcomes' in social work.

One thing emerges clearly. Constraints influence the shape of an outcome. These constraints take various forms. They can be theoretical. For example, it is often impossible to discuss the nature of an outcome without referring to the social workers' perceptions of the aetiology of client's problems. Different causes of problems imply different 'cures' and different evidence of improvement. The constraints can also be contextual. For example, perceptions of success are related to what achievement can be expected in a particular situation. A shortage of resources, or the severity of clients' problems can be an important influence in deciding what is an appropriate outcome. Constraints can also be literally just that – constraints of a legal nature. When, for example, probation officers are working with probationers, or social workers have responsibility for families subject to child care orders. These and other 'constraints' figure prominently in practitioners' discussions of 'outcomes' in social work, and play a decisive part in the form they take. It is to a discussion of these various constraints and the dilemmas they pose that we now direct our attention.

8

Contextual Dilemmas

Practitioners' evaluations are riddled with dilemmas and debates. These tend to revolve round three main issues. There are dilemmas over whether evaluation is or should be concerned with 'process' or with 'outcome', i.e. with the 'doing' of social work, or with 'results'. Even when there is agreement on whether the means or ends are the most important, there are dilemmas over the criteria of evaluation to be taken into account in assessing the success of an intervention. Finally, there exist dilemmas which may best be described as being between ideology and practice. In focusing on these dilemmas we may be better able to understand the difficulties social workers encounter when they attempt to 'weigh their practice'.

Process or outcome?

A number of observers have noted that there have existed in the past two competing orientations towards the purpose of social work interventions (Baird 1976; Levy 1974; Segal 1978). Many articles have been written debating whether the outcome and the achievement of goals, or the process and what takes place in the course of an intervention, should be the focus of evaluation in social work. Weiss (1972) is one writer who believes that it is the results of intervention that are important. Research is a way of measuring the effects of a programme against the goals set out to be accomplished.

Levy (1974), on the other hand, believes that social work evaluation should concentrate on process. He argues that there are inherent limitations, essentially practical in nature, in using outcomes of professional practice in ascertaining professional competence. He feels that 'outcome' studies cannot possibly control all the variables that exist in a given situation. Moreover, he is of the opinion that

> The point – with respect to the determination of the nature of competence and to its assessment – is that the quality of what the social worker can do and has done in a given practice situation is not likely to be attested to in the results, at least not sufficiently to attribute the results to the social worker's qualities, capacities, and interventions (Levy 1974, 378)

In Levy's view, then, it is what social workers possess and what they put into practice that should be the focus of practice evaluation.

116

Opinion is agreed that in the past, 'process' has been seen as the main goal of treatment and the main focus of social work evaluation (Segal 1978). The idea that the main emphasis should be on process still has a strong influence today. However, in recent years more attention has been paid to the outcome of social work interventions (Chommie and Hudson 1974). As a result, research has increasingly been concerned with results and effectiveness, and whether or not a specified set of activities has achieved a set of (usually predetermined) objectives. The current political climate has also had an influence in this debate. Funding bodies' willingness to finance a project is often tied to goals concerning the effects of intervention (Kagle 1978). Partly as a reaction to this latest emphasis on outcome, several writers now argue that both process and outcome are proper concerns of evaluation (Chommie and Hudson 1974).

The dilemma over whether 'process' or 'outcome' is most important also occurs amongst practitioners, with the result that some social workers are geared towards results in social work, while others place more emphasis on the interventive process. No single consideration appears to be of major influence in swaying social workers to one option or another. Rather what seems to be influential is a mixture of the particular ethics, ideals and practice models of social work held by practitioners. Some workers find it *unethical* to talk about 'outcomes' in relation to social work services. Sainsbury describes this position well when commenting on the evaluations of practitioners in a Family Service Unit.

> Success in social work cannot be considered in isolation from ethical and relationship issues. To divorce definitions of success from ethical considerations would leave the social workers at risk of condemnation as cynical manipulators in a professional limbo; to divorce measures of success from considerations of personal relationships would be to deny the validity of experiences, upon which clients themselves placed considerable weight, and which appear to some clients at least, as inseparable from their experiences of, and respect for, ethical values (1975, 110).

This concern that ethical considerations be taken into account when evaluating social work, may have something to do with Nokes's (1967) suggestion that, historically, welfare practice has developed over the years in response to *moral* as well as pragmatic considerations. Originally, the Christian tradition required people 'to give and not to count the cost'. Long after the specifically Christian bases of welfare disappeared, however, these attitudes survive in various secular philosophies and carry on the humanitarian tradition. Social workers and teachers claim their occupations have more than an instrumental status. As Nokes elaborates,

> These people do not see themselves as mere adjustors or social engineers. Indeed their activities seem to be (at least in part) ends in themselves, testimonies of what it is felt right to do, regardless of whether what is done is merely effective in some particular direction (1967, 21).

One of the most regularly heard comments amongst social workers is the denial of any intention to *do* things *to* people. This belief is similar to that found amongst what Rodgers and Dixon (1960) have described as 'natural' social workers. Such workers possess understanding, tolerance, and most important, a sense of vocation. These social workers feel the need to help people on as much emotional as intellectual grounds. Thus doing social work is felt to be worthwhile, whatever the chances of 'improvement' or 'success' − 'not depending for its justification on its results, no "failure" can thus discredit it' (Rodgers and Dixon 1960, 155). Indeed in some circumstances, a social worker may regard discussion of 'results' as objectionable. For example, social work with geriatrics or with people who are terminally ill has more to do with the offering of a warm and sympathetic presence than a 'technical operation to achieve some specifiable goal' (Halmos 1966).

Such beliefs and values have been described by Halmos (1966) as the 'faith' of the counsellors.* This 'faith' sustains workers in the face of lack of evidence of tangible results. Indeed Halmos describes this 'faith' in almost religious terms, and draws a parallel between the outlook of social workers with that of pastoral ministration and its expression of moral concern.

> The failure of prayer to bring about what was prayed for does not revise the belief in the power of prayer. The evidence is simply ignored. It seems to me that the lurking and undeclared faith of the counsellor is that the concern which prompts him to act will overflow into the act, and will never *completely* fail if it is sufficiently steeped in a person-to-person relationship between worker and helped. Neither failure nor success need be recognizable by third parties if the counsellor knows that he can throw himself open to this kind of relationship, and if the client knows that he can partake in that relationship. The service must be rendered even in the face of hopeless odds; there is something inherently proper in the rendering of it irrespective of what difference it would demonstrably make (Halmos 1966, 148).

Such beliefs form part of the altruistic ideology prevalent in the social work field − that professionals must do whatever they can regardless of current knowledge regarding the effectiveness of their intervention strategies (Segal 1978). As Segal (1978) points out, the assumption underlying all this activity is that whatever social workers do, they feel that at best it will be helpful, and at worst, of no consequence. The possibility of negative consequences resulting is seldom considered. But one thing is clear, social workers who perceive their work as a vocation and as more than just a 'job' are unlikely to make a distinction between 'means' and 'ends', or 'process' and 'outcome', in social work. They regard the means as an integral part of the end, and the end consisting in the means.

A second consideration, related to the first, is that some social workers

---

* They are felt to be particularly prevalent amongst those workers who perceive their main function as counselling.

believe the notion of 'outcome' to be a false or misleading one. Halmos (1966) explains that the word 'cure' originally derives from the Latin 'cura', meaning 'care'. Caring is not a finite activity in response to finite needs. Thus some social workers believe that social work is in some sense never-ending. One can always foresee more problems to resolve and ideals to strive towards. If this view is held, talk of 'outcome' is both inappropriate and meaningless.

Whether process or outcome is regarded as the main focus of evaluation also depends on the particular theoretical perspective held by the worker. Kagle (1978) found that amongst her sample of predominantly mental welfare workers, practice principles associated with behaviourism showed a strong orientation towards outcome, while those associated with ego-psychology focused more on process and on the components of practice. When evaluating their practice, behaviourist social workers are more likely to be strongly influenced by the results of intervention. It seems likely too that their methods of social work encourage the learning theorists to consider evaluation as an appropriate exercise, which they would enjoy carrying out. For such quasi-scientific workers, evaluation is an ideologically palatable activity.

Although ethical and ideological considerations play a significant part in practitioners' debates over the relative importance of process and outcome, pragmatic considerations are not to be underestimated. Many social workers are not in a position to know whether or not their interventions have achieved anything. For example, the 'success' of a child care regime may not be evident for many years after the child has left custody. Even if social workers are in a position to get some more immediate feedback on the effects of their interventions, few are clear about what they mean by 'success' or 'failure'. Practitioners often have great difficulty in specifying the desired outcome of a human interaction problem-solving process (Segal 1978). When goals are specified, they are usually of a highly generalized nature, e.g. 'improved social functioning' or 'the gaining of insight'. Such goals are not easily 'measured'. The generalized nature of many social work objectives, combined with the lack of clarity as to what success or failure might look like, means social workers are often left with little guidance as to how they may know whether or not what they have done was done well (Nokes 1967). This is illustrated in a study of British local authority workers (DHSS 1978 – unpublished material). As one worker in a rural team explains 'I've still no objective idea of standards. I don't honestly know whether I'm doing the job properly or not, it's as simple as that.' (DHSS 1978, unpublished material).

One consequence of this uncertainty is that it makes it highly tempting for the social worker to focus on the abstract nature of the helping process, independent of goals or results (Segal 1978). The more one emphasizes the process of social work interventions, the more difficult it becomes to talk about 'outcomes' or 'results' (Sainsbury 1975). Another consequence may be the confusion in the minds of some social workers between 'means' and 'ends', as is sometimes apparent when they talk about 'success' and how it might be achieved. The following quote from a social worker working with a family referred for rent arrears, illustrates how the helping process can become the goal of the intervention. 'We've got to establish relationships with both. And with the young lad in there too. It's not just financial. Probably if we improve the relationship the other side of things would improve too' (Rees 1978, 43).

This confusion explains Nokes's observation that many practitioners are 'unable to make even a conceptual distinction between personal satisfaction and objective success' (1967 25). Thus a 'good' day may be one when the worker has done a 'good day's work', not necessarily one in which some outstanding degree of 'objective good' was achieved (however this term might be defined).

Precisely this criticism has been levelled against the evaluations of social work students by social work supervisors and tutors. Issues involved in the evaluation of social work students are not unconnected with our present discussions of practitioners. To be awarded a qualification in social work, a student has to exhibit competence and ability in fieldwork practice. How this is assessed has been the subject of two pieces of research in which the content of practice evaluation has been examined (Brandon and Davis 1979; Sheldon and Baird 1978).

The findings of these two studies suggest that a great deal of emphasis is placed on the *doing* and performing of social work, rather than on the *effectiveness* of such activities. The three most commonly used criteria amongst tutors from six English training courses were concerned with the social work students' activities with clients and others in a client's environment, the ability to work within the agency and communicate through reports, letters, records, etc. (Brandon and Davis 1979). Attitudes and values expressed in the work, application of relevant theory and professional presentation were other commonly used criteria. Notably, the major content of these criteria is concerned with the process of helping. Sheldon and Baird (1978) have argued that there is too much emphasis on 'process' when evaluating students, and not enough on 'outcome'. Thus situations can arise when trainee social workers are given high praise by their supervisors, when there is sometimes little, if any, evidence that the client has actually benefited from the student's interventions. Although these evaluations of students are perhaps different from the evaluation of practising social workers, they raise interesting questions about the content of practice evaluations, and the relative emphasis placed on 'process' or 'outcome', and the 'means' or 'ends' of social work. A worthwhile study would attempt to answer some of these questions.

Criteria of evaluation

The two previous chapters revealed that social workers differ in their methods of intervention. They also hold differing views as to what constitutes a desirable or undesirable outcome, or 'success', or 'failure'. There is a consequent lack of agreement among social workers over the criteria to be taken into account when making such assessments. Such difficulties have been well documented in the field of medical social work (Butrym 1968), and also in the new area of Community Service Orders (Pease 1974). Indeed such difficulties in arriving at any agreement over, or even making explicit, clear criteria for evaluation are not peculiar to social work practitioners. Discussions of 'success' and 'failure', and 'outcome' in psychotherapy (Luborsky 1971; Mintz 1972) teaching (Elton 1975), and to some extent medical care (Klein *et al.* 1961), have illustrated similar disagreements and debate.

As various observers have noted, different social workers hold to differing theories of social work intervention, which tend to be based generally on different sociological and psychological theories of human functioning. These theories (Goldberg *et al.* 1970; Plowman, 1969) or working ideologies (Smith and Harris 1972), or practice model orientations (Kagle 1978), as they have been variously named, are important because they guide the social worker to a particular perception of the nature of the social problem he or she encounters. Moreover, theoretical considerations, as incorporated in certain ideologies, provide more than a framework for defining the nature of the social work process, they also dictate the form of the desired outcome. Whereas a psychodynamically orientated social worker will seek personal insight in the client as evidence of success, a more politically orientated social worker might look, for example, at a change in social policy or community services as evidence of success. We can only speculate on this. There is an absence of completed and published action/research reports in which the objectives of social workers were to effect some kind of social change, however unambitious.*

One study investigated the effect of what the researcher calls 'interventive models' on social workers' evaluation of social work practice. Kagle's study (1978) of a random sample of 435 from the American NASW Register of Clinical Social Workers set out to discover the respondents' evaluations of case analogues. Each respondent received two case analogues, which were varied in two ways — the goals and 'practice model orientation' of the social worker in the analogue were either stated in the language associated with behaviourism, or in the language associated with ego-psychology. It was

---

* In this respect we have *not* included any analysis of the reported objectives and achievements of community development-type projects.

discovered that in one of the case analogues, the respondent's theoretical perspective was a strong source of variance in statements of evaluation. For example, the behaviourally oriented practitioners were more likely to evaluate positively behaviourally oriented workers and/or positive outcomes. They were also likely to evaluate outcomes negatively if the worker in the case analogue used language identified with ego-psychology. These results could be significant. However, as Kagle herself points out, they were based on simulated analogues and the evaluations were done on unknown workers at the request of a researcher.

A case study of social workers' perceptions of success in a real-life work setting, provides a neat illustration of the influence of 'practice model orientations'. In studying List 'D' Schools in Scotland, Monica Rushforth (1976) studied the staff and interviewed them about their perceptions of success in the school setting. The question of a boy's release posed difficulties for the staff. It was at the time of release that the staff discussed most explicitly whether or not a measure of success was thought to have been achieved with a boy. However, it emerged from the schools studied that two different opinions existed as to what should be taken into account when considering a boy's readiness for release: The staff tended to be either 'treatment' oriented or 'control' oriented in their approach to work. The 'treatment' oriented staff worked for improvement in the boy's relationships at home, or for a development of the boy's sense of responsibility. The 'control' oriented staff, on the other hand, tended to look for improvement in terms of the boy's general behaviour in school, or in his keeping out of trouble while on leave. Thus, even within the same school, a boy's level of 'success' was judged from different standpoints. As Rushforth explains:

> For example, in a control oriented school, behaviour regarded as unacceptable might be called 'disruptive'; while the same behaviour in a treatment oriented school might be described as acting out, or it may even be seen as acceptable behaviour (1976, 10).

As a result of these diverse approaches, different criteria of evaluation are sought as proof of 'success'.

Yet, important as a social worker's theoretical orientation may be in determining the choice of evaluative criteria, for several reasons it cannot in itself constitute a total explanation. Even if social workers share both a general ideology of social work practice and a belief in the desired nature of the outcome of that practice, they may employ different *treatment approaches*, different means of helping and of achieving that outcome. Thus a shared definition of outcome does not always imply a shared definition of the helping process by which the outcome may be achieved. This is a distinction that is rarely made, yet surely one which merits further research. The current fragmented knowledge base of social work is another complicating issue (Mullen *et al.* 1972 a). There is evidence to suggest that many social workers do not stick consistently to one theoretical standpoint. On the contrary, many social workers are 'eclectic' and draw their views from a variety of theories, depending on how they interpret the situation of the client (Carew 1979; DHSS 1978). This implies that criteria of evaluation change depending on the particular social work theory being employed at the time. Other social workers claim they do not use theory in practice (DHSS 1978). They say they tend to work more on an intuitive level in the sense that they respond to an immediate situation without conscious reliance on a theoretical framework (although, of course, they could have 'internalized' some theory).

Such assumptions influence expectations of outcome. One officer in charge of an elderly people's home described the extent to which expectations can influence results: 'If your idea is that once someone is over 75, it's goodbye, then the work is not only slow, it's dead' (Sheldon and Baird 1978, 15). In such a situation, 'staying the same' could be construed as 'success' in that this suggests prevention of the elderly's physical and social deterioration.

The variety of social work approaches employed by social workers with different clients poses a dilemma over what is 'success' in social work. Clearly different social workers employ different criteria of evaluation depending on how they define 'help' and who their client is. Although specific examples of this have been given, we suspect that most social workers are far from clear about the criteria they use in deciding whether or not contact has resulted in anything positive. It is perhaps easier for those workers involved in the techniques of task-centred casework, or contract work, since it is part of those methods to specify specific tasks or goals in advance. This can provide a 'measure' of success or failure. In other situations in which social work methods have less explicitly defined goals, or in which the nature of the problem does not lend itself to specifying goals in advance, the whole business of evaluation is likely to be that bit harder. Highly generalized goals like 'improved social functioning' do not lend themselves easily to 'measurement'. Furthermore, as Sheldon and Baird argue, the beauty of such goals is 'that whatever happens, one can always persuasively claim that they have been at least partially achieved' (1978, 15). They cite the example of one case in which a child with serious behaviour problems was referred to a social services department. At the time of case closure, the child was in care, the father was in prison and the mother was in hospital recovering from a suicide attempt. Yet the social worker retrospectively persuaded himself 'that his [hitherto unrecorded] sub-goal of bringing the latent hostilities within the family system into the open, had at least been achieved.'

Whatever 'measures' practitioners do use, they are unlikely to be constant. Social workers operate in different contexts. These contexts are likely to place pressures of various kinds on social workers' choice of criteria. As one social worker stated,

I often feel that I'm acting more from instinct than from knowledge really or skills – I'm working very intuitively sometimes – when I read the book, I'm often relieved to find that I have done the right thing (DHSS 1978, 191).

In the absence of any explicit theory or practice model of working, on what criteria do these social workers decide whether or not they are effective? Some other criteria, not based on theory must come into operation.

A second consideration which affects a social worker's choice of evaluative criteria is related to the nature of the client group and the social problem at hand. For example, 'client change' may be an appropriate success criterion for interventions with a client with a mental health problem. The same criterion, however, might be completely inappropriate as a measure of success for interventions with the elderly, whose situation often involves deterioration. Cherry Rawlings (1978), in her article on local authority social workers and elderly clients, makes an interesting observation in this connection. According to her study, much of the social work activity with elderly clients is carried out by unqualified workers. Professionally qualified social workers often describe work with the elderly as being 'slow'. Rawlings suggests that part of the reason for this is that 'some workers, albeit unknowingly, hold back from a purposeful and active role *because of their assumptions about the potential for change* in clients who are old and probably also handicapped' (our italics) (Rawlings 1978, 28).

Ideology and practice

The dilemmas involved in the choice of evaluative criteria cannot be divorced from the working context in which practitioners find themselves. The following comment of a social worker illustrates the importance of taking into account environmental and situational factors when researching practitioners' evaluations. This worker refused to take part in an evaluation study because he felt it ignored a lot of relevant issues. He wrote to the researcher on the returned, unanswered questionnaire,

> Why don't you, or someone else do research on the constraints on quality social work practice imposed by budget cuts, increasing job loads, fear of job loss . . .? The evaluations of social work practice in a political and economic vacuum really evaluates a vacuum practice (Kagle 1978, 73).

By examining these constraints, we can see how the existence of a gap between ideology and practice affects social workers' evaluations.

The extensive literature on professionals' roles refers indirectly to the influence of contexts on evaluations. For example, the particular 'role orientation' adopted at a given time has implications for social workers' judgements of their own activities. Given that orientations refer primarily to the views, experiences and intentions of social workers and the range of meanings and interpretations available to them (Whittington 1977), they provide a useful framework for analysing practitioners' evaluative comments (particularly when they do not ignore the importance of the contexts in which such interpretations are made.)

In a review of the literature on such role orientations, Rothman (1974) identified three basic types: (1) the professional orientation, characterized by its concern with professional values and standards (2) the bureaucratic orientation, characterized by a preoccupation with the policies and norms of the employing agency, and (3) the client orientation in which there is primary attention paid to the need of those served by the agency. However, a more recent analysis of practising social workers suggests that such a division is oversimplified. In this study *eight* orientations of practitioners to social work were identified. Whittington (1977) explains 'orientations' as categories of social workers' subjective meanings in respect of clients. Thus:

> Each social work act occurs in the context of some kind of definition of the client. Moreover, the act involves some objective in which the client is implicated. The act may also be conceived as having a focal point, that is, a central area in which problem solving is necessary if the objective is to be realized. These three principal elements comprise the orientation adopted by the social worker in a particular situation (Whittington 1977, 75–6).

If social workers in one situation operate within 'bureaucratic' or 'formalistic' orientation, their main objective is to comply with formal prescriptions and proscriptions, carrying out statutory duties and obligations. In another situation, other workers may work within a 'client-centred' or 'service' orientation, in which their objective may be client satisfaction. The first social workers might be quite satisfied to carry out a statutory duty, perhaps irrespective of client satisfaction. For the latter workers, the reverse might be true. Whittington's observations of social workers' activities and opinions, also suggest that orientations are not *static* – that in fact social workers change their orientation from case to case, or situation to situation. This implies that sometimes the basis of practitioners' evaluations vary from situation to situation. What influences the particular orientation and therefore the choice of evaluative criteria, at any given time?

Various studies have revealed that many social workers feel under considerable pressure of work (Neill, Warburton and McGuiness 1976). Such pressure may be related to heavy caseload, lack of resources or the burden of paperwork (Jordan 1976). In these circumstances the practitioners' concern with professional 'standards' (however they might be defined) can be affected. Certainly, those workers in the nationwide Parsloe/Stevenson project (DHSS 1978 unpublished material), who acknowledged themselves as being under *less* pressure of 'bombardment' were those who expressed *most* anxiety about their standards of work, i.e. they had more time to contemplate the quality and/or efforts of what they do. For example, a worker in one region in which the volume and pace of work was not overtaxing, made the following comment.

I certainly feel that I should do a better job in these circumstances and therefore it's important that I do and that, in a sense, is a pressure. Here I still make plenty of mistakes but I've only myself to blame. In my former authority I did find myself saying when something had gone wrong – 'I didn't have time to do anything else anyway' (DHSS 1978 – unpublished material).

Workers who derive their sense of competence from professional standards may, in some circumstances, have to adjust their ideas depending on what they perceive is possible.

This pressure of work can result in a dilemma. For example, social workers who believe their function is mainly the amelioration of poverty and the general improvement of the clients' situation, may be confronted with a situation in which they find they have little control of the necessary resources (Smith and Harris 1972). In a similar vein, a community worker with a strong commitment to a Marxist position, who believes the only way people's lives can be improved is by a restructuring of the economic system, may find himself or herself 'diverted' into such activities as promoting participation in the local community school or helping residents to gain marginal improvements in their environment (Salmon 1978). This gap between 'ideology' and the 'reality' of compromise can result in the practitioner feeling frustrated, inadequate and even in a state of crisis (Jordan 1976). Such a dilemma is part of what Simpkin (1979) refers to as 'trapped within welfare surviving social work'. The dilemma must be overcome if the worker is to survive. Thus, workers may react in various ways. They may, for example, lower their expectations. Salmon (1978) advocates that community workers carefully examine their expectations of community work. He goes on to say,

> It is equally important to have a realistic appreciation of the limitations both of yourself and of community work. In this way we avoid becoming emotionally drained and depressed by the constant contrast between high expectations and low achievement (1978, 83).

Alternatively, social workers may adopt more formal criteria, such as statutory duties, in assessing the outcome of their interventions. Social workers in a local authority team found themselves caught between conflicting pressures from the clients, on the one hand, and the agency on the other (Jordan 1976). The clients wanted the provision of a variety of material resources, mainly simple aids and adaptations but also resources in the form of residential placements for ageing or ill relatives. The department, however, could not provide all the desired resources. To retain their integrity and to some extent resolve their dilemma, the social workers brought into play some 'defensive manoeuvres' or 'survival mechanisms'. Such mechanisms involved evasive action on the part of the social worker, or the adoption of a passive attitude (the feeling that 'that's how it works') all in some way retreating into the acceptance of the limitations of resources. As a result, these workers became more caseload oriented and less client oriented, and in this way managed to cope with feelings of frustration or inadequacy.

This is very similar to the processes at work in the two studies discussed earlier. In these studies, the workers, over time, came to accept compliance with agency regulations and procedures – by whose standards they could feel they were performing competently and effectively (Blau 1960; Silverman 1969). The adoption of other 'orientations' can also enable social workers to accept, say, the lack of availability of resources more easily. A concern with establishing a client's *eligibility* for material help (Smith and Harris 1972), or a perception that social work is sometimes an agency of social *control* (Smith and Harris 1972), allows a social worker to believe that only those who are largely eligible or who 'conform' or 'behave' or are in genuine need, will receive what resources are available. Thus, a practitioner who is concerned with meeting client needs may at the same time realize that resources are scarce. A moral ideology, (similar to those outlined above) may provide a mechanism for the resolution of such tensions (Smith and Harris 1972, 41). Another 'defence mechanism' in some circumstances could be the workers' acceptance of the clients' definition of need, which we have seen, can often be fairly limited. Demand for services is restricted by accepting the frequently low expectations of clients. The workers' sense of frustration may then be somewhat alleviated, thus allowing him or her to feel that a measure of success has been achieved if the client is happy.

This analysis of the dilemmas caused by the constraints on good or successful social work practice, is as yet, tentative and fragmented. As is confirmed in the impassioned plea of the social worker quoted earlier, researchers interested in evaluations do not always examine the constraints perceived by practitioners as they attempt to carry out their jobs. Some constraints are obvious. Social workers are employed to do a certain job but they are not always given the money or resources to ensure that job is carried out. Some constraints, however, are not so obvious. Any analysis of the ways in which social workers make judgements about the consequences of their efforts must take into account such contextual considerations as the availability of resources, the bureaucratic structure, the pressure of work, the value commitments and competence of individuals. Such considerations are usually incorporated in staff ideologies (See Smith 1980). These could reflect practitioners' values, conservative or otherwise, their imagination or lack of it, their sense of control over their job, their knowledge of resources and how to mobilize them.

Summary

The dilemmas discussed in this chapter, over process and outcome, over criteria of evaluation, and over ideology and practice, testify to the difficulties involved in making decisions as to what is important when evaluating social work. These dilemmas are inevitable. The very nature of social work precludes any 'one way' by which it may be evaluated. A practitioner's evaluative judgements are relative. They are relative to what he thinks he is doing and why he thinks he is doing it. They are relative to what he has been able to do in the past and what he hopes to do in the future with any particular client. They are relative to the particular pressures on him or her at any one point in time.

Evaluation needs to identify the links between ideologies and constraints. It should be confronting the questions whether social workers lower their objectives because of an awareness of constraints, or whether staff objectives were already limited because their personal ideologies matched the unambitious, albeit realistic, goals of the agency. In either case, some documentation of constraints is imperative in evaluation; in the first place because awareness of constraints results in lowering of objectives, in the second place because certain constraints become absorbed as objectives. We need to know more about how social workers evaluate their practice, if indeed they do evaluate it at all. We have to know whether and how evaluation differs depending on the agency in which social workers practice and the clients with whom they work. How does the organizational structure of the agency or department affect the way in which practitioners think about evaluation? What effect does having to justify money grants for the next year have on evaluation in voluntary agencies? Does specialization pin-point criteria of evaluation, whilst attempts to be a generalist diffuse them? What effect does working in a multi-disciplinary team have on evaluation? All these questions and more need to be answered before we can understand more fully how social workers weigh their practice.

Part IV
Conflicting Verdicts

Introduction

At the beginning of this book we discussed the business of accumulating evidence about social work. We also charged certain critics with being selective in the examples they used to promote their version of the consequences of social work. Their pre-judged attitudes have produced only some simple and monolithic arguments, almost as though the correspondence between some findings and the contradictions between others would be too complex to acknowledge.

In our final two chapters we shall highlight the meanings of the criteria used to evaluate social work. We are not arguing that everything is so relative that you cannot reach a conclusion about anything. On the contrary, several firm conclusions can be reached, provided that the criteria being used and the specific activities being referred to are identified. For example, the clients who say they are satisfied do not always mean that they have been helped (Rees 1978, Ch. 4). Evaluations of different forms of intervention seldom refer to exactly the same activities. Surveillance visiting of the frail elderly (Goldberg and Warburton 1979) is not the same as efforts to enlarge the supporting social networks of the aged (Goldberg 1975) or, in total contrast, as initiatives to prevent juvenile delinquency (Wilson 1975). Even the most jaundiced critic of modern medicine does not accuse doctors of dispensing aspirin for everything, yet social work has suffered from such generalizations. Some very different activities are often lumped together indiscriminately under the same label.

In the final two chapters we shall account for the conflicting verdicts on social work in two ways. In Chapter 9, social workers, clients and researchers are shown as disagreeing because they do not value the same forms of intervention, they do not always use the same criteria and they often end up by talking about different things. In Chapter 10 we draw our own conclusions from the findings of research. We question the appropriateness of social workers' activities if they do not result in some permanent changes in otherwise powerless people's circumstances. This perhaps lays us open to the criticism that we have infinite expectations of social work. We will take that risk. Our reference to appropriateness is one way of assessing accountability. There could be others. We could have asked whether social work matched what employers wanted or whether certain professional aspirations were achieved. By comparison with accountability to clients' interests, we have not valued such organizational and professional criteria so highly.

Our conclusions are that certain things can be said with certainty about the processes and outcomes of different kinds of social work. However, the issue of accountability in terms of the appropriateness of social work also raises the question of social work's role in the state. Do social workers collude with various forms of control, albeit in pleasant ways? Are there means of effecting change which would involve social workers in having different self-images, in separating themselves from conventional power relationships and in using different criteria to weigh their practice? Some evaluation of social work's role in the state is a different question from puzzling over the effects of certain social worker activities. This final difficult question will be confronted.

9

Talking about Different Things

This chapter has two purposes. Firstly, it aims to identify conflicting verdicts in evaluations of social work. Secondly, it aims to examine why these disagreements occur. This latter objective is related to our emphasis on the contexts in which social workers and clients meet and researchers carry out their tasks.

With reference to the first objective, the following are the kinds of questions we shall be asking: do the various personnel involved in social work have similar verdicts on the outcome of interventions? Do they agree on the criteria to be utilized when evaluating social work?

The second objective is concerned with the meaning of the criteria of evaluation chosen. In identifying conflicts in evaluation we are not arguing that one person's view is more 'accurate' than another's. Each director, each researcher, each practitioner, each client has a perspective made up of expectations, values and life experiences. These 'views of the world' colour the way in which they think about the helpfulness and effectiveness of social work. Their verdicts differ. Each is nevertheless accurate within his own frame of reference, his own unique way of seeing and interpreting life events.

In exploring the above issues, the chapter is divided into two main parts. Each is concerned with conflicts in evaluation as they occur between

1 researchers, social workers and clients
2 different social workers and different clients

Researchers', social workers' and clients' verdicts

A relatively clear and consistent picture emerges of researchers', practitioners' and clients' verdicts on social work. A diagram summarizes the findings.

Perceived level of success of social work

No success	Mixed verdict	Much success
Some researchers	Most practitioners	Many clients

The results of experimental studies carried out in the 1960s and early 1970s, indicated that there was little evidence to support the notion that social work is effective.* The conclusions of some of these reviews have been contested by a few researchers, e.g. Mullen and Dumpson 1972; Macdonald 1966, but general opinion is agreed that such evaluative studies have pointed to the failure, rather than the success of casework. Studies of the effectiveness of casework intervention in problems of delinquency, programmes for the elderly, rehabilitation and public assistance programmes have produced largely equivocal or negative results (Segal 1978) (although there are a few exceptions).

Fischer's (1973) review of eleven studies designed to evaluate social work concluded that,

> not only has professional casework failed to demonstrate it is effective but lack of effectiveness appears to be the rule rather than the exception across several categories of clients, problems, situations and types of casework (1973, 14).

Furthermore, he goes on to say,

> In a high proportion of psychotherapy studies, as many clients receiving professional services deteriorate as improve. The studies in this review show a parallel phenomenon (1973, 15).

Such findings provide ammunition for social work critics. Even those who are more sympathetic to social work and who believe that the negative findings have much to do with the methodology of the studies reviewed, have indicated that social work must also face the possibility that its personnel and their methods have failed.

> The profession must face the possibility that the reasons so many of the research studies reviewed showed negative outcomes is that the practitioners . . . were not competent (Wood 1978, 455).

Despite these negative findings, social workers still believe that they are achieving something worthwhile. Some rely on 'faith' and carry on irrespective of 'proof' of achievement. Others believe they can provide proof of their effectiveness, and point to tangible outcomes resulting from their interventions. Social workers are thus convinced that they achieve more than the results of evaluative research would indicate.

While social workers believe that their achievements have been underestimated by researchers, their self-evaluations are conservative when compared with the views of clients. The majority of studies which have compared clients' and social workers' perceptions of outcome have revealed that social

---

* The reader is reminded that researchers involved in evaluating social work at this time seemed to focus almost exclusively on one model of research − the group-comparison experimental model. When referring to 'researchers' in this chapter, we are talking primarily about those researchers involved in evaluating social work in the past, the bulk of whom favoured and utilized the experimental or quasi-experimental research model and who regarded social work as synonymous with individual casework or group work.

workers tend to be more cautious in their evaluations than clients. This finding has emerged from a variety of settings in which client and worker have evaluated the same contact, these settings including child guidance agencies, area teams, mental health agencies, medical social work teams and marital counselling agencies. In addition to being more cautious in their verdicts, practitioners are also likely to be less satisfied than clients with what they have been able to do. They often underestimate the strength of clients' satisfaction with service.

To summarize: the results of past evaluative studies have led many researchers to the conclusion that social work as represented by casework is ineffective, indeed sometimes even harmful. Practitioners, on the other hand, believe they achieve some degree of success, while clients' evaluations are even more positive.

Some 'outside' evaluators believe little if anything of value occurs as a result of social work intervention. Yet other, more exploratory, research has revealed both social workers and clients making more positive comments about social work contacts. Researchers, practitioners and clients all talk about the 'effectiveness' of social work. Yet there is little agreement among them as to how successful social work has been. How do they arrive at these differing conclusions? We shall attempt to answer this question by comparing, firstly, the verdicts of researchers and social workers, and secondly, the verdicts of practitioners and clients.

Researchers and practitioners
Research suggests that researchers and practitioners hold divergent views about the effectiveness of social work because they disagree over two main things:

1 the appropriate *methodology* by which social work practice is evaluated, and
2 the appropriate *criteria* by which its success is measured.

Methodology
Agreement over the appropriate research methodology to use is important. If social workers reject the methods by which social work has been evaluated, they may also reject the conclusions resulting from such research.

It is significant that social workers' main criticism of evaluative research is that studies employing strict scientific methods are inimical to therapeutic aims and inappropriate due to the nature of social work. Such methods are also thought to be insensitive to 'intangible' benefits gained by clients.

Until very recently, the popular method of evaluation used by researchers involved an experimental or quasi-experimental design. These researchers' major interest is in selecting variables for research that can be specified, measured and replicated. Criteria that do not lend themselves to this are likely to be rejected (Simmons and Davis 1957). But social workers' thinking is not always in tune with such vocabulary and conceptions as 'criteria', 'measurement', 'control-groups', etc. (Lees and Lees 1975). There is resentment among practitioners that the researcher, with his or her bag of measurement techniques, is introducing alien methods of describing clients and of dealing with them. As a director of a residential treatment centre elaborates:

> . . . the concept of comparison and measurement is threatening. It not only assails the uniqueness of one's own work but also the concept of the uniqueness of the case. Fear for the sacredness of the individual is aroused and the practising psychotherapist feels himself the last high priest of individualization in a world of scientific equalizers (Fanshel 1966, 358).

This quote introduces a key issue in the conflict between researchers and practitioners. The crux of the debate often revolves around whether outcome measures and professional efforts should focus on how an individual improves, or on how society and the community at large benefit (Segal 1978). By a mixture of personality, selection and training, social workers incline to the individual rather than the mass (Anderson 1979). Consequently, they tend to be suspicious of generalizations. This concern of the social worker for the uniqueness of the individual contrasts with the researcher's study of the group, and his or her attempt to document patterns and trends. Thus, the social worker's traditional commitment to the individual contrasts with the 'public health' model of research adopted by many researchers in the 1960s and early 1970s, in which the concern was often to document changes in the incidence or prevalence of some form of behaviour, e.g. delinquency and reconvictions, school truancy and drop-outs (Segal 1978).

Social workers criticize such methods on other grounds. One major requirement, typical of experimental evaluation studies, is that the goals and objectives of an intervention are specified early in contact, so that their achievement may then be measured later. This is unlikely to be popular with many social workers. For example, in some circumstances the social workers feel it is impossible to specify objectives at an early stage. It may take many meetings before a client and social worker agree about the change or improvement they plan to work towards (if, indeed, they do this at all). Other social workers feel that they do not want to commit themselves irrevocably to some initial goal, when at a later stage of contact, a problem may be redefined and another goal then becomes more appropriate. Seen in this light, 'research' becomes synonymous with 'interference' in the helping process.

Other social workers believe that, in any case, quantitative measurements of progress are difficult or impossible to apply to practice. Social workers do not see people's complex and interrelated problems as lending themselves readily to such measures. For example, in short-term casework, some benefits to clients are small. In the view of the practitioners, it would be difficult to include such benefits in a formal rating scale. The social caseworkers in an American Family Agency argue that the value of specific improvements in an area of client social functioning is dependent 'not on the magnitude of the changes but rather on the leverage they provide for coping with immediately pressing problems' (Sacks *et al.* 1970, 85). That is, the perceived value of a change may depend not on its size, but on its contribution to solving a particular problem. The value of such measures and scales is also questioned. In some cases 'improvement' may consist of a degree of psychological adjustment in the client. Social workers do not always believe that such a subtle change can be measured in any systematic way. Other considerations are also mentioned in the practitioner's argument against oversimplified measures – the circumscribed focus and diversity of gains, and the multiplicity of problems and their interrelated nature.

For many workers, however, the above objections are subsumed by moral considerations. Many practitioners find it difficult on ethical grounds to accept a study using experimental and control groups, in which for example, a group of clients may be deliberately deprived of a much needed service (Aronson and Sherwood 1967). Alternatively, they worry about exposing their clients to the 'wrong' treatment just for the sake of the researcher's experiment (Clarke and Cornish 1975). Practitioners are thus reluctant to pursue research requirements which they feel should not take precedence over the client welfare (Hoffman 1975). The more researchers in the past have insisted on adherence to a specific research design, the more open they have been to practitioners' accusations that academics are 'more interested in research than in people' (Aronson and Sherwood 1967, 95). Objections of a similar nature have also been raised over follow-up studies. Some social workers feel that such studies unnecessarily dredge up the past, which could have painful consequences for the client (Rodman and Kolodny 1971). A typical reaction of a social worker to such research aims is, 'When are you going to stop experimenting with people and let us start helping them?' (Aronson and Sherwood 1967, 92).

These disagreements described above have been named as conflicts between the 'feeling' caseworker and the 'rational' researcher (Berleman, 1969); the 'intuitive' versus the 'logical' (Mitchell and Mudd 1957); the 'helping' versus the 'controlling' (Casselman 1972); and even 'practice art' versus 'science' (Segal 1978). Many social workers see practice resting on the vagaries of intuition and feeling which cannot be researched in any objective, rational way. They feel that the researcher's orientation is too cold and contrived. The researcher, on the other hand, feels that social workers 'can't see the wood for the trees', and that their orientations are subjective and hopelessly 'involved' (Simmons and Davis 1958).

Criteria
In evaluations of social work, there are few cut and dried definitions of 'success' and 'failure'. Defining social work goals is far from easy. There is often disagreement between researchers and social workers, and between practitioners themselves concerning the objectives of social work intervention. This disagreement is reflected in controversies over the criteria to be utilized as 'measures' of the degree of attainment for these objectives.

Researchers' and practitioners' criteria of evaluation need not be the same. Although it is quite common for researchers to discuss the difficulties they have in identifying 'successful' social work, rarely do they make it clear whether or not they consult social workers as to the criteria eventually chosen. On the occasions when social workers are consulted about objectives and criteria of evaluation, they have been shown to be preoccupied with the *components* of social intervention (Aronson and Sherwood 1967). They have appeared less concerned with describing the relationship between these components and the outcomes they are intended to achieve. When encouraged to define criteria of success, they usually refer to generalized objectives, e.g. 'helping people' (although what is meant by 'help' is not always clarified) (Aronson and Sherwood 1967). On the other hand, those researchers involved in effectiveness studies tend to be preoccupied with more specific definitions of intervention outcomes. When studying an American Opportunities for Youth Programme (OFY), Aronson and Sherwood found a good illustration of what can happen when practitioners and researchers disagree over the nature of the criteria of evaluation.

> a summer camp programme designed by OFY has as its outcome variable better school work (in subsequent academic years). Success to the camp staff, on the other hand, meant that all the boys expected arrived and all were returned home, that no one drowned, there were not too many fights, everyone seemed to have fun and the boys respected the counsellors. This definition of success was manifested in a brief speech made by a camp director at a meeting of camp staff at the end of the summer. He announced to his colleagues that he suspected that the researchers would soon declare his programme a failure but that he *knew* that it had triumphed, and that he could see its achievements 'in the smiling faces of the campers' (1967, 94).

The authors state that the researchers did not doubt that the boys smiled frequently, but this was not how they felt an outcome should be assessed.

The above example also suggests that researchers' choice of goals and the criteria used to assess these goals are more ambitious than those used by social workers. They are more ambitious in two ways. Firstly, they appear to expect that social work interventions will have relatively long-lasting effects on the client. For example, researchers have been concerned with following up the effects of various treatment programmes up to 30 years after the client terminated contact (McCord 1978). However much they may wish it, few social workers seriously expect that their efforts have such long-lasting consequences. Secondly, researchers have higher expectations than practitioners of what social work can achieve, even in the short term (Meyer *et al.* 1965).

An example of the conflict that can arise over these differing expectations is provided by a piece of research carried out in Britain into residential 'care' as a means of dealing with delinquents (Clarke and Cornish 1975). The relative effectiveness of two differing forms of interventions, one 'training' and one 'treatment' oriented, were compared. The criterion selected by the researchers to determine the effectiveness of the two methods under study was that of subsequent convictions for a two-year period immediately following the boys' stay in the school. No significant difference between the performance of the two groups of boys appeared. The researchers, sensitive to the criticisms that such a measure was too crude, introduced 'refinements' in their assessments and included such criteria as the length of time between release and first conviction, the number of subsequent court appearances, and the 'seriousness' of the first offence after release. No significant difference between the two groups were found on these measures either. The researchers subsequently arrived at the conclusion that there was little to indicate that the interventions had achieved anything at all but the staff in the residential centre were critical of the criteria used by the researchers to measure success. They believed the wrong things were being measured and the researchers' conclusion (that treatment was ineffective) implied that nothing of value was being done in the home. The staff were convinced that positive things had been achieved. They pointed to success in the areas of health and education, e.g. when the boys put on weight and increased their reading attainments; they pointed to the formation of mutually satisfying relationships between staff and boys; they pointed to success in settling the boys into their new environment. The researchers viewed these 'achievements' with scepticism. They believed that the practitioners' rejection of reconviction rates as a criterion measure was their particular way of 'rationalizing failure'. Neither researchers nor practitioners felt each other's criteria were valid. Although they both used the word 'effective' they clearly had different ideas about what this meant.

This disagreement between the two parties as to what should be a measure of success is not peculiar to social work research. Similar arguments have occurred between researchers and practitioners in the field of psychiatric hospitalization (Schuerman *et al.* 1967) and also psychiatric rehabilitation (Simmons and Davis 1957).

Why should social workers and researchers disagree so often about how the effectiveness of social work is best measured? Two issues seem to be relevant. Essentially they are concerned with the social worker's level of involvement in research, and more importantly, the differing 'orientations' or styles and modes of thinking, between researchers and practitioners.

Generally, social workers have a low level of involvement in research. For example, practitioners are rarely involved in setting up their own research. A study of 470 members of the American NASW, found that very few practitioners produce research (Kirk, Osmalov and Fischer 1976). In Scotland, a member of a research funding body said that few research proposal applications are sent in by practitioners.* Research still tends to be carried out *on*

---

* From conversation with representatives from Social Work Services Group, Scotland, 1979.

social work rather than within it, although a few recent studies are redressing this imbalance (Davies 1975).

One consequence of research being an activity in which practitioners are seldom directly involved, is the absence of any obvious link between research and practice. For example, observers have found that few social workers consult research material. At least two American studies report that professionally qualified social workers feel that reading research articles is one of the least helpful activities in formulating a treatment plan (Casselman 1972; Rosenblatt 1968). Moreover, research is regarded as contributing least to improvement in practice (Casselman 1972), or to improvement in social work skills (Rosenblatt 1968). Another study has confirmed that British social workers also place a low priority on assimilating the results of research projects (McCulloch *et al.* 1968). This sceptical attitude of social workers to research may have something to do with the previously mentioned failure of research projects to demonstrate clearly either the effectiveness of various social work interventions, or the superiority of qualified over untrained social workers. It is probably more than this. Although many, perhaps most, researchers are careful and thorough in their attempts to communicate their findings, some, in particular in the USA, do use a statistical and technical jargon, which is alien and incomprehensible to most social workers (Editorial Comment, *Social Work Today*, 1979). It is little wonder that practitioners are confused, as one social worker remarks on his reading of research,

> The journals I read contained a number of articles using various scales and measures, such as 'Response sets and the Maudsley Personality Inventory' and 'A comparison of the Rosenweigh P-F Study and the Brown Inter-Racial Version (Hawaii)'. While some of the subjects for these articles sound fascinating, and they sound like they might be extremely relevant to something (although to what is not always clear), our training, happily, does not go into these things in much detail. This makes it difficult to understand the articles and leads to a great deal of frustration − so much that I felt the percentage of such articles in journals was very high (Rothman 1974, 550−1).

To rub salt in the wound, some researchers' critical evaluations have been regarded as showing little appreciation 'of the real problems with which the practitioner is faced and the limited resources and authority he has available to cope with them' (Rothman 1974). Such an attitude does not foster a climate of cooperation.

One of the paradoxes of social work research is that it 'denotes a combination of two professional orientations which so far have been antagonistic to one another' (Pollak 1956). Social workers have little experience in research. They are suspicious of it. Research scientists may or may not be trained social workers. But in adopting the role of 'researcher', their orientation differs from that of the practitioner.

This difference manifests itself in various forms. For example, the practitioner tends to want answers to practical problems.* However, only a little of social science is immediately practical. (Wilensky and Lebeaux 1958). A social work student comments:

> I have had a very difficult time finding social science articles that were of real relevance to me. Most of the articles contained information which might be necessary background but which was not of immediate applicability (Rothman 1974, 549).

Social workers are often sceptical, even resentful, of the spending of money on research, which is felt to be 'unproductive', i.e. which does not seem to help them in practice. These feelings are intensified when the social worker is asked to be involved in a research project, but only indirectly. Such a request might involve filling in forms or giving up valuable time to be interviewed. Social workers want to know what they stand to gain by cooperating in such a manner and it is usually far from clear what benefits they will receive.

If social workers are of the opinion that research is an extra burden, they are likely to be irritated by the continual questioning of researchers. The researcher's persistent request for *evidence* rather than *impressions* 'may be felt as carping or quibbling by the practitioner with a host of patients and clients to be seen' (Rodman and Kolodny 1971).

Other social workers regard such probing and questioning not only as a nuisance, but also as a personal threat. As one observer has noted, social work may be one of the most intensively supervised professions,

> ... as they are often driven beyond their limits of tolerance by their inter-professional contacts and intra-professional supervision, it was perhaps unfortunate that social workers met research scientists in the particular context of evaluative studies such as measuring social work effectiveness. Thus social work encountered social research in one conspicuous instance as a potential threat rather than a potential sources of assistance (Pollak 1956, 298).

This sense of threat largely arises from researchers' scrutinization of activities which practitioners had previously accepted on faith (Berleman 1969). It would be difficult for a social worker to sustain any belief in his effectiveness and competence if on questioning, he can only say 'I don't know what makes clients improve and I don't really know if they would be better off not seeing me.' (Rosenblatt 1968, 57–8). In this situation, researchers should not be expected to disguise the fact that what is being evaluated is not only the impact of a programme or a particular intervention, but also certain aspects of personal ability and competence. But such frankness may be seen as threatening. In this respect Aronson and Sherwood (1967) described the conflicts which developed between the practitioners responsible for the

---

* In their concern with practice, many practitioners, (not just in social work) complain that research reports are so long that they would never have time to read them let alone consider the implications for practice. See, Wilson, S., 'Explorations of the Usefulness of case study evaluations'. *Evaluation Quarterly*, **3** (3) August 1979 p. 446–59.

design and implementation of an American anti-delinquency project, and the researchers responsible for monitoring the effectiveness and efficiency of the project. One of the sources of conflict arose over practitioners' doubts about the use of detailed clients' records for research purposes. As Aronson and Sherwood explained,

> Uneasiness about records (also) results from the fact that the practitioner often fears that records will be used as a projective device to tell about him, that they will be used as a measure of his ability as a diagnostician or of his judgement in devising treatment methods (1967, 92).

Even if social workers do not feel threatened, many remain ambivalent towards research which aims to assess their effectiveness (Rodman and Kolodny 1971). Although the researcher's concern may have nothing to do with 'evaluation' or 'effectiveness', social workers remain suspicious of the former's intentions. In a review of 49 research projects (some concerned with evaluation, others not), almost all of the practitioners viewed the studies 'as a challenge to their professional competence' (Kandel and Williams 1964, 50). In a specific study (Rodman and Kolodny 1971) a researcher entered a social work agency with the aim of exploring what was researchable in that setting. This intention was made explicit on at least two occasions by the researcher and an administrator, yet a questionnaire later illustrated that almost one-third of the 25 social workers mentioned 'evaluation' as a function of the researcher's job.

Discussion and implications

Social workers' lack of in-depth involvement in research, the contrasting modes of thinking between themselves and researchers, combined with the former's ambivalence over the aims of evaluative research explain, to some extent, why practitioners and researchers have come to different conclusions about the effectiveness of social work. They have different interpretations of 'success' and 'failure' and mean different things when they talk about 'effectiveness' or 'outcome'. Contrary to the belief of some researchers that social workers' views represent a 'rationalization of failure', practitioners' evaluations are based on different assumptions and presumptions from those of academic researchers. This explains social workers' insistence that they have achieved more than the bulk of the research studies on their effectiveness would indicate.

Our documentation of several comments which are critical of researchers is not intended to imply that any future improvement in practitioners' involvement in research will depend only on having sympathetic and flexible researchers. The problem lies elsewhere, in the two-world view of research and practice which has been promoted by far too many educators. These problems have been recognized (Fanshel 1980) and have been debated at length in articles and correspondence in some professional journals (Hudson 1978; Wertkin, Gyarfas and Hudson 1978). In a summary of the future of social work research, Fanshel observed that formidable institutional barriers stand in the way of collaboration between researchers and practitioners. He also reported that a national conference in the USA had recommended as a priority that the artificial barriers between research and practice should be ended (Fanshel 1980). We take this point very seriously.

In drawing our own conclusions on researchers' views of the consequences of social work we shall argue (in Chapter 10) that in several important respects evaluation and practice could become synonymous. It is desirable that all trained social workers should possess a taken-for-granted knowledge of the nature of evaluative research and should have some idea of the chequered record of social work as reported in research findings. As and when such basic information is required, the staff who see themselves as mainly practitioners will not feel so threatened by researchers, and the staff who see themselves as mainly researchers will be gratified by knowing that some of their work is widely taught and read and some of it influences practice.

Social workers and clients

A variety of explanations have been used by researchers to account for the discrepancies in evaluations between social workers and clients. These explanations are of two kinds. They involve clients' and social workers' differential access to information, and differences in their perceptions of the nature and number of problems requiring attention.

Two studies concerned with casework agencies have suggested that when social workers make lower estimates than clients of the effectiveness of an intervention, this is partly due to what has been called 'information gap'. It is felt that, particularly in short-term casework, social workers rarely get feedback on the client's situation. They are therefore not always in a position to know what has happened to the client. A study of short-term casework with people with severe marital problems provides an example of this (Sacks *et al.* 1970). The researcher found that client and social worker agreement on the level of progress with a number of problems varied.

> For example, agreement was higher on topics normally close to the central themes of treatment, such as the marital relationship, and especially low on changes involving the functioning of family members not seen or relationships outside the home (Sacks *et al.* 1970).

A similar explanation for the discrepancy has been offered in another study involving longer, more sustained contact (Maluccio 1977). These findings seem to support the idea that social workers are not always aware of positive changes in clients and their circumstances when these occur outside their immediate scope of contact.

Another explanation has concentrated on clients' and social workers' perceptions of the problems for which help is sought. A number of studies have shown that although workers and clients often identify a considerable number of the *same* problems, workers tend to identify somewhat *more* (Taber 1970; Beck 1962). Practitioners are more likely to have a long-range view of people's problems than the clients have themselves. As two

American researchers have observed, with regard to a voluntary agency's services for low-income unmarried mothers,

> Clients accustomed to their circumstances might not define themselves as having as many as or as serious problems as workers would. Or unlike workers, clients might only define as problems those circumstances with which they think a worker might be of help (Rubenstein and Bloch 1978, 74).

Many poor black clients at a Boston multi-service neighbourhood centre presented one problem even though they were 'experiencing difficulties in several areas of living' (Perlman 1975, 26) In addition, Perlman comments on the tendency of the centre's professional staff to perceive several problems because they were trained to think and act in terms of 'the whole person and the whole family' or 'the total situation' (ibid). Such potential for disagreement regarding the number of problems increases when a large proportion of clients expect complete resolution of their difficulties in contrast to social workers who feel that neither immediate nor complete solutions are available (Morris, P. *et al.* 1973)

Rubenstein and Bloch indicated that some social workers perceive more problems in *different areas* from clients. Their research, concerned with the contacts of 50 unmarried mothers attending a family agency, provides an illustration of this (Rubenstein and Bloch 1978). Although the mothers' and the social workers' perceptions of problems often tallied, there were areas in which their perceptions of the most important problems differed markedly. High disagreement occurred over issues of family planning, financial assistance, the mother's relationship with the alleged father and other persons, and intra-personal functions. In all of these, except financial assistance, the difference was the result of the worker's defining a problem not identified by the client. In identifying factors believed to be contributing most to client problems, workers gave relatively more emphasis to intra-personal and interpersonal factors than to lack of resources and tangible goods and services (although these were not ignored). The clients, on the other hand, tended to emphasize their lack of resources and interpersonal rather than intra-personal problems.

Other studies have revealed similar perceptual difference between workers and clients. These views are significant for evaluation because perceived differences in the number and nature of problems implies the existence of disparate notions of what might constitute 'improvement'. For example, in discussing people with family problems attending a family agency, Sacks *et al.* (1970) found that clients and workers had differing expectations of what constituted progress. The workers tended to search for some basic change in the behaviour of parents towards their children, or alternatively for a change in parents' perception as to the root cause behind their child's behaviour. The parents' definitions of improvement, in contrast, involved less significant changes. They felt better because they had been given the chance to express their feelings, which gave them much emotional relief and resulted in some of the tension being alleviated in the home situation. Just as researchers' criteria of evaluation were more ambitious than the practitioners in the effectiveness studies, social workers' criteria here were more ambitious than those of the clients.

The reason why this discrepancy occurs may be related to social workers' training and 'knowledge'. This is not to assume that there is always a visible link between training and practice. Nevertheless, as a result of 'training' and social work experience, practitioners' thinking is sometimes characterized by an assumed superiority over clients' understanding and definitions of needs, problems and help required. Whittington (1977) has identified this mode of thinking and action, and has named it the 'expert' orientation in social work. Practitioners who adopt this mode of thinking and acting assume that they 'know better' than their clients. This is because social workers perceive themselves as having access to expert knowledge to define and effect the help or treatment needed. In turn, this knowledge affects judgements about outcome. Because social workers are sometimes reluctant to deal with the problem as the clients present it, they often have higher expectations and aspirations of what is necessary for a desirable outcome. It follows that more has to be achieved before a social worker is willing to admit some improvement has occurred.

But even if clients' and social workers' judgements of the degree of improvement achieved are similar, their satisfaction with that outcome need not be the same. This is illustrated in the following comments of a client/worker 'pair' on termination of their counselling casework contract. The social worker is clearly dissatisfied with not getting to the 'root of the problem'. He or she is also either unaware of many positive things happening in the women's life, or does not believe such things to be important or fundamental enough to constitute a great 'improvement'.

Client	Worker
Miss Becker: The counselling was worthwhile. It felt good – because it was the first time in years I could talk to someone about what's on my mind – she helped me to gain confidence. I began to get out more with people to get along easier – I still have a long way to go – but I speak out more for my rights.	We were still in the beginning phase of treatment when she pulled out. Some important things got out on the table, but we didn't really deal with them – I was dissatisfied – because we couldn't get in and deal with these issues. I couldn't penetrate her defenses – I didn't feel that we were making any progress, that things were happening.

(Maluccio 1979)

On the rare occasions when clients and social workers have made similar assessments of outcomes, the context in which these evaluations occurred proved significant. Quite close agreement on improvement and verdicts on outcome occurred when in an American agency, workers and clients agreed about limited objectives and about the number of meetings required to attain those objectives (Reid and Shyne 1969).

One of the distinguishing features of this contract method is that it involves much discussion, explanation and clarification between client and social worker – on the nature of the presenting problem, on the problem-solving activity in which they will engage and on the task or goal they hope to achieve. In such circumstances, there is less likelihood of the worker being the victim of an 'information gap' about what has happened to the client. Also, when social worker and client discuss and agree to work towards a specific goal, there is less chance of their expectations of what can be achieved being out of step with one another.

Similar to the discrepancy in verdicts between researchers and practitioners, social workers and clients disagree over what constitutes 'progress' or 'improvement'. We can now see why the general pattern on outcomes (described at the beginning of the section) has emerged. Researchers' evaluations of 'success' and 'improvement' tend to involve fairly ambitious criteria, certainly more ambitious than those used by many social workers. Academics' research methods are criticized by practitioners for not taking into account 'progress' of a more tangible but nevertheless important nature. Yet in turn social workers are sometimes unwilling to believe that fairly small changes in the client or his situation constitute 'success'. The client, however is often satisfied with less than the worker. To the individual who has perhaps suffered a difficulty for a long period, or who has been unsuccessful with help-seeking experiences elsewhere, any change, however small, any attention, however fleeting, can be regarded as significant. The social worker may be unaware, for example, that clients' emotional relief on being able to talk to someone, can have an effect on the clients' relationship with others, unseen by the practitioner.

Although researchers, social workers and clients are all talking about the 'effectiveness' of social work and the success it can achieve – they seem to have differing interpretations of what these terms might mean. They have differential access to information, they perceive different criteria as being important or significant in any evaluation of social work. Although they may be using the same vocabulary, when referring to the 'effectiveness' of social work, they are often talking about different things.

Conflicts between different social workers' and different clients' verdicts.

The last section may have given the impression that all practitioners' and all clients' verdicts are similar. This is not completely true. Clients' views differ. People approaching or being referred to a social work agency do not all share the same expectations, values and assumptions about the help they are going to receive. Not surprisingly, they do not all make similar evaluations. Just as clients are not an homogeneous group, neither are social workers. Social workers differ in the level and nature of their training and work experiences. They work in different agencies with differing duties, obligations and working philosophies. It is the examination of these diversities, between clients, and between social workers, and how they affect evaluations, that is the concern of this section.

Workers
Whether or not social workers have been trained affects whether their views differ. The evidence is tentative, nevertheless it has been suggested that social worker qualifications can influence their evaluation of outcome. In her study of the elderly in a London borough, Goldberg *et al.* (1970) found that the two qualified staff, both trained as psychiatric social workers, perceived more problems and therefore more need for social work among the elderly, than did the unqualified workers. Whereas the trained workers estimated that 33 per cent of the elderly were in very great need of social work, the untrained workers assessed only 16 per cent as being in need of such help. The qualified workers were also more likely than the unqualified workers to perceive more problems involving emotional or mental disturbances. Training thus had altered and sensitized the qualified workers to less 'obvious' needs in the community. At the end of the study, the qualified workers' judgements of outcome were more conservative than the unqualified workers. This occurred even though the clients of the trained workers had received more help in the form of time and services than the other clients in the study.

We should be cautious about generalizing too readily from this study as it included only two professionally qualified workers. However, a similar link has been made in another piece of research carried out in Britain. Barker's study (1974) of a city area team revealed some discrepancies between the 32 clients and their social workers over whether or not they felt aspects of the service could have been improved. In cases where there was least discrepancy between client and social workers, 73.3 per cent of the practitioners had no formal social work training. Where there was highest discrepancy, 58.9 per cent of the workers had received such training. Together these studies suggest that different verdicts on outcome among social workers may be accounted for by their level of training.

But the trained and the untrained have to work within particular contexts. In our analysis (in Chapters 7 and 8) the evidence suggested that the constraints of staff's working situations were as important, if not more important in affecting practice than the influence of training or the lack of it. For example, the level of improvement expected by caseworkers working in a specialized agency and concentrating on the clients in their relatively limited caseload, may be quite different from the expectations of social workers in a public agency with heavy caseloads struggling to keep their heads above water and to cope with all the demands of their diverse caseloads. Social workers working in the first context may seek proof of fairly significant changes in the client or his situation, before feeling that a measure of success has been achieved. Social workers in the latter setting, with less time and resources, may have expectations which amount to achieving only very limited change. Slight improvement could mean enormous success if the initial expectations are low.

In one study social workers actually rated a greater level of success than clients. Here the practitioners' working context proved significant (Jordan 1976). In this study, although the 16 clients and their 10 qualified workers in a local authority department were mainly agreed about the definitions of the problem requiring help, there was far less agreement about the action required and the degree of satisfaction with outcome. Most of the workers expressed satisfaction at the end of the contact, but few clients were happy. The workers were under a lot of pressure and had a notable lack of autonomy, particularly in relation to the availability of expensive resources. They also had many individual records to keep, due to their particular agency's policy (as outlined in a complex guide book, 25 pages long). Most seemed to be at least superficially content with providing the minimum of service – this was all that could be expected *given the circumstances*. Simpkin (1979) has described well the effects on individual social workers of so many conflicting demands and so many built-in frustrations. Clients are often trapped within welfare and social workers have to learn, for very good psychological and other health reasons, how to survive with them in such a system.

Clients

> There appears to be an association between the ways in which people approach and use the social services agencies and the outcomes they experience. The process is a complicated one in which clear cut 'causes' and 'effects' are hard to come by (Perlman 1975).

Perlman's quote describes neatly the link between the differing values, attitudes and expectations of clients seeking help, and the varying nature of their contact outcomes. In Chapter 4 we identified clients' different 'problem solving' orientations, and how these coloured what people thought was appropriate or inappropriate help. The way in which people think about help and the manner in which they relate to social service personnel influences also their opinions of the usefulness and effectiveness of contacts.

To repeat our previous statement, clients are not homogeneous. They bring to an agency differing beliefs and assumptions, as well as a variety of knowledge and experience about what they can get out of the personal social services. This is one area which has been well researched and which has produced remarkably similar findings. Researchers in Britain, North America and Australia, unaware of each other's studies, have quite independently made common observations about the ways in which people approach agencies for help. Although the researchers use different terminology, the characteristics of the three client groups they identify have much in common with one another. We need to describe these typologies further to understand why they account for different assessments of outcome.

The first group of people identified by the researchers has been variously named the 'defeated' (Silverman 1969), the 'buffeted' (Perlman 1975), and the 'passive' (McCaughey and Chew 1977; Rees 1978). (Indeed, two researchers quite independently used this last term). These people are typically financially poor. Many are single parents and the majority are unemployed and dependent on welfare benefits. Their financial difficulties compound other problems in the areas of health, family welfare and relationships. These problems have usually existed for a long time and life is felt to be a never-ending struggle against forces largely out of their control. These families usually have little education and often lack the support of neighbours and friends, who are often in a similar plight and unable to help. Not surprisingly, many of these people are subject to depression and feelings of helplessness. They make no plans for the future, about which they tend to be pessimistic. They are resigned to their life and passively accept their situation. As a result of this, as well as some unsuccessful experiences of seeking help in the past, they expect little from the social services and take very few, if any, initiatives to improve their conditions. Generally they regard it as either inappropriate or pointless to challenge those in positions of authority. They are either unable or reluctant to evaluate critically those services offered them. Indeed, some are in such a desperate plight they gladly accept any financial or other help they are given, however inadequate it may be. As one of the single parents in an Australian study remarked, 'I was just relieved that the kids would be fed for the next week' (McCaughey and Chew 1977, 98).

It is fairly obvious that these people's low expectations of service, the resignation of their life situation, and the precariousness of their very existence are likely to produce a very limited view of what constitutes a 'successful' social work intervention. They are satisfied with very little, and are unlikely to express discontent if help is either not forthcoming, or is inappropriate or inadequate.

Contrast the help-seeking orientations of this 'passive' group with another client group clearly identified by researchers. This second group has been named the 'copers' (McCaughey and Chew 1977) the 'circumspect' (Rees 1978), the 'problem solvers' (Perlman 1975) and the 'rational' (Silverman 1969). In contrast to the passively oriented families, these people manage to function reasonably well. As many of them are in employment they have a sense of security derived from having an adequate and regular income. Unlike the first group, many of these families enjoy support from friends, relatives and neighbours. They have a sense of autonomy and control over their lives and do not feel trapped and helpless. Their sense of security and autonomy allows them to make plans for the future. They are optimistic about their own and their children's future. They have far higher aspirations than the 'passive' families. They persistently seek solutions to their problems and are willing to explore various avenues of help. They possess self-confidence and are often articulate and assertive when dealing with people in positions of authority. These confident and active people are the most critical of the three groups identified. They evaluate services critically and seek alternatives if not satisfied. One can see that their reactions to service and their assessment of the success achieved are likely to be quite different from that of the more passive and resigned families.

There is less similarity between the people who make up the third group identified by the different researchers. Generally, however, they can be placed somewhere between the two groups just discussed. They are more confident and aggressive than the 'passive' group, but have less security and ability to manage relationships with people in authority than the 'copers'. This intermediate group has been called the 'vulnerable' (McCaughey and Chew 1977), the 'resource seekers' (Perlman 1975), the 'magical' (Silverman 1969) and the 'assertive' (Rees 1978). Some of this group have employment (although often lowly paid work) and some are unemployed. They are subject to economic pressures, but not to the same extent as the passive families. They take some initiatives to help themselves and to organize their lives but rarely do these steps alleviate their situation to any great extent. Many have experienced some problems for a fairly long time, and as a result, are less optimistic than the 'copers'. Common to these people is a sense of grievance or anger, of entitlement to services, but not always satisfaction with services. As McCaughey and Chew (1977) (talking about services in Melbourne) explain 'they were sufficiently critical to be dissatisfied with many services but not sufficiently confident to demand a better service, so they frequently simply withdrew and did not go back.'

Although most of these studies are concerned with clients from the lower-middle socioeconomic groupings, we can see that a diversity of approaches and orientations exists amongst these people. Just as it would be misleading to say that all social workers think similarly about 'success' and 'achievement' in social work, it would be inaccurate to state that all clients have common notions of what these terms represent. Economic circumstances have much influence on people's attitudes and actions. The more hopeless the person's life situation, the more conservative are their expectations. It is the desperately poor – the most depressed and needy people – who tend to be satisfied with little. Clients whose economic circumstances are brighter can afford a measure of optimism. They can and often do expect more from their contacts with social workers.

Summary

The material in this chapter affirms our observation of the directors' comments, that evaluation means 'different things to different people'. Although researchers, social workers and clients all talk about the 'effectiveness' or the 'success' of social work interventions, they attribute different meanings to these terms. Their particular interpretations are inextricably linked to value judgements about how social work should be evaluated and what it should be capable of achieving. Their interpretations are also influenced by various contextual constraints, which largely determine their particular 'frame of reference'. It is clear that researchers, practitioners and clients are either not always aware of each other's perspective on social work, or do not regard these perspectives as being particularly valid. In a way, they are each 'trapped' within their own particular way of looking at the world. The results of the studies reviewed in this chapter would seem to provide grounds for optimism. They indicate that contrary to the results of experimental studies, social work *is* achieving something, however limited. This is shown in the evaluations of social workers and of clients. Contrary to those studies which have said social work is ineffective, full stop, our findings could be said to be optimistic in that the people at the grass-roots level of social work are making statements about 'helping' and 'being helped'. On the same topic (in Part III) we reported social workers as saying that interaction with clients and others affected their judgements about outcomes. We also identified how a social worker's practice-oriented ideologies affected the choice of priorities and thereby their selection of criteria for job effectiveness.

However, there comes a point at which the relativity of judgements ceases to give much guide as to the grounds for continuing a service or for changing the content of training or for redirecting an occupation's goal. Not every criterion of evaluation can be weighted equally. Even an aggregate of research findings does not necessarily give clear implications regarding future developments, and especially if the finding have not been related to wider social and economic issues. For these reasons and with regard to these issues in the following (and final) chapter we draw our own conclusions and reach our own verdict.

10

Appropriateness and Accountability

Introduction

In this final chapter we shall be summarizing the verdicts of clients and social workers. It is a chequered picture. There are some important achievements and some serious shortcomings.

We shall also be drawing our own conclusions about these verdicts and about the research from which they were derived. The linked criteria of appropriateness and accountability are our yardsticks for determining where social workers should be concentrating their existing resources and what extra resources they should aim at developing. Our choice of appropriateness and accountability and our definition of such criteria only follows from analysing the research which has produced such conflicting verdicts. Such an evaluation will also involve answering the important policy-related question, what role should social workers be playing in what remains of any country's welfare state.

Some achievements, some shortcomings

Our analysis produces a picture from others' research, of clients being referred apparently to seek some resolution of a problem and social workers with a habit of responding mostly to people as individuals. We are aware of another literature which warns social workers against any preoccupation with individual models of explanation of behaviour and individual forms of 'treatment' (Philp 1979). Nevertheless we have been analysing social work which is carried out usually in terms of individual face-to-face encounters.

Existing research provides more information about the helpful and unhelpful qualities displayed in the *processes* of services than about the permanence of certain outcomes achieved by social workers. In this information about processes, considerable reliance is placed on clients' points of view. Three points stand out. Firstly, certain people value highly receiving personal interest and support at certain stressful times in their lives. Secondly, the prompt provision of material aid, in cash or in kind, is highly regarded by clients. Thirdly, certain people appreciate initiatives on their behalf, as demonstrated by the social workers' willingness to use skills in advocacy and negotiations.

Personal interest and support

The changes achieved by social workers' personal interest and support were hardly the kind to excite outside evaluators. Nevertheless, clients claimed that such social work enabled them to make plans and manage a sense of oppression or depression when they would otherwise have felt powerless and friendless. 'Personal interest and support' refers to skills in caring through listening and an ability to put people at ease, as well as evidence of being willing and able to do things. For example, even elderly people who had assumed that 'help' could refer only to the delivery of some material aid, also came to appreciate the more personal forms of social workers' support provided that support was regular and frequent (Jordan 1976). On the other hand, many elderly people who were also poor had low expectations of help and tended to be satisfied easily (Rees 1978).

The natural parents of children in care valued personal involvement and support from social workers not least because the parents themselves were sensitive to notions that they were bad (Aldgate 1978; Oxley 1977). People suffering depression, sometimes described as having suicidal tendencies, identified the importance of task-centred casework which provided emotional relief (Gibbons *et al.* 1979). Yet others who sought help with interpersonal problems and who evaluated favourably social workers' response, were those who possessed a particular orientation to solving problems. These people had some capacity to consider how their own actions contributed to their problem (Gurin *et al.* 1960).

Children in residential care appreciated social workers' support provided that each individual worker was not seen merely as one of too many functionaries involved in those childrens' welfare (Page and Clark 1977). To these children, support involved a genuine sense of consultation leading to desired changes, such as removing them from a foster home to residential care, or vice versa (Bush *et al.* 1977).

Faced with complex regulations and large bureaucracies, not all of them related to welfare, people without specialized information or experience in negotiations often feel powerless. The positive evaluations of social workers who showed themselves as openly partisan in clients' interests, were made often by clients who had previously received indifferent responses from other officials in positions of authority. In this respect it is inaccurate to say that people were satisfied because the social workers were able to meet the clients' objectives in seeking help. That is the oversimplified model which is too often imposed by naive researchers searching for clear statements of objectives, input and outcomes. These are stages which might occur later when precise objectives may have been defined. They may be so defined following an encounter with someone willing to take an interest. Many social workers' first achievements involved conveying to people that their enquiries were legitimate, that the solution to some sort of problem could be pursued with enthusiasm and without cost.

Prompt material aid

A social worker's display of personal interest and support can also be made manifest to clients by the provision of tangible aid. Many families' satisfaction with social workers is directly related to their receiving the material help which they expect and want. This refers not only to financial aid (Mayer and Timms 1970) but also to the prompt provision of aids and adaptations for client groups such as the physically handicapped (Butler 1977). Many clients are poor, have inadequate housing, limited job opportunities and have other problems in addition to their material needs. Such people value having their material needs dealt with early on in the help-seeking process. People appreciate financial help when it is given spontaneously, when they do not have to bargain for it, when they are not put in a position of having to earn entitlements through proof of an inability to cope (George and Wilding 1972; Rees 1978).

There are other qualifications to make about clients' appreciation of tangible aid. The first concerns the grounds for clients' positive evaluations. A second refers to the cash-help policies of agencies whose major function is not income maintenance.

Clients often make positive evaluations of material aid from social workers merely because it seems more generous than that received previously from other official sources and/or from their personal network. On the other hand, some studies suggest that material help from social workers is relatively insignificant compared to that received from relatives and friends (George and Wilding 1972). The giving of financial help by social workers is haphazard largely because it depends on social workers' different practice-oriented ideologies. There is neither coordination between agencies over the giving of financial help nor is there much relationship between clients' income and the amount of assistance that they will be given (See Commonwealth of Australia 1976, Chapter 3).

Negotiation and advocacy

Negotiation and advocacy overlap. Negotiation refers here to a social worker presenting a particular position or point of view as a basis for changing another party's views to correspond to his (the social worker's) own or as a basis for reaching some compromise solution. This method of working could also refer to the ability to tease out information and so define the needs or tasks which different parties see as a priority. This is equally relevant to interpersonal difficulties as to more widely shared social problems. Advocacy is an activist trait which refers not only to the explicit pursuit of some resource or the redress of some grievance but also to the ability to unravel difficulties, as might an advocate in preparing a case or cause. Advocacy is as relevant to the business of carefully articulating the alternatives to resolving some difficulty, as it would be to pursuing one line of action rather than another. Social work educators, social workers and related professionals should listen to clients' judgements on these topics.

Parents of mentally handicapped children value social workers who not only have information but who also show initiatives in obtaining information which they do not have (Hewett 1970). The ability to negotiate also involves an ability to differentiate between clients' needs and available resources, and not merely those agency resources which were known about as a matter of routine. This involved taking seriously individuals' points of view and refusing to lump together indiscriminately all the people with apparently the same problems. For example, handicapped adults want more than places in day care centres. They want to be in association with people of the same age (Hammersmith SSD 1979). They want to be involved in activities which they find self-fulfilling, which do not involve routine tasks (Wandsworth SSD 1977).

Foster parents expect social workers to be partners in discussions about the care of foster children (Shaw and Lebens 1977). In these parents' terms the negotiations relating to the placing of foster children cannot be concluded satisfactorily if the social workers are themselves not well prepared and are not able to brief adequately the foster parents (Jones 1975).

The ability to be an advocate depends on the sustained commitment of one person to a particular interest. Clients of all kinds are highly critical when their hopes for interest and commitment are met by routine responses or a frequent change-over of staff. Such change-over suggests to the individuals that they are unimportant, that the agency as well as its staff are disinterested (Shaw and Lebens 1977; Bandcroft 1970).

A different weighting of the value of advocacy skills has occurred between prisoners and probationers on the one hand and their respective social work supervisors on the other. Probationers and parents of probationers value the mediating role of the probation officer (Gandy *et al*. 1975). Prisoners who want expert advice appreciate social workers who are prepared to be their arms and legs. Thought is no substitute for action. The social workers who are unwilling or who are unable to put themselves out and thus demonstrate their separateness from the system employing them and which certain individuals see as oppressing them, are regarded at worst as useless and at best as people who make unconvincing gestures about helping.

Negotiation and advocacy skills are appreciated by people who feel powerless partly through lack of information. At the point at which they feel able to take action on their own behalf, advocacy by others becomes less important. This raises the point that evaluations at one point in time do not hold forever. For example, children who viewed fostering negatively at the beginning of a·study changed their views before that enquiry finished (Page and Clark 1977).

Clients' emphasis on negotiation and advocacy has implications not merely for giving individual social workers a sense of purpose in acting in some people's interests. It also has the potential to give agencies with too many functions a greater sense of direction. In relation to community action, Marris and Rein concluded that only as an agency became partisan and chose between its possible roles, could it recover its coherence (1973, 230). For our purposes, a further implication of this conclusion concerns the inter-relatedness of the policies from which social work tasks derive and the importance of choosing which policies to promote in the interests of which groups of people. We return later to the inter-relatedness of policy and practice.

Social workers' competence

Cutbacks in services in education, health and welfare have heralded a potentially pragmatic and selfish decade. These cutbacks have been based on ideological commitments to a free market and the value of less public intervention in citizens' lives. However, the evidence exists that certain social work services sustained partly by a set of values which are different from those which prompt cutbacks, are helpful to certain vulnerable groups of people. Unless that evidence is spelled out, politicians might be excused for assuming public indifference to social work.

Clients who had formulated their views were clear in their definitions of helpful and unhelpful skills and services. By contrast, social workers were reluctant to define competence. Senior staff would not commit themselves, almost as though the absorption of non-judgemental attitudes meant that, in particular regarding peer evaluations, potentially controversial issues as in assessment of standards of work, should be avoided. The Scottish directors were confident about whom they would promote, yet they were hesitant to evaluate one set of services and practitioners by comparison with others.

> . . . We had a survey of effectiveness of services . . . we told staff that this wasn't intended to be an evaluation of them . . . we endeavoured to make the staff feel that this wasn't the spirit of the operation. (See Chapter 2)

Similarly, in an Australian study in 1976 in which 15 agencies were approached, few members of any agency could identify any formal evaluation procedures. The authors reported, 'The evaluation of the activities of each agency was performed very largely by personal and individual self-examination' (Howlett *et al.* 1976).

In some accounts, social workers identified their sense of competence as being related to specific knowledge in a particular field. Their sense of power to act depended on control over information. The corollary of this premise was the clients' sense of ignorance about health and welfare services contributed to their sense of powerlessness.

The absence of studies which relate competence to input and outcome is a serious omission in research and apparently does not feature in agencies' deliberations about their practice. Without such information it is unlikely that social workers will identify good and bad practice except on the basis of hunch and intuition. Their reluctance to define competence has something to do with the notion that familiarity with research findings is somehow separate from the other ingredients of potentially good practice. If social workers and educators would only listen to the volume of client opinion about the importance of case-by-case advocacy and negotiation and, by implication, how such roles would provide rehearsals for confronting wider issues, they would not continue an uncritical commitment to some of the more traditional activities. Yet when social workers weighed their own practice, they valued objectives and skills which were not so important to clients.

In our account of social workers' valued images and activities, we found them with goals which sounded worthy yet esoteric, representing humanitarian gestures. But major social issues affecting people's lives were not addressed. For example, people who are poor or unemployed or homeless generally feel at a loss in the social service market place, trying to find their way in a maze of alleged social service entitlements. In relation to people with such difficulties some social workers acknowledged that their objectives referred to talking about feelings and heightening self-awareness! (Maluccio 1977; Silverman 1969).

Other objectives concerned the carrying out of agency residual-type policies; in fulfilling supervisory responsibilities, staff acknowledged social and moral control objectives. They aimed to keep their charges out of further trouble.

Some social workers did try to stick with clients' objectives and use the clients' criteria as measures of successful social work. Even this is no guarantee of the development of a competence that matches some notion of accountability to clients' best interests. Some clients' goals were not ambitious. Old people's passive acceptance of little has been noted (See pp. 46–8 Chapter 4). Families with multiple problems judged the usefulness of social work, not in relation to whether that social work intervention permanently improved their circumstances, but according to some assessment as to how they fared in comparison to other groups whom they had heard had received help (Jackson 1973). Prisoners who held a sympathetic view of the limited powers of welfare officers expected them to act only as a messenger-mediator. They did not expect such social workers to effect change in the penal system (Holborn 1975, see p. 68–72 Chapter 4).

These last examples introduce the issue of accounting for social workers' achievements, as reported by researchers, in terms of their appropriateness to clients' long-term interests. But how to judge clients' long-term interests? The answer will vary according to ideological stances and related interpretations of the roles of social workers. In this respect the criterion of accountability emerges as a means of questioning the effects of any particular intervention but always in relation to the more general question of the relevance of social work at all.

Appropriateness and accountability

In our view, social work's major function involves responding to problems which have been thrown up largely by an economic and cultural system which operates for the considerable benefit of some and consequently results in the exploitation and suffering of others. In response to these problems the most appropriate objectives for social workers are to work according to socialist principles for a more equal and just society in which poverty would be eliminated and equality of access would exist in key services such as housing, health, education and the administration of justice. In the pursuit of such objectives, social workers' priorities would be focused not just on policies concerned with the distribution of resources but also on the quality of human relationships in a variety of contexts, and in all transactions related to personal services. Such goals could not be achieved by social workers acting alone but would require them to make alliances with those who shared the same concerns, including client groups and, of course, colleagues in social welfare whatever their status or professional standing.

Our own criteria for sifting and sorting social workers' reported achievements and shortcomings derive inevitably from the ideologically based point of view which we have just expressed. Our criteria would focus on accountability to clients' interests and, most important, to those people least able to help themselves. These are the groups whom Morris alleges 'cannot care for themselves but must be cared for' (Morris 1977). With reference to intake and long-term social work in one local authority area in Britain, Goldberg and her colleagues identified powerless people as the frail elderly, the physically and mentally disabled and children (Goldberg *et al.* 1979). However these categories would vary from one agency context to another.

We have deliberately linked accountability to appropriateness. In this respect the most telling means of assessing accountability is in terms of the appropriateness of social work to the interests of the most powerless citizens. Such a statement implies the desirability of explicit ideologically based commitments which enable social workers to say what their priorities are and on what grounds they have chosen them. Adherence to accountability alone would not necessarily mean this. Used loosely it is only a term of convenience.

References to accountability which do not confront questions of appropriateness can produce many conflicting goals, with social workers attempting to use several frames of reference and go in several directions at once. For example, in our earlier account of interviews with Scottish Directors of Social Work, they described their sense of accountability in terms of the necessity to play to several different audiences, to present their work to different publics: media, elected members, colleagues and some client groups. Such audiences did not all have the same interests.

In the discussion in Chapter 7, which was part of social workers' evaluations, four particular constraints were identified as controlling the outcomes of social work. Only some of these outcome criteria referred directly to clients' interests. Although 'client change' and 'client satisfaction' were seen as important, so too were 'bureaucratic obligations' and the need to exert 'social and moral control'. Accountability for outcomes could therefore be judged in different ways.

In Chapter 8, the varying responses to the contextual dilemmas of social work were elaborated with reference to different role orientations: the bureaucratic, the professional and the client. In terms of accountability to the most vulnerable people's interests, bureaucratic and professional considerations would not necessarily assume importance. But equally the reference to client orientations and clients' interests must be more than a slogan. It requires some justification in terms of equity. In this respect, social workers should take seriously clients' appraisal of negotiation and advocacy by seeking a fairer distribution of social workers' existing resources and the development of precise strategies to provide care for those who are usually the most vulnerable. In no way should social workers be colluding with a set of arrangements which merely amount to the humanitarian handling of a continuous sense of oppression felt by people who become clients. Social workers might avoid such co-optation by examining critically their role in the welfare state and by identifying collectively the ways to change the operation of their own agencies and the means of effecting alliances to attain even wider social objectives. That would be an appropriate use of time and other resources.

A testing of social workers' achievements through some appraisal of accountability in terms of appropriateness should involve social workers in questioning their objectives in relation to powerless groups in general and not merely with reference to particular cases. This task requires some familiarity with existing evaluations of social work. It also raises the importance of addressing questions about the function of social work in the state. What political and related functions does this occupation perform? To what extent can it be charged with performing society's 'dirty work'? (Hughes 1971).

The first task will be discussed in terms of evaluation being seen as part of practice; the second in terms of the relationship between policy and practice. Both tasks involve some familiarity with the politics affecting the running of welfare organizations and the political debates affecting the future direction of social work.

Evaluation as practice
Researchers usually address their conclusions to other people whose business is the generation of information. This seems pointless. There is little purpose in marshalling others' conclusions if social work practitioners at all levels feel that evaluation and research is carried out only by specialists within their organization and/or by specialists outside it.

In emphasizing the importance of regarding evaluation as a part of practice, we are not suggesting that a future social work may merely concentrate on the most laudable practices as reported in research. Any such recommended technical solutions should always be evaluated in relation to the contexts of deep-seated social and political considerations. We will return to this contention about avoiding technical solutions later in the chapter. At this point we will give an example of what we mean, by evaluating the usefulness and appropriateness of a case review system, as documented in Goldberg and Warburton's research *Ends and Means* (1979). The research methods used in this study appear impeccable. The result was the production and refinement of a case review system which, in terms of its apparent clarity, could have been exported immediately to other agencies. Some of the findings present an optimistic picture of social work. They showed that the majority of 2,000 clients in one years' referrals received what they hoped for and the help received made a difference to their lives. The case review system provided the practitioners with a means for assessing their work, and management with information on how best to employ scarce manpower resources.

In terms of management efficiency, the value of developing a case review system seems sensible but should it be introduced at the expense of other goals? Were the social workers and researchers so absorbed by this activity that they ceased to raise the question of how important it was in relation to other initiatives? The momentum behind a successful project can hinder the subsequent questioning of a particular activity in comparison with other ways of spending time and money. The question of appropriateness is not addressed specifically. In consequence a new fashion – the case review system – developed following impressive research into the relationship between input and output, is in danger of gathering momentum.

Social workers have had their share of sacred cows, a fascination with Freud, unitary methods, behaviourism and various therapies. The input-output model as an appropriate means of evaluating client/worker relations may produce similar passing fascinations but yet ignore as many issues as it covers. For example, inter-professional and inter-organizational conflicts and their effects on social work may not even be considered, nor may the broader socioeconomic context be taken into account.

In Chapter 9 we discussed the finding that researchers, social workers and clients differ in their evaluations of social work because they are talking about different things. This process is almost inevitable if there is little dialogue between parties who might claim to have things in common. For example, researchers and practitioners seem determined to keep their worlds separate, addressing their own reference groups, hiding behind symbols such as alleged scientific methods on the one hand and the mysteries of arcane skills on the other.

There is a peculiar masochism in social workers finding themselves easy targets for almost any critics (more so than doctors or lawyers) yet wishing to distance themselves from some of the information which would enable them to develop their roles and enhance their usefulness. Perhaps some of them remain ambivalent about their objectives and others do not think their positions worth defending? There is something lemming-like about this stance. Employers and client groups might expect to receive continuous evidence to support social workers' roles, or at least some of them with certain people in specific contexts. Research findings can be presented in readable, relevant ways although we have observed that agencies' own reports, in the form of in-house evaluations, are often so long and tedious that practitioners would never find time to read them and should be excused from doing so. However, very useful summaries of key issues in the evaluation of human services do exist (Rossi 1978; Sarri 1979).

Professionals' worlds are built up often at the expense of one group and for the benefit of another. The worlds of evaluators and practitioners should merge by demystifying notions of research and evaluation and by social workers having a greater familiarity with the conflicting verdicts about the consequences of social work.

Demystification

Consideration of the findings of evaluation-type research is often blocked by practitioners' assumptions about the distinctions between objectivity and subjectivity. The notion that evaluators are objective and practitioners are subjective is a fallacy. Social workers' documentation of what they do and why they do it may be subjective but it still represents data. Social workers' documentation does not have to be as ambitious as Goldberg and Warburton's impressive case review system (1979). There is no need to jump from doing nothing to trying to do everything.

Evaluations of social work should aim at achieving a greater understanding of which particular activity has some desired effect in some individuals' lives. The interests of evaluators differ only from the clients making judgements in that the evaluators are using their several criteria in a more disciplined and patterned way, by seeing, in Schutz's words, that 'the activities of people cannot be understood, apart from their placement within the scheme of motives, beliefs, plans and purposes of those who perform them' (Schutz 1962).

One of the authors has earlier concluded that values are at the hub of social workers' decisions about resources, and are represented by a whole series of moral calculations. Clients used similar criteria (Rees 1978, Chapter 5). Others have shown that value judgements which reflect the worth of something affect decisions about the outcome of services, whether in education, health or welfare. For example Gorry and Goodrich (1978) describe their experiences with evaluation in a multi-disciplinary biomedical research centre. They argue that subjective judgements of worth should and can be explicitly stated so that they can be openly discussed, monitored, changed over time, recognized as a source of conflict and identified as a major influence in programme evaluation.

Faithful accounts

In courts of law there are rules of procedure for identifying admissable evidence, for ensuring proper documentation and for establishing the means of verification. Verdicts about social work have been made often without reference to similar procedures. Some have argued that social workers have been judged inefficient in relation to goals they never held and activities they never intended to fulfil (Macdonald 1966).

To come to any verdict about social work requires a sharp profile of who was doing what to whom and with what objectives in mind. Distinctions need to be made between the giving of advice and the giving of tangible items, between work limited to one interview and the achievement of some sense of alliance between worker and client.

Social work and welfare are often lumped indiscriminately together. Clients with experiences of Australian welfare agencies were regarded as highly critical of social work (Bryson 1979), yet a careful reading of this research shows that many of these people seem never to have met anyone who would have identified themselves as a social worker.

Those who sweep away social work because experimental studies have judged casework to be ineffective demonstrate how little they have paid attention to the research completed over the last 10 years. Casework represents only a small part of social work. For example, Goldberg and Warburtons' detailed analysis of one year's social work in an English town distinguished between short-term and long-term work. Short-term work involved different activities: exploration and assessment, information and advice giving; mobilization of resources. The long-term provided protective services for the very young, very old and the disabled. They concentrated on surveillance and review visiting. An up to date account of social work requires distinguishing features and not undiscriminating stereotypes sustained by reference to a formless and misleading label.

Not surprisingly, accounts of social work show a chequered record of achievements and shortcomings. Such accounts describe different activities. They use data obtained by different methods. The conclusions derived from explorative research merit different weight from those derived from experimental studies, but they are not necessarily less important. Wyatt Jones has recently summarized the considerations affecting the choice of methods (1980). He quotes others who argue that designed experiments 'seek to confirm that we have the right answer', but exploratory data analysis 'help assure us that we have the right question' (Bennett and Lumsdaine 1975).

The choice of 'the right question' may depend on the different objectives of clients, social workers and researchers. Such 'participants' make different judgements about a social work service, often because they are talking about different things and have different goals. Clients may hope for total resolution of a problem whereas practitioners aim at only partial resolution or some relief. Researchers want to evaluate outcomes, practitioners are concerned more about the processes associated with their work.

However, 'the right question' should refer to some test of social work's ability to shift power relationships in the interests of client groups, to respond to those, potentially, most useful of all evaluative-type questions, 'where does power rest and how it is denied to some?' With a few notable exceptions these questions have seldom been posed (Bennington 1975; Liffman 1978).

A test of accountability should require asking whether any form of social work was an appropriate response to clients' interests, given the various forms of powerlessness which they share. The linking of accountability and appropriateness will involve some evaluation of client/social worker encounters *and* policy considerations. Just as we have argued earlier that evaluation and practice can be merged, so we find it difficult to assess accountability to clients' interests by analysing something called practice as though it is separate from management and policy objectives.

Policy and practice

Although the policies of social work agencies have been potentially innovative, in practice they have fulfilled residual functions. Social workers have provided services as a last resort and even then could often provide only band-aids. This process has occurred partly because social workers have operated as though they could serve client's best interests without some front-line staff in each agency having a responsibility for devising policies to develop resources for specific powerless groups.

The objective of developing policies and practices which are appropriate in terms of the priority needs of certain clients is insufficiently specific to be operationalized. One needs to adopt Blau and Scott's means of appraising the objectives of any organization, and ask the question 'who benefits?' (1963). In this respect the appropriateness of social workers' activities is often assumed, seldom checked, and rarely evaluated.

The Scottish directors felt accountable to ordinary people yet seldom planned how to ensure that some sense of accountability was initiated and maintained. In none of the Scottish regions was there regular machinery for recording clients' views. By contrast, in all of the regions there was a pre-occupation with the accountability to political and bureaucratic superiors.

Running an organization with the least amount of trouble can suggest a concern only with staff peace of mind. Demonstrating the virtuous effect of activities suggests only some awareness of a public comprised of potential critics and paymasters. The preoccupation with keeping an organization alive hardly suggests space for thinking about choices and about objectives which might reflect the interests of the most powerless groups. Even the current fascination with cost effectiveness is no guarantee that client interests will influence the pruning of one activity and the reinvestment in another.

Some front-line social workers may be involved in policy-making and be able to assess their work with client groups in relation to such policies. However, research seldom shows whether they do this. Neither do we have much of a picture of the relative impact of social work activities in relation to other services or in relation to the economic and political circumstances affecting a local population at a particular point in time. Too often, social work research gives an impression of agency-only considerations and even these make little reference to local social policies. We are referring to a shortcoming of research. This may not be a faithful representation of practice.

Avoiding political naviety

We would be blurring the issues if we did not make clear our own views about the priorities of social workers. We would be naive if we did not recognize the day to day dilemmas involved in trying to implement such priorities. It is not easy to make explicit an alternative and, some would say, radical ideological basis for practice let alone to develop policies, strategies and legislation in specific areas, for example, womens' and childrens' rights, job creation schemes, the reform of the administration of justice and of penal systems. Although familiarity with research findings should provide a baseline from which to develop practice and plan educational objectives, the future direction of social work does not depend only on an improvement of competence in those areas which clients have found helpful. The implications of negative conclusions should also be taken seriously. Such conclusions are as follows:

1   Certain forms of competence are identified in clients' evaluations but social workers are reluctant to make such judgements.
2   Clients have valued highly negotiation and advocacy on their behalf, or in association with them, but social workers have not considered such roles to be so important.
3   By placing themselves in a position of reacting to client needs, social workers have colluded with their agencies in the development of conservative, residual functions and policies.
4   Social workers have known about client interests only in terms of individual cases and caseloads and in consequence they have concentrated on services which were not necessarily geared to effecting any form of social change.
5   Social workers do not check whether their agency's objectives are attained.
6   It is often assumed, rather than tested, that agency goals are appropriate in terms of the needs of the most vulnerable groups.

These conclusions imply the need for social workers to address questions about social change, starting with the objectives of their employing agencies. Even if social workers valued acting collectively, they would be unable to effect lasting changes if they did not confront the relationship between themselves, their employers, other employees and client groups such as the unemployed. The unwillingness and inability to confront such issues is born of a political naivety to which even the most competent practitioners might plead guilty. We will say what we mean by this.

In their apparent concentration on work with individual clients, social workers have been relatively artless in their understanding and management of other public affairs. These other public affairs include the operation of agencies; the links between policy objectives and the needs of client groups; the means of making alliances with other interested parties such as pressure groups or trade unions; the need to articulate publicly, and therefore to test openly, the role of social work in the state. Each of these areas of public affairs concerns relationships between the powerful and the less powerful, between people who possess information and other resources and those who are relatively ignorant and without resources. To be able to shift such power relationships in some ordinary people's interests requires some commitment and competence in developing resources and in limiting constraints. Such objectives cannot be attained if social workers are ingenuous about the contexts in which they work. Attempts to attain such objectives require, in addition to the radical commitment referred to above,* an understanding of policies and the management of power relationships. At the very least social workers should avoid being politically naive.

We are arguing that social workers should operate both at the short-term individual level *and* at the long-term social/political level. In saying this, we are addressing the problem of 'how to engage in small-scale changes in an overall political context' (Corrigan and Leonard 1978, 141). Despite the considerable difficulties of combining these actions, we believe that the pursuit of both short-term and the long-term goals is possible, desirable and not necessarily contradictory. The alternative, concentrating on the long term at the expense of the short term, or vice versa, is untenable. We shall explain how we have reached this conclusion.

We want to repeat our view that accountability to clients is not synonymous with slavishly following their views by concentrating on those services which they have identified as helpful. Individuals' aspirations are often circumscribed by their limited knowledge of what is available, a point which we will elaborate in our discussion of the notion 'clients' interests'. Another reason for caution in concentrating on various 'helpful' forms of intervention, as identified by clients, is that these helpful activities may actually contribute to some clients' continued suffering in the long term if it means that broader political issues are ignored. We do not want to be guilty of the assumption of many evaluators accused by Simpkin of 'technical tinkering', i.e. we do not believe that the problems which many clients face are going to be solved by any technical solution provided by the social workers alone. Clearly, many clients' difficulties are beyond this. Hence our belief that social workers should direct much of their attention to broader sociopolitical issues.

At the same time, however, we are not advocating a concentration on social change while writing off all small-scale interventions and goals. We take note of practitioners' accusations of academics that 'It's all right for you to talk – we have to work where the heat is' (Cohen 1975). Immediate human suffering is painful and should be alleviated, at once if possible. It is

---

* See also the definition in Chapter 1, p. 3.

no use telling a family who come into a social services department late on a Friday afternoon, penniless and homeless, that sorry they cannot be helped, they'll have to 'wait and work for the revolution' (Simpkin 1979). But skilled humanitarian activities can be facilitated by an understanding of the workings of the state, its institutions and its representative; and should be associated with longer-term social change objectives, a marrying of the personal and the political.

By way of conclusion we will develop this argument with reference to three areas of public affairs: the relationship between social workers' aspirations and those of ordinary people; the challenge to agency and related constraints; participation in agency and public debate about the economics and efficiency of the personal social services.

Clients' interests

Radical social workers' attempts to articulate policy goals with clients' interests in mind are not necessarily shared by the people concerned let alone by politicians and civil servants. The values which prompt practices in clients' interests have to be made explicit. Subsequently, a test of the appropriateness of social work activities would involve the skill of linking client considerations to policy developments, and policy considerations to evaluations of practice. That process involves having 'an eye for evaluation' (Moller and Graycar 1981).

Even the spelling out of innovative goals is hardly justified merely on the basis that they are novel or will effect change. The potential conflict between the goals of social workers and the interests of ordinary people will always require exploration. Bitensky (1975) has shown how the aspirations of some social and community workers gloss over the difficulties of bringing ordinary people from apathy to activism. Pinker (1971) has been concerned with the disparity between some academics' attitudes and the conservatism of the 'working class'. Similarly Tulloch (1978) contrasts the prescriptions of professionals and the subjective perceptions of reality of ordinary citizens. She asks what is the moral basis of an ideology which demands a utopia unwanted by those it claims to represent?

But we would argue that ordinary people's passivity and alleged conservatism is not surprising given the ways in which the media of many countries promote one-sided versions of society and encourage readers and viewers to be unquestioningly grateful in their attitudes and expectations. In this respect Freire has highlighted how, in industrialized societies, a culture of silence threatens to dominate an over-consuming and over-managed population, where education too often means merely socialization (1972). Radical social workers should not feel constrained by academics' observations concerning the gap between some social workers' goals and the compliance of the most vulnerable people. It is part of a radical social work to raise people's consciousness of conditions affecting them, to enable people, and women in particular, to redefine their assumptions about roles within families and the functions of families within a wider economic order. In that way radical social work should have a liberating function and its success should be measured accordingly.

Constraints of practice
Accountability even to clients' low expectations, let alone to egalitarian socialist objectives, is unlikely even to be addressed if staff accept the constraints on their practice. Restraints are part of practice and affect its goals. They can become almost a preoccupation in practice itself.

We have seen how constraints operate at different levels. On one level, clients' low expectations can constrain a practising social worker intent on more ambitious goals. On another level, the worker him/herself is frequently constrained by the hierarchy within which he or she operates. Even the directors, at the top of such hierarchies, referred to the constraints of budgets, of an uninformed public, of media interests in sensations, of the energy required merely to keep an organization functioning in some way. We argue that such constraints do not have to be accepted with such a sense of resignation. For example, through information and enlightenment, clients' expectations can be raised; decisions about economic resources are negotiable, both within and without the social work arena; at least some of the media can be handled differently and encouraged to analyse social workers' activities not merely to stereotype them. Education and consultation are valued social work methods and can be directed towards public opinion.

Social workers should be involved in debates about the merits of welfare state services of which they are only a small part. It is not true that they cannot have a voice because of statutory constraints. They can challenge the point of view that the public and private sectors of each nation's economies are separate. They can test and resist the notion that it is always better to invest in services for groups who can repay in some way.

Some economic literacy
Measures of accountability do not involve only the values of accountants. For example, in any calculation of fairness, the value of services for the aged or the handicapped can be measured, albeit not so easily as in the other side of the cost benefit equation.

Some of the recent controversies over social work have concerned the costs of government-sponsored social work services as opposed to the alleged savings made by relying on private individuals' initiatives or (which may amount to the same thing) doing nothing. Social workers are regarded as being in the middle of such trade-offs between considerations of equity and the economics of efficiency (Jones 1980). Yet social workers have been silent in such debates, as though they have been taught that economic and other policy considerations are somehow separate from the resources available in practice. A certain political and organizational naivety shows if social workers insist on the alleged benefits of their services without knowing much about the economic costs.

Benefits from social welfare expenditure can be advocated in terms of relative costs. Choices about the development of home help services for the aged or concerning the creation of experimental hostel schemes for the adult mentally handicapped will be made partly on actuarial grounds. However, social workers' involvement in decisions about money is usually confined to the matter of whether to give a very small grant to certain deserving families. The costs and benefits of long-term care could be as much a part of social workers' stock-in-trade information as is their concern with accounting in families' budgeting, or their familiarity with attractive (to them) models of explanation of behaviour. Social workers' references to accountability in terms of appropriateness would be strengthened if they could also include some economic considerations affecting the policies which they interpret and implement.

Summary and conclusions

Over the past 20 years, research of various kinds gives a chequered verdict on the achievements and shortcomings of social workers. Those practitioners who possessed a certain competence, often illustrated by skills in advocacy and negotiation, were able to effect changes which clients valued at the time. Conversely, other clients found themselves disappointed by social workers' attitudes, relative ignorance and inactivity. The meaning and weight of such conclusions varied according to the contexts in which such social work was carried out and in which the research was conducted.

Some negative views on the consequences of social work have been derived from an uncritical reliance on the conclusions of experimental research. For several reasons this has provided a narrow and often inaccurate source of information. These experimental studies were concerned to measure the effects of casework. More recent research shows that social workers' activities seldom resemble such a rarified form of casework. However, a major difficulty in encouraging forms of practice identified as useful by researchers is social work education's proclivity for continuing to teach a type of individual casework that is rarely ever encountered in the practice of most social workers in most agencies. In this respect university and college departments which ought to be contributing to solutions are in reality part of the problem.

Other evaluative findings can be derived from studies which were not experimental in design and which did not focus exclusively on intervention labelled casework. For example, there is a correspondence in the conclusions of exploratory studies, some of them unpublished, carried out in different agencies in different countries.

Some application of criteria of appropriateness and accountability point to the relative conservative nature of social workers' objectives and achievements. Yet, ironically, assumptions about clients' interests as one form of accountability may leave social workers seriously adrift with aspirations which do not match those of ordinary people. Some solution to this mismatch will depend on raising clients' expectations and making explicit the ideological commitments affecting social workers' priorities. Such practitioners, sandwiched as they are between powerful institutions and relatively powerless people, have to decide whose side they are on. They can and should be unapologetic and unashamed in their commitment to meeting the short and long-term needs of client groups. By contrast, organizational, professional and other considerations will always be incorporated in ideologies which produce pragmatic allegiances in which accountability to clients' interests is given only lip service.

Criteria of appropriateness and accountability are not easy to apply. Even if research produced a favourable verdict on social workers' activities, critics might still argue that such activities amounted to poor use of time. In relation to the continuing poverty of large numbers of people, social workers are seen as having concentrated on inappropriate tasks. By contrast, if research showed social workers addressing social and political issues in attempting to effect change but achieving little, critics might still argue that such pessimistic findings were incentives to social workers to do more. That is our point of view.

Social work should not exist merely to soften the sense of powerlessness felt by millions of people. Social workers' tasks should involve commitments to providing services effectively and to effecting changes that would improve permanently the living conditions of particular people. In the process of effecting such change, social workers and powerless clients' interests become common. Traditional social work/client distinctions can and should be eliminated in most contexts.

Social workers can influence their terms of reference. To do this involves access to information, as in the preparation of evidence and the marshalling of arguments to ensure the best use of existing resources and the development of new ones, both within and outside agencies. Deciding whose side you are on involves knowing who your allies are and this is especially pertinent in a time of economic cutbacks.

The apparent simplicity of economic measurements is currently attractive to those who wish to evaluate social welfare expenditure in terms of costs. However, in the debate about priorities in social policy expenditure, those who value highly some apparently uneconomical services seldom make their own criteria clear. Partly in consequence, politicians, industrialists, hostile journalists and executives of social work agencies show some preoccupation with economic efficiency. This could anaesthetize a gullible public into thinking that these are either the only or the most important yardsticks for evaluating the activities of social workers. This, in our view, is not the priority direction either for evaluation or for practice.

There is room for the development of ideals and goals to match clients' interests. The struggle to implement such goals would be a desirable feature of policy-making and a key to social workers' future priorities. The challenge is wider than attempts to encourage one occupation to be held accountable for ordinary people's interests. We are drawing these conclusions at a time of economic recession when there has been a strident search for scapegoats. The verdicts-on-social-work debate occurs in a wide political arena. The struggle to define and implement appropriate goals is crucial in any society in which gross forms of inequality are maintained and in which it is often argued that economic stability demands a certain amount of human suffering.

Regarding the debate about social work's future we have found that some social workers achieve certain things. There is no reason why they should not be known for such achievements. For several reasons, the achievements can be seen to be conservative. Many clients expect little and make unambitious demands. Many social workers accept too easily the constraints of their jobs. Perhaps their greatest constraint has been a certain artlessness regarding the contexts of their employment, as is evident in the lack of familiarity with techniques to effect changes in their own organization let alone strategies to influence policies related to larger social issues. A means of overcoming such political naivety is to acknowledge how priorities and interests are affected by ideologically based commitments.

In achieving even unambitious social changes on behalf of certain client groups, the development of a competence in skills and interaction is not unimportant. The evidence in this book implies that such competence is only a first step. The development of objectives in association with relatively powerless people and the strategies to sustain particular initiatives requires of social work that it embrace ideologies, roles and self-images which differ from those involved in the traditional provision of services. Such services can continue to be provided in a sensitive and humanitarian way but they will not disturb existing power relationships. A radical alternative would involve identifying the grossest inequities which arise from capitalist economies and developing strategies to enable ordinary citizens to have more influence in the policies and other institutional arrangements which have previously asked that they be motivated, skilful and grateful recipients. Only a conservative and compliant social work would be content to sustain such arrangements no matter how outwardly efficient or professional these practices might be claimed to be.

The most telling criterion of evaluation of social work concerns some examination of accountability in terms of certain vulnerable groups' long-term interests. That is the challenge for an imaginative and radical social work. The major question for all social workers should be 'what kind of social work is wanted, in what kind of society?' It can never be merely the more narrow goal of trying to maximize competence in terms of objectives which even the most cautious supporter of social work would find neither imaginative nor inspiring.

References

Adams, P.L. and McDonald, N.F. 1968: Clinical cooling out of poor people. *American Journal of Orthopsychiatry* **38**(3), April, 457–63.

Adamson, G. 1969: How children's departments treat their foster parents. *Case Conference* **15**(10).

Aldgate, J. 1978: Advantages of residential care, *Adoption and Fostering* **92**(2), 29–33.

Alexander, D.A. 1973: Yes, but what about the parents? *Physiotherapy* **59**(12), 391–3.

Alexander, J. and Sutton, J. 1980: Family support services scheme 1979–1980. *Evaluation Report*, Sydney: Family support management committee.

Anderson, D. 1979: Enabling practitioners to contribute to practice. *Social Work Today* **10**(39) 12 June, 15–17.

Anonymous 1973: Another sleepless night: a parent's viewpoint. *Social Work* **18**(1), January, 112–14.

Aronson, A. and Sherwood C. 1967: Research versus practitioner: problems in social action research. *Social Work* **12**(4), October, 89–96.

Backner, B.L. and Kissinger, R.D. 1963: Hospitalised patients' attitudes toward mental health professionals and mental patients. *Journal of Nervous and Mental Diseases* **136**, 72–5.

Bandcroft, A. 1970: Hostel – follow-up study. *Case Conference* **16**(9), 364–8.

Baird, P. 1976: Process or outcome? *Social Work Today* **7**(1), 10–11.

Barker, P.J. 1974: The discrepancy between what clients and social workers think is helpful. *Unpublished 1974 project*, National Institute for Social Work.

—— 1975: Clients' likes and dislikes. *Social Work Today* **6**(3), 77–8.

Barnet Social Services Department 1979: *Consumer study of day centre for the elderly.*

Bayley, M. 1973a: *Mental handicap and community care.* London: Routledge & Kegan Paul.

—— 1973b: The mentally handicapped and their professional helpers. *British Journal of Social Work* **3**(3), 349–63.

Beck, D.F. 1962: *Patterns in the use of family agency service.* New York: Family Service Association of America.

—— 1975: Research findings on the outcomes of marital counselling. *Social Casework* **56**, March, 153–81.

Beck, D.F. and Jones, M.A. 1973: *Progress on Family Problems – a nationwide study of clients' and counsellors' views on family agency services.* New York: Family Service Association of America.

Becker, H. 1971: 'Who's side are we on?' in *Sociological work, method and substance.* London: Allen Lane.

Bedfordshire Social Services Department 1978: *Handicapped children.*

Begley, E. and Lieberman, L. 1970: Patient expectation of therapist's techniques. *Journal of Clinical Psychology* **26**, 112–16.

Beker, J. 1965: Male adolescent inmates' perceptions of helping persons. *Social Work* (USA) **10**(2), April, 18–25.

Bennett, C.A. and Lumsdaine, A.A., eds., *Evaluation and experiment: some critical issues in assessing social programs.* New York: Academic Press.

Bennington, J. 1975: The flaw in the pluralist heaven. In Lees, R, and Smith G., *Action Research in Community Development*, London: Routledge & Kegan Paul.

Ben-Sira, Z. 1976: The function of the professional's affective behaviour in client satisfaction: a revised approach to social interaction theory. *Journal of Health and Social Behaviour* **17**(3).

Bergin, A. 1971: The evaluation of therapeutic outcomes. In Bergin A.E. and Garfield S.L., eds., *Handbook of psychotherapy and behaviour change*, New York: John Wiley & Sons, 217–70.

Berkowitz, N.H., Malone, M.F. and Klein, Malcom W.: Patient care as a criterion problem. *Journal of Health and Social Behaviour* **3**, 171–6.

Berleman, W.C. 1969: Practitioners and research: first questions. *Social Casework* **50**(8), 461–6.

Bernstein, I. and Freeman, H. 1976: *Academic and entrepreneurial research.* New York: Russell Sage.

Billingsley, A. 1964: Bureaucratic and professional orientation patterns in social casework. *Social Service Review* **38**(4), 400–7.

Bitensky, R. 1969: Social action – the therapy of poor folk, *Mental Hygiene* **53**(4).

—— 1975: From apathy to activism. *Inquiry* **18**, 213–23.

Bittner, E. 1973: Objectivity and realism in sociology. In G. Psathas, ed., *Phenomenological sociology*, New York: John Wiley, 109–25.

Black, J.M.M. 1978: Families with handicapped children – who helps whom and how? *Child-Care Health and Development* **4**(4), July/August, 239–45.

Blau, P.M. 1960: Orientation toward clients in a public welfare agency. *Administrative Science Quarterly* **5**, 341–61.

Blau, P. and Scott N. 1963: *Formal organizations.* London: Routledge & Kegan Paul.

Blaxter, M. 1976: *The meaning of disability.* London: Heinemann.

Blenker, M. 1950: Obstacles to evaluative research on casework: parts I and II. *Social Casework* **3**, 54–60.

Bloom, M. and Black S.R. 1977: Evaluating one's own effectiveness and efficiency. *Social Work* **22**(2), 130–6.

Blumberg, D.D., Ely, A.R., and Kerbeshian, A. 1975: Clients' evaluation of medical social services. *Social Work* **20**(1), 45–7.

Borgatta, E.F., Fanshel, A. and Meyer, H.J. 1960: *Social workers' perception of clients*. New York: Russell Sage Foundation.

Brandon, J. and Davies, M. 1979: The limits of competence in social work: the assessment of marginal students in social work education. *British Journal of Social Work* **9**(3), 295–347.

Brewer, C. 1977: Are social workers really necessary? *Community Care* **152**, March 16, 14–15.

—— 1976/77: Social workers – benefit or bane? *Age Concern Today* **20**, 25–26.

Brewer, C. and Lait, J. 1980: *Can social work survive?* London: Temple Smith.

Briar, S. 1966: Welfare from below: recipients' views of the public welfare system. In Ten Broek, J., ed., *The law of the poor*, San Francisco: Chandler Publishing Co.

Brown, G.E., ed., 1968: *The multi-problem dilemma*. Metuchen, NJ: Scarecrow Press.

Bryson, L. 1979: The views of clients: what people think of welfare services. In Commonwealth of Australia, *Through a glass darkly*, Canberra AGPS, 1–22.

—— 1981: Abuses and uses of evaluation. *Australian Journal of Social Issues* **16**(2), 103–13.

Buchanan, S.W. and Marofsky, L.F. 1970: The fearlessness of revision. *Public Welfare* **28**(2), 141–57.

Burck, C. 1978: A study of families' expectations and experiences of a child guidance clinic. *British Journal of Social Work.* **8**(2), 145–58.

Bush, M., Gordon, A.C. and Le Bailley, R. 1977: Evaluating child welfare services: a contribution from the clients. *Social Service Review* **15**(3), 481–501.

Butler, N. 1977: Uncovering a gap in the service. *Community Care* 3 August, 14–16.

Butler, J., Bow, I. and Gibbons, J. 1978: Task-centred casework with marital problems. *British Journal of Social Work* **8**(4), 393–409.

Butrym, Z. 1968: *Medical social work in action*. London: Bell.

Bywaters, P. 1975: Ending casework relationships (1). *Social Work Today* **6**(10), 301.

Campbell, L.A. 1979: Consumer participation in planning social service programs. *Social Work* **24**(2), 159–63.

Caplan, E.K. and Sussman, M.B. 1966: Rank order of important variables for patient and staff satisfaction with outpatient service. *Journal of Health and Human Behaviour* **17**.

Carew, R. 1979: The place of knowledge in social work activity *The British Journal of Social Work* **9**(3).

Carpenter, P. 1977: A view of the client/worker encounter. *Smith College Studies in Social Work*, Northampton, Mass. **47**(3), June, 167–80.

Carter, M. 1966: *Into work*. London: Penguin.

Casselman, B. 1972: On the practitioner's orientation towards research. *Smith College Studies in Social Work* **42**(3), June, 211–33.

Chambers, R. 1978: Young views on residential care. *Community Care*, **205**, March 22, 20–1.

Chommie, P.W. and Hudson J. 1974: Evaluation of outcome and process. *Social Work* **19**(6), November, 682–7.

Clarke, R.V.G. and Cornish, D.B. 1972: *The controlled trial in institutional research – paradigm or pitfall for penal evaluators?* Home office Research Study (15), London: HMSO.

—— 1975: *Residential treatment and its effects on delinquency*. Home office research study (32), London HMSO.

Coates, K. and Silburn, R. 1970: *Poverty: the forgotten Englishman*. London: Penguin.

Cockburn, C. 1977: *The local state*. London: Pluto Press.

Cohen, A. 1971: Consumer view: retarded mothers and the social services. *Social Work Today* **1**(12), 35–43.

Cohen, S. 1975: It's all right for you to talk: political and sociological manifestos for social work action, in Bailey, R. and Brake, M., eds., *Radical Social Work*, London: Edward Arnold.

Collins, S. 1977: Casework – more than good intentions? *Social Work Today* **8**(31), 11–12.

Commonwealth of Australia 1976: *Commission of inquiry into poverty*, Community Services: four studies, Canberra AGPS.

—— 1979: *Through a glass darkly* evaluation in Australian Health and Welfare Services, Canberra AGPS.

Condie, C.D., Hansen, J.A., Lang, N.E., Moss, D.K. and Kane, R.S. 1978: How the public views social work. *Social Work* **23**(1), 47–53.

Corrigan, P. and Leonard, P. 1978: *Social work practice under capitalism*. London: Macmillan.

Creer, C. 1975: Living with schizophrenia. *Social Work Today* **6**(1).

Culyer, A.J. 1976: *Need and the national health service*. London: Martin Robertson.

Dailey, W.J. and Ives, K. 1978: Exploring client reactions to agency service. *Social Casework*, New York, **59**(4), April, 233–45.

Dartington, T. and Miller, E. 1977: A brave face for the handicapped? *Social Work Today* **9**(11) 9–10.

Davies, M. 1975: You and research. *Social Work Today* **6**(16) 510–11.

Davies, M. 1979: Through the eyes of the probationer. *Probation Journal* **26**(3), 84–8.

Day, P.R. 1972: Perception and social work tasks. *Probation* **18**(3), November.

Deisher, R.W., Engel, W.L., Speilhols, R. and Standfast, S.J. 1965: Mothers' opinions of their pediatric care. *Pediatrics* **35**(1), Part 1, January, 82–90.

Dennis, N. 1970: *People and planning*. London: Faber & Faber.

Department of Health and Social Security 1978: *Social Service Teams: The Practitioner's view*. London: HMSO.

Eaton, J. 1958: Science, art and uncertainty in social work. *Social work* **3**, July.

Editorial Comment 1979: Research and long term strategy. *Social Work Today* **10**(39), 12 June.

Eisenthal, S. and Lazare, A. 1976: Evaluation of the initial interview in a walk-in-clinic (the patient's perspective on a 'customer approach'). *Journal of Nervous and Mental Disease* **162**(3), 169–76.

Elton: L.R. 1975: Is it possible to assess teaching? In *Evaluating teaching in higher education*, a collection of conference papers, the University of London Teaching Methods Unit.

Fanshel, D. 1966: Sources of strain in practice-oriented research. *Social Casework* **47**, June.

Fanshel, D. 1980: The future of social work research: strategies for the coming years. In Fanshel D., ed., *Future of social work research*, Washington DC: NASW, 3–18.

Fischer, J. 1973: Is casework effective? *Social Work* **18**(1), 5–20.

—— 1976: *The effectiveness of social casework*. Springfield, Ill: Charles C. Thomas.

—— 1978: Does anything work? *Journal of Social Service Research* **1**(3), Spring, 215–43.

—— 1979: Isn't casework effective yet? *Social Work* **24**(3), 245–7.

Freidson, E. 1960: Client control and medical practice. *American Journal of Sociology* LXV (65), 376–7.

—— 1961: *Patients' view of medical practice*. New York: Russell Sage.

Fowles, A.J. 1978: *Prison welfare: an account of an experiment in Liverpool*. Home Office Research Study (45), London: HMSO.

Fox, R.C. 1959: *Experiment perilous*. New York: Free Press.

Frank, H. 1979: Taking up research in practice. *Social Work Today* **10**(39), 12 June, 13–15.

Freire, P. 1972: *Pedagogy of the oppressed*. London: Penguin.

Fry, A. 1978: Finding the right balance. *Community care* **197**, 17–19.

Fry, A. and Cockburn, R. 1980: Study on social work is to start. *Observer* 21 September.

Fry, L.J. 1973: Participant observation and program evaluation. *Journal of Health and Social Behaviour* **14**, September, 274–8.

Galper, J. 1980: *Social work practice, a radical perspective*. Englewood Cliffs, NJ: Prentice Hall.

Galtung, J. 1967: *Theory and method in social science*. London: Allen & Unwin.

Gandy, J.M., Pitman, R., Strecher, M. and Yip, C. 1975: Parents' perceptions of the effect of volunteer probation officers in juvenile offenders. *Canadian Journal of Criminology and Corrections* **17**(1) 5–19.

George, V. 1970: *Foster care*. London: Routledge & Kegan Paul.

George, V. and Wilding, P. 1972: *Motherless families*. London: Routledge & Kegan Paul.

Gibbons, J.S., Bow, I., Butler, J., and Powell J. 1979: Clients' reactions to task-centred casework: a follow-up study. *British Journal of Social Work* **9**, Part 2, 203–16.

Gilbert, P. 1979: Socking the social services. *Community Care* **249**, 1 February, 17–19.

Gilmore, D.W. and Oates, R.K. 1977: Counselling about Down's syndrome: the parents' viewpoint. *Medical Journal of Australia* II (18) October 29, 600–3.

Giordano, P. 1977: The client's perspective in agency evaluation. *Social Work* **22**(1) 34–9.

Glampson, A., Glastonbury, B. and Fruin, D. 1977: Knowledge and perceptions of the social services. *Journal of Social Policy* **6**(1), June.

Glampson, A. and Goldberg, E.M. 1976: Post-Seebohm services (2) the consumer's viewpoint. *Social Work Today* **8**(6), 9 November.

Glaser, G. 1964: *The effectiveness of a prison and parole system*. Indianapolis, Indiana: Bobbs-Merrill Co. Inc.

Glastonbury, B., Burdett, M. and Austin, R. 1973: Community perceptions and the personal social services. *Policy and Politics* **1**(3).

Goffman, E. 1952: Cooling the mark out: some aspects of adaptations to failure. *Psychiatry* **15**, 451–63.

Goldberg, E.M. 1970: *Helping the aged*. London: Allen & Unwin.

Goldberg, E.M. and Neill, J.E. 1972: *Social work in general practice*. London: Allen & Unwin.

Goldberg, E.M. and Warburton, R. 1979: *Ends and means in social work*. London: Allen & Unwin.

Goode, W.J. 1960: The profession: reports and opinion. *American Sociological review* **25**, 902–14.

Gorry, G.A. and Goodrich, T.J. 1978: On the role of values in program evaluation. *Evaluation Quarterly* **2**(4).

Gorst, A. 1978: Who's being exploited? *Social Work Today* **9**(40), 4 April.

Gostick, C. 1976: The intake phenomenon. *Social Work Today* **8**(10), 7–9.

Gottesfeld, H. 1965: Professionals and delinquents evaluate professional methods with delinquents. *Social Problems* **13**.

Goyne, J.B. and Ladoux, P. 1973: Patient's opinions of outpatient clinic service. *Hospital Community Psychiatry* **24**, 627–8.

Grann, R.P., Olerïdzki, M.C. and Goodrich, C.H. 1972: How well does the system work? Welfare clients speak out. *Public Welfare* **30**(3), 34–8.

Gray, C.M., Conover, C.J. and Hennessey, T.M. 1978: Cost effectiveness of residential community corrections. *Evaluation Quarterly* **2**(3), 375–400.

Graycar, A. 1979: Political issues in research and evaluation. *Evaluation Quarterly* **3**(3), 460–71.

Greenaway, W.K. 1976: Faith and science in the professional ideology of Canadian social caseworkers, *Canadian Review of Sociology and Anthropology* **13**(1), 106–13.

Greenberg, R.P. 1966: Effects of pre-session information on perception of the therapist and receptivity to influence in a psychotherapy analogue. *Journal of Consultative Clinical Psychology* **33**, 425–9.

Greenberg, R.P., Goldstein, A.P. and Perry M. 1970: The influence of referral information upon patient perception in a psychotherapy analogue. *The Journal of Nervous and Mental Disease* **150**, 31–6.

Grey, A.L. and Dermody, H.E. 1972: Reports of casework failure. *Social Casework* **53**, November, 534–43.

Gunzberg, H.C. 1977: Guided or unguided adjustment to life in the community: an evaluation. *Journal of Practical Approaches to Developmental Handicap* **1**(1), 31–6.

Gurin, G., Veroff, J. and Feld, S. 1960: *Americans view their mental health.* New York: Basic Books.

Gurland, B., 1977: The comprehensive assessment and referral evaluation – rationale, development and reliability. *International Journal of Aging and Human Development*, New York, **8**(1), 9–42.

Guttentag, M. and Struening, E.L., eds., 1975: *Handbook of evaluation research*, Vols. 1 and 2. Beverley Hills: Sage publications.

Hall, A.S. 1974: *The point of entry.* London: Allen & Unwin.

Halmos, P. 1966: *The faith of the counsellors: a study in the theory and practice of social casework and psychotherapy.* New York: Schocken books.

Hammersmith Social Services Department 1979: *Clients' views of day centres for the elderly and physically handicapped.*

Handler, E. 1973: The expectations of day-care parents. *Social Service Review* **47**(2), 266–77.

Handler, J.F. 1974: *The coercive social workers: British lessons for American social services.* New York: Academic Press, Inc.

Handler, J.F. and Hollingsworth, E.J. 1971: *The 'deserving poor'.* Institute for research on poverty. Monograph Series, Chicago: Merkham Publishing Company.

Harbert, W.B. 1976: Who checks the checkers? *Health and Social Service Journal* **26**(86).

Harris, S. 1978: Perth prison welfare project, *unpublished report*, Aberdeen University.

Hart, J. 1973/74: Is it success? *Social Work Today* **4**(2), 53–6.

Haug, M. and Sussman, M.B. 1969: Professional autonomy and the revolt of the client. *Social Problems* **17**, 153–61.

Heilbrun, A.B. Jr. 1972: Effects of briefing upon client satisfaction with the initial counselling contact. *Journal of Consulting and Clinical Psychology* **38**(1),.50–6.

Heraud, B.J. 1970: *Sociology and social work*. Oxford: Pergamon.

Hewett, S. 1970: *The family and the handicapped child*. London: Allen & Unwin.

Heywood, J.S. and Allen, B.K. 1971: *Financial help in social work*. Manchester University Press.

Hill, J.A. 1969: Therapists' goals, patient aims and patient satisfaction in psychotherapy. *Journal of Clinical Psychology* **25**, 455–9.

Hillingdon Social Services Department 1973: *Report on a pilot study survey to examine the public's awareness of an attitude toward social services department.*

—— 1974: *Client opinions: a report on a pilot study to find the view of 50 elderly people referred to the social services department.*

Ho, M.R. 1976: Evaluation: a means of treatment. *Social Work* **21**(1), 24–7.

Hoffmann, Walter, P.F. 1975: Expectations of mental health centre clients related to problem reductions and satisfaction with services. University of Pennsylvania DSW, May, from *Abstracts for Social Workers* **11**(3), No. 700.

Holborn J. 1975: Some male offenders' problems. *Homeless offenders in Liverpool. Casework with short-term prisoners.* Home Office Research Study (28), London: HMSO.

Holman, R. 1965: How children see fostering. *New Society* **6**(164), 22–3.

—— 1968: Client power. *New Society* **12**(318), 645–6.

—— 1975: The place of fostering in social work. *British Journal of Social Work* **5**, 3–30.

Home Office Studies 1974: *IMPACT – intensive matched probation and after-care treatment.* vol. I&II. Home Office Research Study No. 36. London: HMSO.

Horan, P.M. and Austin, P.L. 1974: The social bases of welfare stigma. *Social Problems* **21**(5), 648–57.

Horenstein, D., Houston, B. Kent, and Holmes, David, S. 1973: Clients', therapists', and judges' evaluations of psychotherapy. *Journal of counselling psychology* **20**(2), 149–53.

Hornstra, R.K. and Lubin, B. 1974: Relationship of outcome of treatment to agreement about the treatment assignment by patients and professionals. *Journal of Nervous and Mental Disease* **158**(6), 420–3.

Howe, M.W. 1974: Casework self-evaluation: a single-subject approach. *Social Service Review* **48**(1), 1–23.

—— 1976: Using clients' observations in research. *Social Work* **21**(1), 28–32.

Howlett, J., Lorenz, S. and Walters, J. 1976: *Manpower in social welfare:*

a study of social workers. Institute of Applied Economic and Social Research, University of Melbourne.

Hudson, W.W. 1978: First axioms of treatment. *Social Work* 23(1), January, 65–73.

Hughes, E. 1958: *Men and their work.* Illinois: The Free Press of Glencoe.

—— 1971: Professions, in E. Hughes, *The sociological eye,* Chicago: Aldine.

Hulya, B.S., Zyxanski, S.J., Cassel J.C. and Thomson, S.J. 1971: Satisfaction with medical care in a low income population. *Journal of Chronic Diseases* 24(661).

Huxley, A. 1932: *Brave New World.* London: Chatto & Windus.

Humphries, B. 1978: What do they think of me? *Social Work Today* 9(22), 16–18.

Hunt, L. 1978: Social work and ideology, in Timms, N. and Watson, D. eds., *Philosophy in social work,* London: Routledge & Kegan Paul.

Jackson, F. 1973: Families and workers in Islington. *FSU Quarterly* 5, 1973.

Jason, L.A. and associates 1980: Decreasing dog litter: behavioural consultation to help a community group. *Evaluation Review* 4(3), 355–69.

Jeffreys, M. 1965: *An anatomy of social welfare services.* London: Michael Joseph.

Jemelka, R.P. and Borich, G.D. 1979: Traditional and emerging definitions of educational evaluation. *Evaluation Quarterly* 3(2) 263–76.

Jenkins, S. and Norman, E. 1975: *Beyond placement: mothers view foster care.* New York: Columbia University Press.

Jones, B. 1976: Social workers at risk. *Social Work Today* 6(25), 780–1.

Jones, E.O. 1975: A study of those who cease to foster. *British Journal of Social Work* 5(1), 31–41.

Jones, M.A. 1980: *The Australian welfare state.* Sydney: Allen & Unwin.

Jones, R. 1978: Intermediate treatment and adolescents' perceptions of social workers. *British Journal of Social Work* 8(4), 425–38.

Jones, W. 1980: Evaluation research and program evaluation: a difference without a distinction. In Fanshel, D., ed., *Future of social work research,* New York: NASW.

Jordan, B. 1979: *Helping in social work.* London: Routledge & Kegan Paul.

—— 1980: Why social work should survive. *New Society* 54(94), 416–17.

Jordan, M.B. 1976: *Social workers and clients: expectation and experience.* Thesis submitted for the degree of MA, University of Kent at Canterbury.

Kagle, J.D. 1978: A survey experimental study of social work practitioners' evaluation of social worker performance. Illinois, Urbana – Champaign, DSW, May 1978, from *Social Work Research and Abstracts* 14(3), 778.

Kandel, D.B., and Williams, R.H. 1964: *Psychiatric rehabilitation: some problems of research.* New York: Atherton Press.

Keith, P. 1975: Evaluation of services for the aged by professionals and the elderly. *Social Service Review* **49**, June, 271–8.

Kennedy, M.M. 1979: Generalizing from single case studies. *Evaluation Quarterly* **3**(4), 661–78.

Kirk, S.A. and Fischer, J. 1976: Do social workers understand research? *Journal of Education for Social Work* **12**(1), Winter 1976, 63–70.

Kirk, S.A., Osmolov, M.J. and Fischer, J. 1976: Social workers' involvement in research. *Social Work* **21**, March.

Kisch, A.I. and Reeder, L.G. 1969: Client evaluation of physician performance. *Journal of Health and Social Behaviour* **10**(1).

Klein, M.W. *et al.* 1961: Problems of measuring patient care in the outpatient department. *Journal of Health and Social Behaviour* **2**, 138–44.

Kline, F., Adrian, A. and Spevak, M. 1974: Patients evaluate therapists. *Archives of General Psychiatry* **31**(1), 113–16.

Korte, O.G. 1977: The perception of four relationship factors as related to outcome scores in social casework treatment. University of Columbia, DSW May 1977, from *Social Work Research and Abstracts*, **13**(3).

Kuhn, M.H. 1962: The interview and the professional relationship. In Rose, Arnold M., eds., *Human behaviour and social processes*, London: Routledge & Kegan Paul.

Landsberg, G. 1973: Consumers appraise store front mental health services. *Evaluation* **I**, February, 66–8.

Larsden, D.E. and Rootman, I. 1976: Physician role performance and patient satisfaction. *Social Science and Medicine* **10**(29).

Lees, R. and Lees, S. 1975: Social science in social work practice. *British Journal of Social Work* **5**(2), 161–74.

Lehmann, S. 1970: Selected self-help: a study of clients of a community social psychiatry service. *American Journal of Psychiatry* **126**(10), 1444–54.

Leigh, A. 1975: You and research: the problem of the 'presenting problem'. *Social Work Today* **5**(20).

Levy, C.S. 1974: Inputs versus outputs as criteria of competence. *Social Casework* **55**(6), 375–80.

Liffman, M. 1979: *Power for the poor.* Sydney: Allen & Unwin.

Lishman, J. 1978: A clash in perspective? A study of worker and client perceptions of social work. *British Journal of Social Work* **8**(3).

Luborsky, L. 1971: Perennial mystery of poor agreement among criteria for psychotherapy outcome. *Journal of Consulting and Clinical Psychology* **37**(3), 316–19.

Lukhard, W.L. 1976: Involving the client. *Social and Rehabilitation Record*, Washington, **3**(2), 2–4.

McCaughey, J. and Chew, W. 1977: The family study. In McCaughey J., Shaver, S. and Ferber H. *Who cares – family problems community links and helping services,* Institute of applied economic and social research, University of Melbourne: Sun books.

McCord, J. and McCord, W. 1959: *Origins of crime.* New York: Columbia University Press.

McCord, J. 1978: Thirty year follow up: treatment effects. *American Psychologist* **33**(3), March, 284–9.

McCoy, T., Penick, E.C., Powell, B.J. and Read, M.R. 1975: Clients' reactions to an outreach program. *Social Work* **20**(6), 442–4.

McCulloch, W. *et al.* 1968: A national social work inter-disciplinary study of reading behaviour and helpful factors in professional practice, *unpublished study,* University of Bradford.

Macdonald, M.E. 1966: Reunion at vocational high. *Social Service Review* **40**, June.

McIsaac, H. and Wilkinson, H. 1965: Clients talk about their caseworkers. *Public Welfare* **23**, 147–54.

McKay, A., Goldberg, E.M. and Fruin, D.J. 1973: Consumers and a social services department. *Social Work Today* **4**(16).

McKinlay, J.B. 1972: Some approaches and problems in the study of the use of services. *Journal of Health and Social Behaviour* **13**, June, 115–52.

—— 1973: Social networks, lay consultation and helpseeking behaviour. *Social Forces* **51**(3), March.

McKinlay, J.B. and Mitchell, D. 1975: Socio-psychological factors affecting health service utilization – some doubts about 'patient satisfaction'. *Galley,* **104.**

McWhinnie, A. 1978: Support for foster parents. *Adoption and Fostering* **92**(2), 15–21.

Mahoney, S.C. 1966: Number magic: the oversimplified quantification of complex problems. *Social Science Review* **40**, 64–70.

Maluccio, A.N. 1977: As client and social worker see it – an exploratory study of their perception of casework. University of Columbia, DSW, May 1977, from *Social Work Research and Abstracts* **13**(3) No. 778.

—— 1979: *Learning from clients: interpersonal helping as viewed by clients and social workers.* New York: Free Press.

Mansfield, P. and Smith, J. 1974/75: What a reception. *Social Work Today* **5**(12), 354–6.

Marris, P. and Rein, M. 1973: *Dilemmas of social reform,* second edition. Chicago: Aldine.

Marsden, D. 1969: *Mothers alone, poverty and the fatherless family.* London: Allen & Unwin.

Mayer, J.E. 1967: Disclosing marital problems. *Social Casework,* **48**(6), 342–51.

Mayer, J.E. and Timms, N. 1970: *The client speaks.* London: Routledge & Kegan Paul.

Meeaghan, T. and Mascari, M. 1971: Consumer choice and consumer control in service delivery. *Social Work* **16**, October.

Meyer, H.J., Borgatta, E.F. and Jones, W.C. 1965: *Girls at vocational high: an experiment in social work intervention.* New York: Russell Sage Foundation.

Mintz, J. 1972: What is 'success' in psychotherapy. *Journal of Abnormal Psychology* **80**(1), 11–19.

Mitchell, H.E. and Mudd, E.H. 1957: Anxieties associated with the conduct of research in a clinical setting. *American Journal of Orthopsychiatry* **27**.

Moller, J. and Graycar, A. 1981: *An eye for evaluation,* unpublished paper, Social Welfare Research Centre, University of New South Wales.

Morris, P., Cooper, J. and Byles, A. 1973: Public attitudes to problem definition and problem solving. *British Journal of Social Work* **3**(3), 301–20.

Morris, R. 1977: Caring for versus caring about people. *Social Work* **22**(5).

Mullen, E.J., Chaxin, R.M. and Feldstein, D.M. 1972: Services for the newly dependent: an assessment. *Social Service Review* **46**(3), 309–22.

Mullen, E.J. and Dumpson J.R., eds., 1972: *Evaluation of social intervention.* San Francisco: Jossey Bass.

Mulvey, T. 1977/78: Aftercare – who cares? *Concern,* Part 26, 26–30.

Neill, J., Fruin, D.J., Goldberg, E.M. and Warburton, R.W. 1973: Reactions to integration. *Social Work Today* **4**(15), 458–65.

Neill, J., Warburton, R.W. and McGuiness, B.J. 1976: The social worker's viewpoint – perceptions of social workers in four area offices in 1972 and 1975. *Social Work Today* **7**(2), and **8**(5), 9–14.

Nokes, P. 1967: *The professional task in welfare practice.* London: Routledge & Kegan Paul.

Orlinsky, D.E. and Howard, K.J. 1967: The good therapy hour: experimental correlates of patients' and therapists' evaluation of therapy sessions. *Archives of General Psychology* **16**, 621–32.

Overall, B. and Aronson, H. 1963: Expectations of psychotherapy in patients of lower socioeconomic class. *American Journal of Orthopsychiatry* **33**, April, 421–30.

Owtram, J. 1966: Nine points for the disabled. *Case Conference* **13**(1), 3–7.

Oxley, G.B. 1977: Involuntary clients' responses to a treatment experience. *Social Casework* **58**(10), 607–14.

Page, R. and Clark, G.A. 1977: *Who cares?* London: National Childrens Bureau.

Pahl, J. 1978: *A refuge for battered women – a study of the role of a women's centre.* London: HMSO.

Parlett, M. and Hamilton, D. 1976: Evaluation as illumination: a new approach to the study of innovatory programs. In Tawney, D., ed., *Curriculum evaluation today: trends and implications,* London: Macmillan.

Parkinson, G. 1975: I give them money. *New Society* **15**(334), 131.

Parsloe, P. and O'Boyle, F. 1980: *Monitoring community service orders.* Unpublished research, University of Aberdeen.

Parsloe, P. and Stevenson, O. 1978: *Social service teams: the practitioners view*. London: HMSO.

Pearson, G. 1975: *The deviant imagination*. London: Macmillan.

Pease, K. 1974: *Observations on community service orders 1974*. Draft of a talk given to a conference of the Probation and Aftercare Services, 19 April at Moreton-in-Marsh, England.

Pease, K. and McWilliams, B. 1977: Assessing community service schemes: pitfalls for the unwary. *Probation Journal* **24**(4), December, 131–9.

Perlman, H.H. 1968: Casework and the case of Chemung county. In Brown, G.E., ed., *The multi-problem dilemma*, Metuchen, NJ: The Scarecrow Press.

Perlman, R. 1975: *Consumers and the social services*. New York: John Wiley & Sons Inc.

Philp, M. 1979: Notes on the form of knowledge in social work. *Sociological Review* **27**(1), 83–111.

Piliavin, I. 1963: Conflict between cottage parents and caseworkers. *Social Service Review* **37**(1), 17–25.

Pinker, R. 1971: *Social theory and social policy*. London: Heinemann.

Piven, F.F. and Cloward, R.A. 1971: *Regulating the poor: the functions of public welfare*. New York: Pantheon Books.

Plowman, D.E.G. 1969: What are the outcomes of casework? *Social Work* **26**(1).

Pohlman, E. and Robinson, F. 1960: Client reactions to some aspects of the counselling situation. *Personnel and Guidance Journal* **38**, 546–51.

Pollak, O. 1956: Comments in *Social Service Review* **30**, September, 296–9.

Powell, B.J., Shaw D. and O'Neil, C. 1971: Client evaluations of a clinic's services. *Hospital and Community Psychiatry* **22**, June, 189–90.

Powers, E. and Witmer, H. 1951: *An experiment in the prevention of delinquency* – the Cambridge-Somerville Youth Study. New York: Columbia University Press.

Pritlove, J.H. 1976: Evaluating a group home: problems and results. *British Journal of Social Work* **6**(3), Autumn, 353–76.

Rawlings, C. 1978: *Social work with the elderly: some problems and possibilities*. University of Keele social work research project.

Raymond, F.B. 1977: A changing focus for the profession: product rather than process. *Journal of Social Welfare* **4**(2&3), 9–16.

Reeder, L.G. 1972: The patient-client as a consumer: some observations on the changing professional/client relationship. *Journal of Health and Social Behaviour* **73**, December, 406–12.

Rees, S.J. 1974: No more than contact: an outcome of social work. *British Journal of Social Work* **4**(3), 255–79.

—— 1975: How misunderstanding occurs. In Bailey, R. and Brake, M., eds., *Radical social work*, London: Edward Arnold.

Rees, S.J. 1978: *Social work face to face*. London: Edward Arnold.

Reid, W.J. and Epstein, L. 1972: *Task-centred casework*. New York: Columbia University Press.

Reid, W.J. and Shapiro, B.L. 1969: Client reactions to advice. *Social Service Review* **43**(2), June, 165–73.

Reid, W.J. and Shyne, A., 1969: *Brief and extended casework*. New York: Columbia University Press.

Rein, M., 1970: *Social policy*. New York: Random House.

Reith, D., 1975: I wonder if you can help me? *Social Work Today* **6**(3), 66–9.

Report of the Evaluation Unit, 1979: Family & Children's Services Agency, Appendix 4, Sydney, May.

Roberts, R.W., 1968: Social work: methods and/or goals? *Social Service Review* **42**(3).

Robinson, J., 1971: Experimental research in social casework. *British Journal of Social Work* **1**(4).

Robinson, T., 1975: The tarnished image of social work. *Community Care*, 8 January.

—— 1978: *In worlds apart*. London: Bedford Square Press.

Rodgers, B.N., and Dixon, J., 1960: *Portrait of social work* London: Oxford University Press.

Rodman, Hyman and Kolodny, Ralph, 1971: Organisational strains in the researcher–practitioner relationship. In Francis G. Caro, ed., *Readings in evaluative research*, New York: Russell Sage Foundation.

Rondeau, G. 1976: *Evaluative Research with Clients on the Services Received in the Family Agencies of Metropolitan Montreal*. University of Pittsburgh.

Rosenblatt, A. 1968: The practitioner's use and evaluation of research. *Social Work* **13**(1), 53–9.

Rosenfield, J.M., 1964: Strangeness between helper and client: a possible explanation of the non-use of available professional help. *Social Service Review* **38**(1).

Rossi, P.H., 1978: Issues in the evaluation of human services delivery. *Evaluation Quarterly* **2**(4), 573–99.

Rothman, D., 1978: The state as parent: social policy in the progressive era. In Gaylin, W., Glasser, I., Marcus, S., and Rothman, D. eds., *Doing good: the limits of benevolence*, New York: Pantheon Books.

Rothman, J., 1974: *Planning and organisation for social change*. New York: Columbia University Press.

Rubenstein, H., and Bloch, M.H., 1978: Helping clients who are poor: worker and client perceptions of problems, activities and outcomes. *Social Service Review* **52**(1), 69–84.

Runciman, W.G., 1966: *Relative deprivation and social justice*. London: Routledge & Kegan Paul.

Rushforth, M., 1976: Success in List D. schools. *Focus*, on social work and service in Scotland, November, **55**(1), 9–11.

Sacks, J.G., Bradley, P.M., and Beck, D.F., 1970: *Clients' progress within 4 interviews – an exploratory study comparing workers' and clients' views.* New York: Family Service Association of America.

Sainsbury, E., 1975: *Social work with families,* London: Routledge & Kegan Paul.

Sainsbury, E. and Nixon, S., 1979: Organizational influences on the ways in which social work practice is perceived by social workers and clients. Unpublished first draft, University of Sheffield.

Salmon, Harry, 1978: Ideology and practice. In Paul Curno, ed., *Political issues and community work,* London: Routledge & Kegan Paul.

Sarri, R. 1979a: History and development of evaluation in human services: a view from the United States. In Commonwealth of Australia, *Through a glass darkly,* Canberra: AGPS, 61–75.

Sarri, R. 1979b: Methods of evaluating effectiveness of human services. In Commonwealth of Australia, *Through a glass darkly,* Canberra: AGPS, 76–84.

Schmidt, J.T. 1969: The use and purpose in casework practice. *Social Work* (USA) **14**(1), 77–84.

Schuerman, J.R. 1975: Do family services help? An essay review. *Social Service Review* **49**(3), 363–75.

Schuerman, J.R., Shaw, D.A. and Magner, G.W. 1967: Changes in social functioning of hospitalized psychiatric patients. *Social Service Review* **41**, 371–8.

Schutz, A. 1962: Collected papers I, *The problem of social reality,* edited by M. Natanson, The Hague: Martinus Nijhoff.

Schwartz, C.G. 1970: Strategies and tactics of mothers of mentally retarded children for dealing with the medical case system. In Norman R. Bernstein, ed., *Diminished people – the problems and care of the mentally retarded,* Boston: Little, Brown & Company.

Schwartz, M.C. 1974: Importance of the sex of worker and client. *Social Work* **19**(2), March, 177–86.

Scott, R.W. 1969: Professional employees in a bureaucratic structure: social work. In A. Etzioni, ed., *The semi-professions and their organization: teachers, nurses, social workers,* New York: The Free Press.

Seed, P. 1980: *Mental handicap in the Highlands and Western Isles.* Research project, University of Aberdeen.

Segal, S.P. 1972: Research on the outcome of social work therapeutic interventions: a review of the literature. *Journal of Health and Social Behaviour* **13**, March, 3–17.

—— 1978: Issues in the utilization and evaluation of social work treatment. *International Social Work* **21**(1).

Shaw, I. 1975: Consumer opinion and social policy: a research review. *Journal of Social Policy* **5**, 19–32.

Shaw, M. 1974: Social work in prison. *Home Office Research Study* No. 22. London: HMSO.

Shaw, M. and Lebens, K. 1976: Children between families. *Adoption and Fostering* **84**.
—— 1977: Foster parents talking. *Adoption and Fostering* **88**(2), 11–16.
Sheldon, B. and Baird, P. 1978: Evaluating student performance. *Social Work Today* **10**(16).
Sheppard, M.L. 1967: The social worker's use of material and practical aid. *The British Journal of Psychiatric Social Work* **8**(3), 28–34.
Shyne, A.W. 1960: Former clients evaluate a youth service program. *Children* **7**, 175–9.
Shyne, A.W. and Kogan L.S. 1958: A study of components of movement. *Social Casework* **39**, June.
Silverman, P.R. 1969: *The client who drops out: a study of spoiled helping relationships*. Ph.D. The Florence Heller Graduate School for Advanced Studies in Social Welfare, Brandeis University.
—— 1970: A re-examination of the intake procedure. *Social Casework*, December, 625–34.
Simmons, O.G. and Davis, J.A. 1957–58: Interdisciplinary collaboration in mental illness research. *American Journal of Sociology* **63**, 297–303.
Simpkin, M. 1979: *Trapped within welfare – surviving social work*. London: Macmillan.
Singer, J.W. 1979: When the evaluators are evaluated, the GAO often gets low marks. *National Journal*, October, 1889–92.
Smith, G. 1980: *Social Need, Policy, Practice and Research*. London: Routledge & Kegan Paul.
Smith, G. and Harris, R. 1972: Ideologies of need and the organization of social work departments. *British Journal of Social Work* **2**(1), 27–45.
Social Work (Scotland) Act, 1968, London: HMSO.
Stanton, E. 1970: *Clients came last*. Beverley Hills: Sage.
Stark, F.B. 1959: Barriers to client-worker communication at intake. *Social Casework* USA 1959 **40**(5), April, 177–83.
Stevenson, O. and Parsloe, P. 1978: *Social service teams: the practitioner's view*. London: Department of Health and Social Security, HMSO.
Stimson, G. 1974: Obeying doctor's orders: a view from the other side. *Social Science and Medicine* **8**, 97–104.
Strupp, H.H. and Bergin, A.E. 1969: Some empirical and conceptual bases for coordinated research in psychotherapy. *International Journal of Psychiatry* **7**, February.
Strupp, H.H., Fox, R. and Lessler, K. 1969: *Patients view their psychotherapy*. Baltimore: Johns Hopkins Press.
Strauss, A. 1964: *Psychiatric ideologies and institutions*. New York: Free Press.
Stuart, A. 1975: Recipient views of cash versus in-kind benefit programs. *Social Service Review* **49**(1), 79–91.
Taber, M. 1970: Social work as interference in problem definitions. *Applied Social Studies* **2**, 59–68.

Taylor, H. 1978: *An evaluation of the effectiveness of social services provision in a rural area*. University of Birmingham, Department of Social Administration, Social Services Unit in collaboration with Hereford and Worcester County Council social services department.

Tessler, R.C. 1975: Client's reactions to initial interviews: Determinants of relationship-centred and problem-centred satisfaction. *Journal of Counselling and Psychology* **22**, May, 187–91.

Thomas, E., Polansky, N. and Kounine, J. 1955: The expected behaviours of a potentially helpful person. *Human Relations* **8**, 165–74.

Thorpe, R. 1974: Mum and Mrs So and So. *Social Work Today* **4**(22).

——— 1980: The experience of children and parents living apart. In Triseliotis, J., ed., *New developments in fostering and adoption*. London: Routledge & Kegan Paul.

Timms, N. 1973: *The receiving end*. London: Routledge & Kegan Paul.

Toch, H. 1967: Prison inmates' reaction to furlough. *Journal of Research in Crime and Delinquency* **4**(2), July.

Truax, C.B. and Carkhuff, R. 1967: *Towards effective counselling and psychotherapy*. Chicago: Aldine Publishing Company.

Tulloch, P. 1978: Normative theory and social policy. *Australian New Zealand Journal of Social Policy* **14**(1), 65–74.

Varon, E. 1962: *The client of a protective agency in the context of the community*. Unpublished Ph.D. dissertation, Forence Heller Graduate School for Advanced Studies in Social Welfare, Brandeis University.

Wallace, A. 1981: *Social work: the client's verdict*. M. Litt. Thesis, University of Aberdeen.

Wandsworth Social Services Department 1977: Project '74: A research study in which mentally handicapped speak for themselves, *Clearing House for Local Authority Research*(1).

Wasserman, H. 1971: The professional social worker in a bureaucracy. *Social Work* (USA), 16 January, 89–95.

Weed, P. and Greenwald, S.R. 1973: The mystics of statistics. *Social Work* **18**(2), March, 113–15.

Weiss, R.S. 1972: Helping relationships: relationships of clients with physicians, social workers, priests and others. *Social Problems* **20**(3), 319–28.

Wells, R.A., Dilkes, T.C. and Trivelli, N. 1972: The results of family therapy: a critical review of the literature. *Family Process* **11**(2).

Wertkin, R.A., Gyarfas, M. and Hudson, W.W. 1978: Points and viewpoints, *Social Work*, November, 517–19.

White, D. 1973: Receptionist power. *New Society* **26**(581), 453–4.

Whittington, C. 1977: Social workers' orientations: an active perspective. *British Journal of Social Work* **7**(1), Spring, 73–97.

Who cares? Young people in care speak out, *Social Work Today*, 4 October 1977, 14–18.

Wigan Social Services Department 1979: A survey of the visually handicapped, part II.

Wikler, Lyn 1975: Consumer involvement in the training of social work students. *Social Casework* **60**(3), 145–9.

Wilensky, H.L. and Lebeaux, C. 1958: *Industrial society and social welfare.* New York: Russell Sage Foundation.

Williams, W. and Elmore, R. 1975: *Social program implementation.* New York: Academic Press.

Wilson, H. 1975: Parenting in poverty. *British Journal of Social Work* **4**(3), 241–54.

Wilson, S. 1979: Explorations of the usefulness of case study evaluations, *Evaluation Quarterly* **3**(3), 446–59.

Wootton, B. 1959: Contemporary attitudes in social work. In Wootton, B., *Social science and social pathology,* London: Allen & Unwin.

Wood, K.M. 1978: Casework effectiveness: a new look at the research evidence. *Social Work* **23**(6), 437–56.

Worby, M. 1953: The adolescent's expectations of how the potentially helpful person will act. *Smith College Studies in Social Work* **26**(19), 59.

Wright, H. 1977: Evaluation study of the exploratory visit: an innovative outreach activity of the ILGWU's friendly visiting program. *International Journal of Aging and Human Development,* New York, **8**(1), 67–82.

Younghusband, E. 1959: *Report of the ministry of health working party on social workers in the local authority health and welfare services.* London: HMSO.

Index